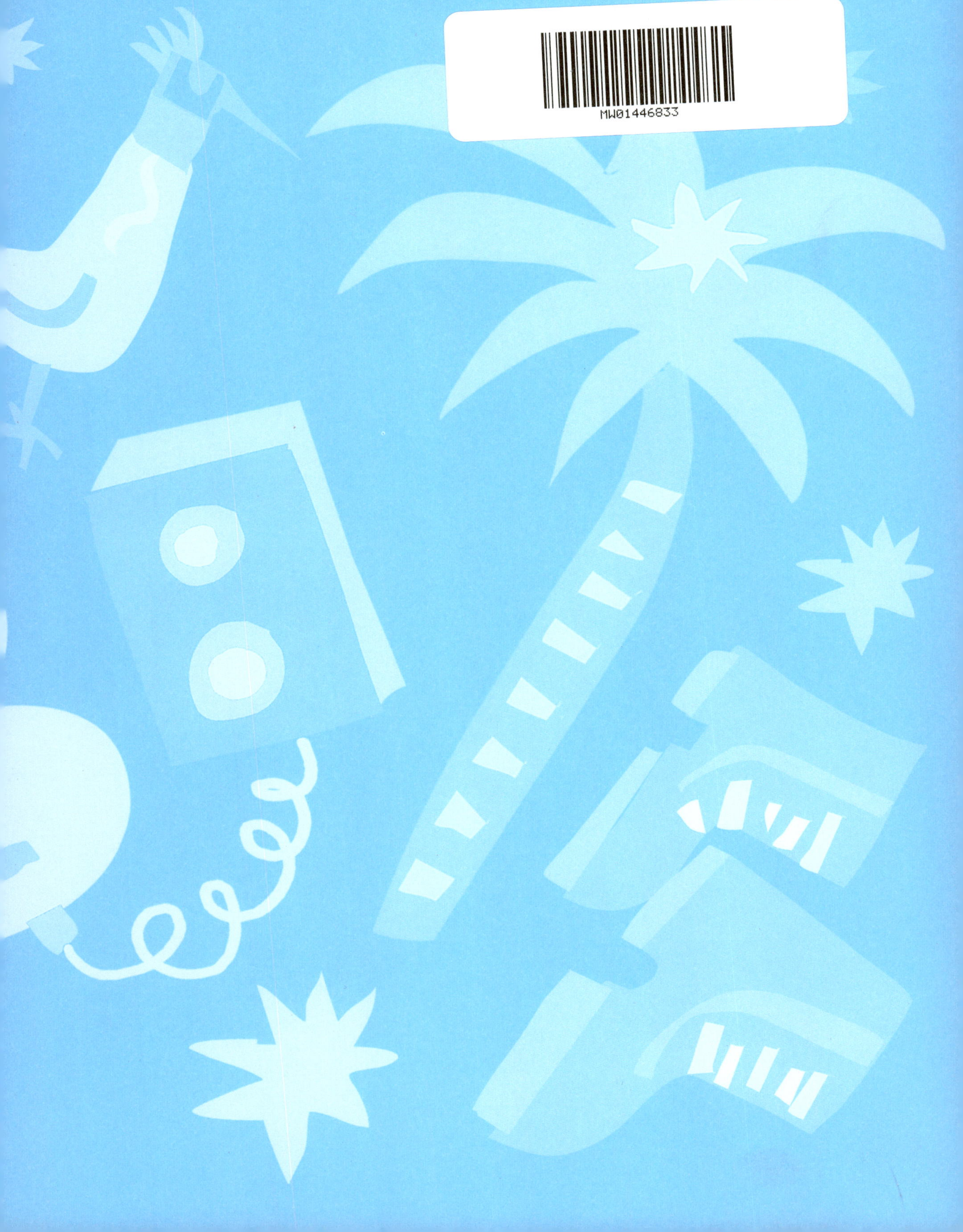

THE INTREPID LIST*

*NOT A BUCKET LIST

THE INTR

100 UNCOMMON EXPERIENCES TO CHANGE THE WAY YOU TRAVEL

EPID LIST

Hardie Grant
EXPLORE | Intrepid

Bay bathing on the Adriatic Coast

CONTENTS

INTRODUCTION viii
THE INTREPID LIST xi
WHAT'S ON THE INTREPID LIST? xi
TRAVELLER ETHICS xii
WORLD MAP xvi

FOOD & DRINK 1
ACTIVITIES & SPORTS 31
WILDLIFE 53
NATURE 89
ART & CULTURE 135

The Okavango Delta, Botswana

FESTIVALS & EVENTS 177
SLOW TRAVEL 197
RESPONSIBLE TRAVEL 229
ARCHITECTURE 249
HISTORY 265

INDEX 284

ABOUT THE AUTHORS 288

INTRODUCTION

As the world's largest purpose-led adventure travel company, Intrepid Travel has been taking travellers around the globe since 1989.

On hundreds of trips in over 100 countries, Intrepid brings small groups of like-minded travellers together with a locally based leader. Intrepid itineraries weave the highlights into the hard-to-forget moments in hard-to-find places. From homestays to Indigenous community-led experiences, between the hidden noodle bars and backstreet bodegas, Intrepid experiences are built to keep the economic benefits of travel where they belong.

It all stems from a simple mission: create positive change through the joy of travel. As a B Corp, Intrepid is committed to balancing purpose and profit by operating equitably, sustainably and transparently. The Intrepid Foundation, established in 2002, gives travellers a way to give back to the places they've visited, by supporting organisations around the world that are making a difference in their communities.

At Intrepid, travel is about more than just seeing the world, it's about experiencing it and sparking connections with Intrepid people wherever you go.

Learn more at intrepidtravel.com.

Kornati archipelago, Croatia

Finding the best sunset vantage point near Aït Benhaddou, Morocco

THE INTREPID LIST

The world is at our fingertips like never before in history. We can slip instantaneously across the planet right from our desks or the palms of our hands. Yet the more connected we become digitally, the more something inside us yearns for deeper interaction and exchange. We need to breathe and be present in a place to really experience it. This is how those of us touched by the spirit of discovery and adventure are lured out onto the road.

But it's not always easy to track down engaging travel experiences – the kind that will offer more than just a popular Instagram post. Enter *The Intrepid List*. Here we've gathered experiences from 48 adventurous travellers, including travel experts, locals and writers from within the Intrepid family. All of them passionate about meaningful, ethical, engaging and intrepid travel.

We asked them to write about incredible travel experiences that they've encountered in this wonder-filled world. *The Intrepid List* is not a bucket list; it's almost the opposite. This is a curation of precious moments experienced by our travellers that have never been forgotten. It aims to inspire you to explore a little further and delve a little deeper, to engage with communities, look below the surface and open yourself to new learnings. This is the way to find the kinds of experiences that will stay with you forever so you can form your own personal Intrepid List.

WHAT'S ON THE INTREPID LIST?

Within our 10 themed sections are experiences from more than 55 countries worldwide. They range from daring to caring, wild to mild. We'll take you to Ireland to celebrate literature and Iceland to celebrate lava. We'll sleep under the stars in Egypt and listen to LPs in a record bar in Seoul. We'll sample cicheti in Venice and enter 13th-century churches carved into rock trenches in Ethiopia. We'll learn LGBTQIA+ history in New York City and dip into the sapphire-pure waters of the remote Cocos Keeling Islands. And so much more!

TRAVELLER ETHICS

The world may be your oyster, but that doesn't mean you need to slurp it up in a greedy rush and let it dribble all over your shirt. At its best, travel promotes respect and understanding between cultures, educates and activates people and connects communities across large distances. Here are some of the ways you can ensure you have a positive impact on the communities and places you visit.

WILDLIFE AND PLACES

Wilderness Unfortunately, tourism can have a large and negative environmental impact, but it doesn't have to be that way. With simple strategies that you probably use at home you can reduce your impact, like pack out everything you pack in.

Stay Wild Keep your distance from wild animals – for your safety and theirs. Avoid petting zoos and animal experiences that incentivise keeping animals in captivity.

Reduce, Reuse and Recycle Discarded plastic is a huge issue around the world often linked to tourism. You can make a significant impact by bringing your own shopping bag and avoiding purchasing bottled water. Instead you can purify your water by boiling it or using a filtration system (such as LifeStraw) or a UV light treatment system (such as Steripen).

Count Your Carbon Travel has a large carbon footprint, especially air travel. It's not always easy to see your carbon footprint while travelling, but there are tools such as the calculator on Sustainable Travel International (sustainabletravel.org/our-work/carbon-offsets/calculate-footprint/) to learn your personal impact. You'll soon see how quickly alternatives like taking a train or bus, or better yet a sailboat or bicycle, can lower your footprint. Other carbon-footprint reducers include flying economy, booking nonstop flights, using public transport, choosing electric buses, cars and tuk tuks, remembering to turn off air-conditioning and electricals in hotel rooms, and avoiding buying souvenirs and gifts you and your friends really don't need.

Bonding through shared experience in India

PEOPLE AND COMMUNITY

Shop Local Seek out small local businesses to spend your valuable foreign funds, such as small stores, artisan-run market stalls and local family restaurants. You can often make an even larger difference in communities by choosing to support women-owned businesses.

Honour Your Word If you say you'll stay in touch with the people you meet, make sure you do. If you say you'll send photos, follow through on it.

Donate Responsibly You can also donate responsibly by planning your giving – many people decide to support an NGO or conservation initiative rather than giving ad-hoc donations on the ground.

Dress Appropriately You can signal your respect for the values of the communities you visit by adopting a similar dress code. Check what the locals are doing – are they wearing bikinis? Shoes? Hats? Shorts? If not, follow their lead. This is particularly important in sacred places.

Stay Calm and Flexible Travel can be stressful and there are plenty of times when you're not quite sure what's going on. Keep an open mind and avoid being aggressive or showing anger. In many parts of the world, these are considered extremely confronting behaviours.

Learn a Few Words in the Local Language This can be a huge sign that you're keen to engage, and not just consume. Even just a few words, like 'thank you', 'delicious' and 'beautiful' can help you connect on a different level.

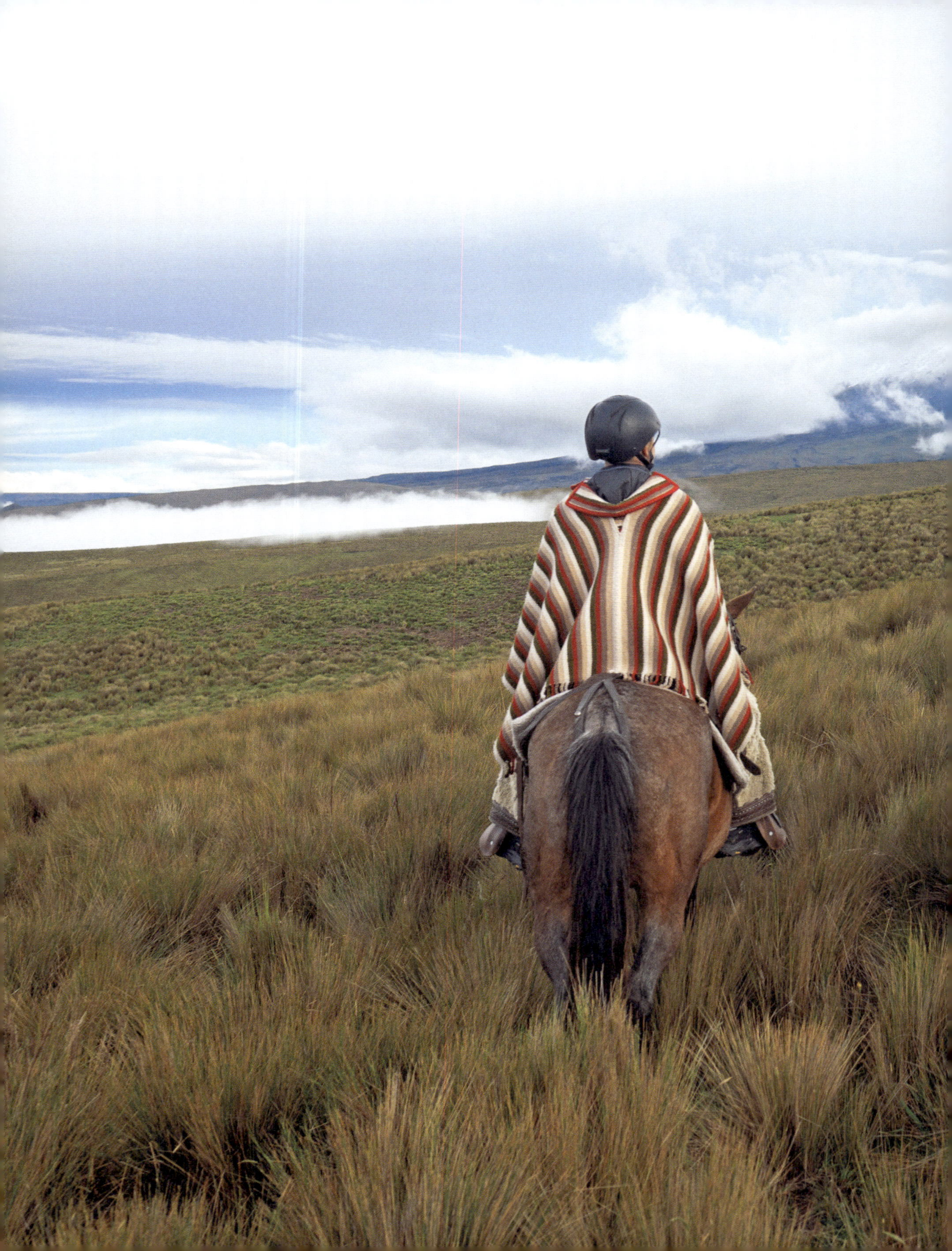

Horse riding with a view of Cotopaxi, Ecuador

WORLD MAP

1	Oaxaca, Mexico – p. 5
2	Gaziantep, Türkiye – p. 6
3	Bangalore, India – p. 8
4	Lima, Peru – p. 10
5	Nuwara Eliya, Sri Lanka – p. 13
6	Plzen and Ceske Budejovice, Czechia – p. 18
7	Venice, Italy – p. 20
8	Dublin, Ireland – p. 25
9	Tennessee, Missouri and Texas, USA – p. 26
10	Dublin, Ireland – p. 35
11	Marburg, Germany – p. 36
12	Soweto, South Africa – p. 39
13	Dalmatia, Croatia – p. 40
14	Cocos Keeling, Australia – p. 42
15	Boston and Chicago, USA – p. 46
16	Nazaré, Portugal – p. 49
17	Tokyo, Japan – p. 50
18	Nauta, Peru – p. 56
19	Johnstone Strait, Canada – p. 59
20	Sumatra, Indonesia – p. 63
21	Tonlé Sap, Cambodia – p. 65
22	Alaska, USA – p. 66
23	Manghopir, Pakistan – p. 69
24	Galápagos Islands, Ecuador – p. 70
25	Maria Island, Australia – p. 75
26	Okavango Delta, Botswana – p. 76
27	Punta Norte, Argentina – p. 81
28	Niue – p. 82
29	Cuyabeno National Park, Ecuador – p. 84
30	Cosigüina, Nicaragua – p. 92
31	Aotea/Great Barrier Island, Aotearoa/New Zealand – p. 94
32	Simien Mountains, Ethiopia – p. 98
33	Southern Utah, USA – p. 100
34	Vik and Reykjavik, Iceland – p. 104
35	Phong Nha-ke Bang National Park, Vietnam – p. 108
36	Delta el Tigre, Argentina – p. 100
37	Dead Sea, Jordan – p. 113
38	Kilimanjaro National Park, Tanzania – p. 114
39	Moalboal, Philippines – p. 117
40	Santo, Vanuato – p. 118
41	Yucatan, Mexico – p. 119
42	White Desert, Egypt – p. 122
43	New England, USA – p. 124
44	Finland and Norway – p. 127
45	Salar de Uyuni, Bolivia – p. 128
46	Lukla, Nepal – p. 131
47	Marrakech, Morocco – p. 139
48	Painted Desert, USA – p. 140
49	Tbilisi, Georgia – p. 143
50	Rio de Janeiro, Brazil – p. 144
51	Fremantle, Australia – p. 147
52	Hiroshima, Japan – p.148
53	Hydra, Greece – p. 150
54	Oslo, Norway – p. 152
55	Paso Robles, USA – p. 155
56	Seville, Spain – p. 156
57	Seoul, South Korea – p. 159
58	Chamula, Mexico – p. 162
59	San Francisco, USA – p. 165
60	Sydney/Warrang, Australia – p. 166
61	Morocco – p. 170
62	Timor-Leste – p. 173
63	Nunavut, Canada – p. 174
64	Mexico City, Mexico – p. 181
65	Bangkok, Thailand – p. 182
66	Cusco, Peru – p. 185
67	India – p. 186
68	Dublin, Ireland – p. 189
69	Ouarzazate, Morocco – p. 190
70	Wellington, Aotearoa/New Zealand – p. 195
71	Isle of Skye, Scotland – p. 200
72	Udaipur, India – p. 205
73	Chicago, USA – p. 207
74	Avignon, France – p. 210
75	Gubeikou, China – p. 213
76	Ta Xua, Vietnam – p. 214
77	St Moritz, Switzerland – p. 217
78	Whanganui River, Aotearoa/New Zealand – p. 218
79	Coastal California, USA – p. 220
80	Sydney/Warrang, Australia – p. 225
81	Torres del Paine, Patagonia – p. 227
82	Camino de Santiago, Spain – p. 232
83	Bali, Indonesia – p. 235
84	New Norfolk, Australia – p. 236
85	Levanto, Italy – p. 241
86	Copenhagen, Denmark – p. 242
87	Plateau Mountain, Svalbard – p. 244
88	Old Pejeta Conservancy, Kenya – p. 247
89	USA – p. 253
90	Phnom Penh, Cambodia – p. 254
91	Hukeng, China – p. 257
92	Lalibela, Ethiopia – p. 258
93	Zipaquirá, Colombia – p. 262
94	Doha, Qatar – p. 269
95	Sassi di Matera, Italy – p. 270
96	Famagusta, Cyprus – p. 272
97	Vienna, Austria – p. 273
98	Nemrut Dag, Türkiye – p. 277
99	Jodhpur, India – p. 278
100	New York City, USA – p. 282

NORTH AMERICA

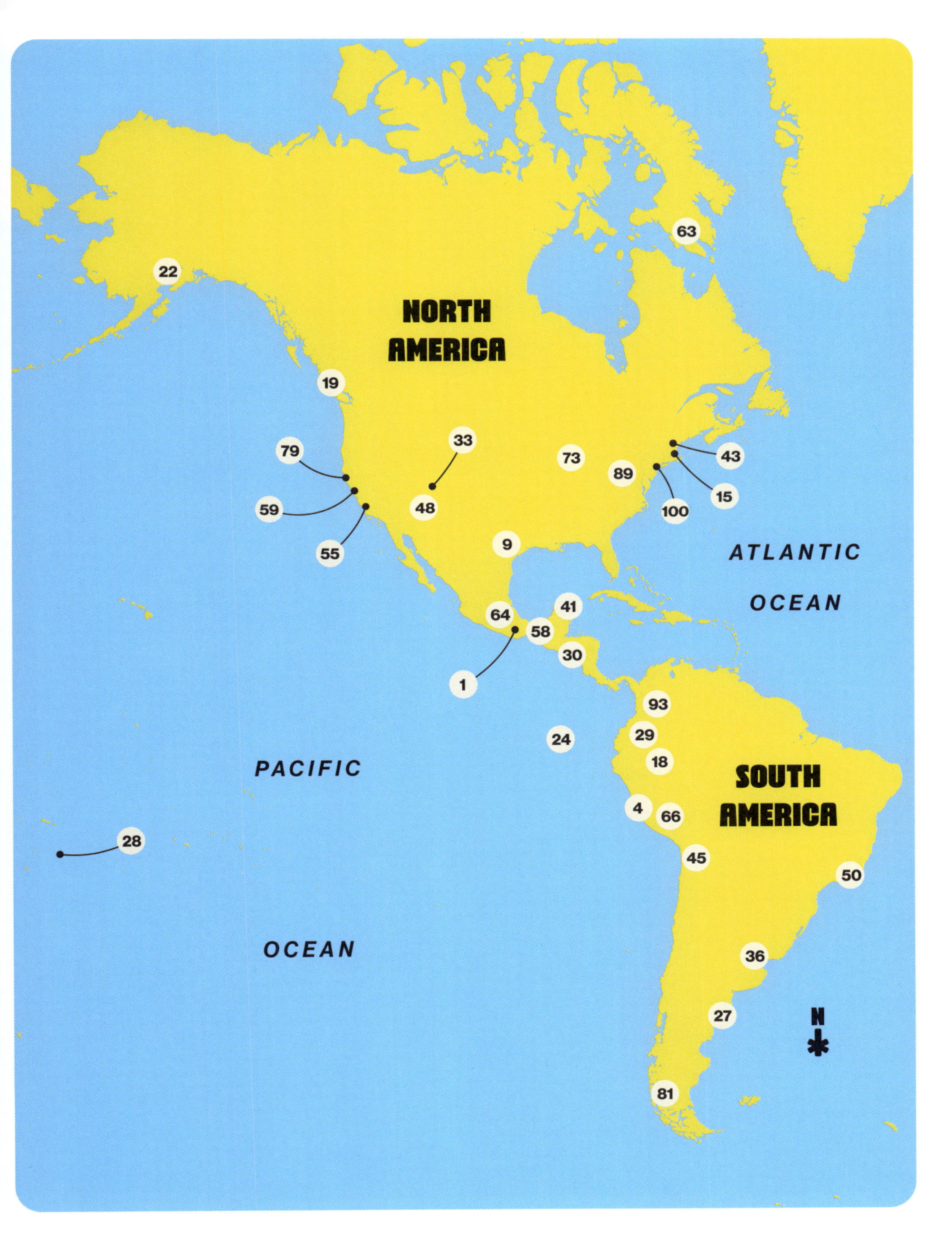

ATLANTIC OCEAN

SOUTH AMERICA

PACIFIC OCEAN

N

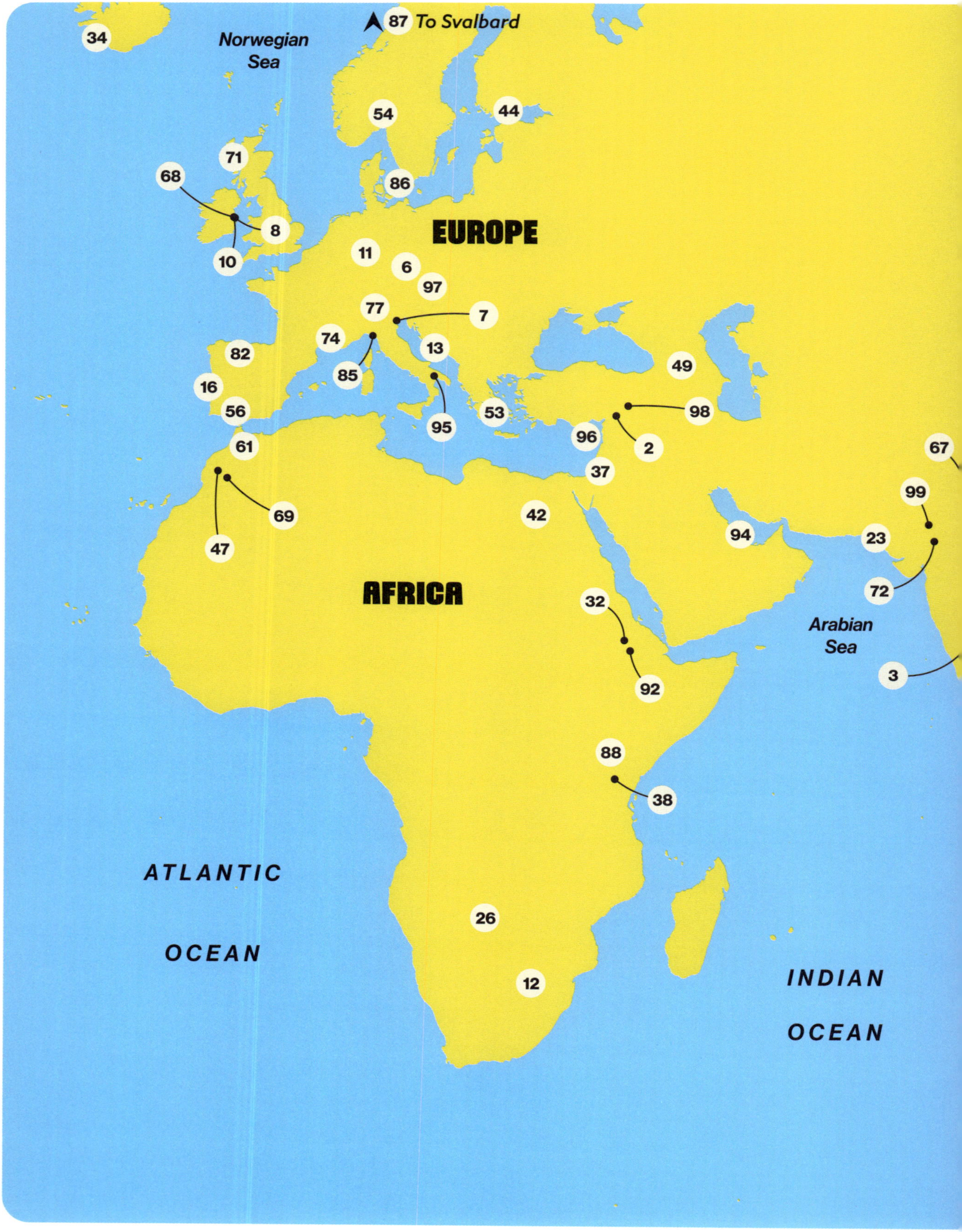
87 To Svalbard
34
Norwegian Sea
54
44
71
68
86
EUROPE
8
10
11
6
97
77
7
74
13
82
85
49
16
95
98
56
53
96
2
61
37
67
69
42
99
47
94
23
AFRICA
72
32
Arabian Sea
92
3
88
38
ATLANTIC OCEAN
26
12
INDIAN OCEAN

ASIA

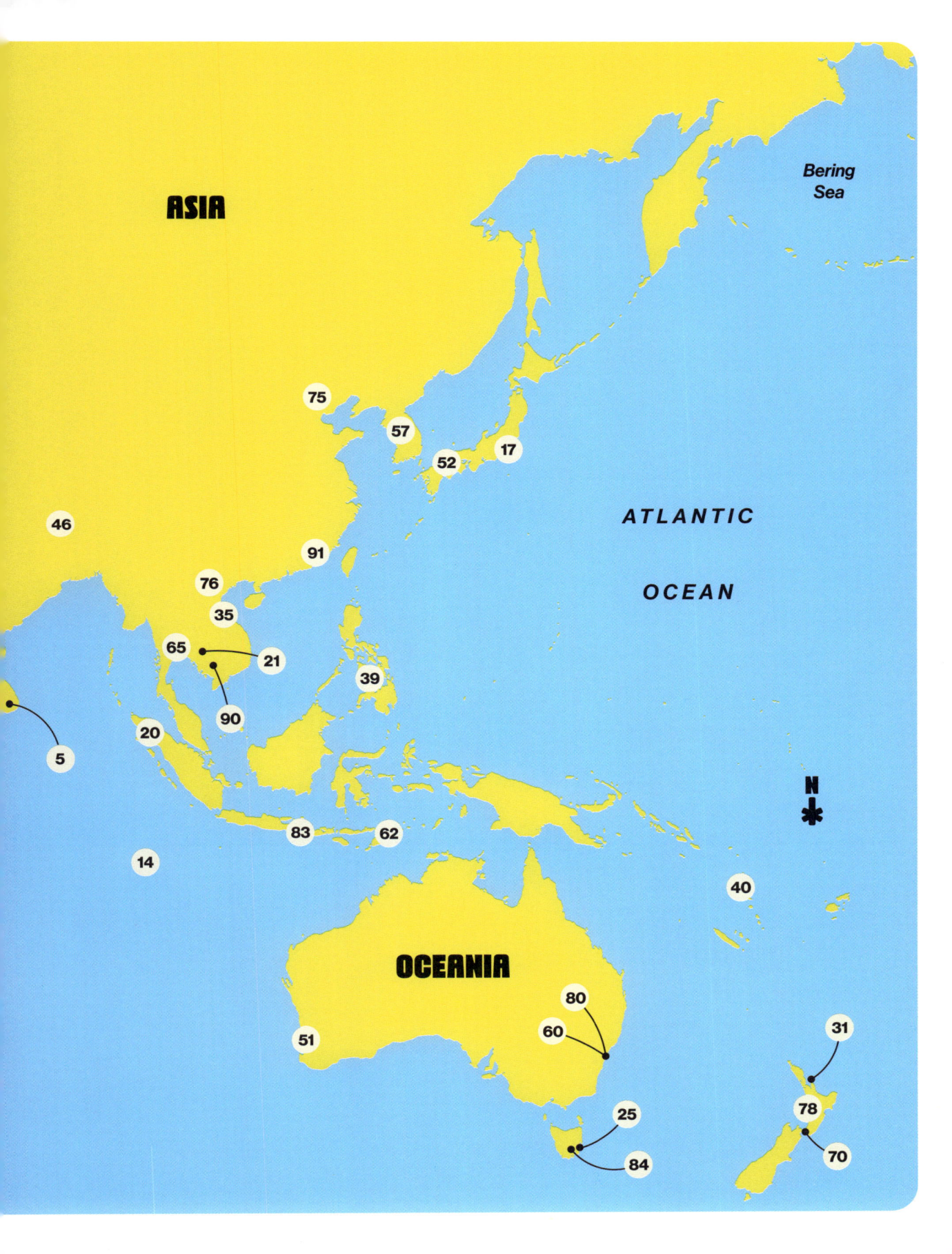

Bering Sea

ATLANTIC OCEAN

OCEANIA

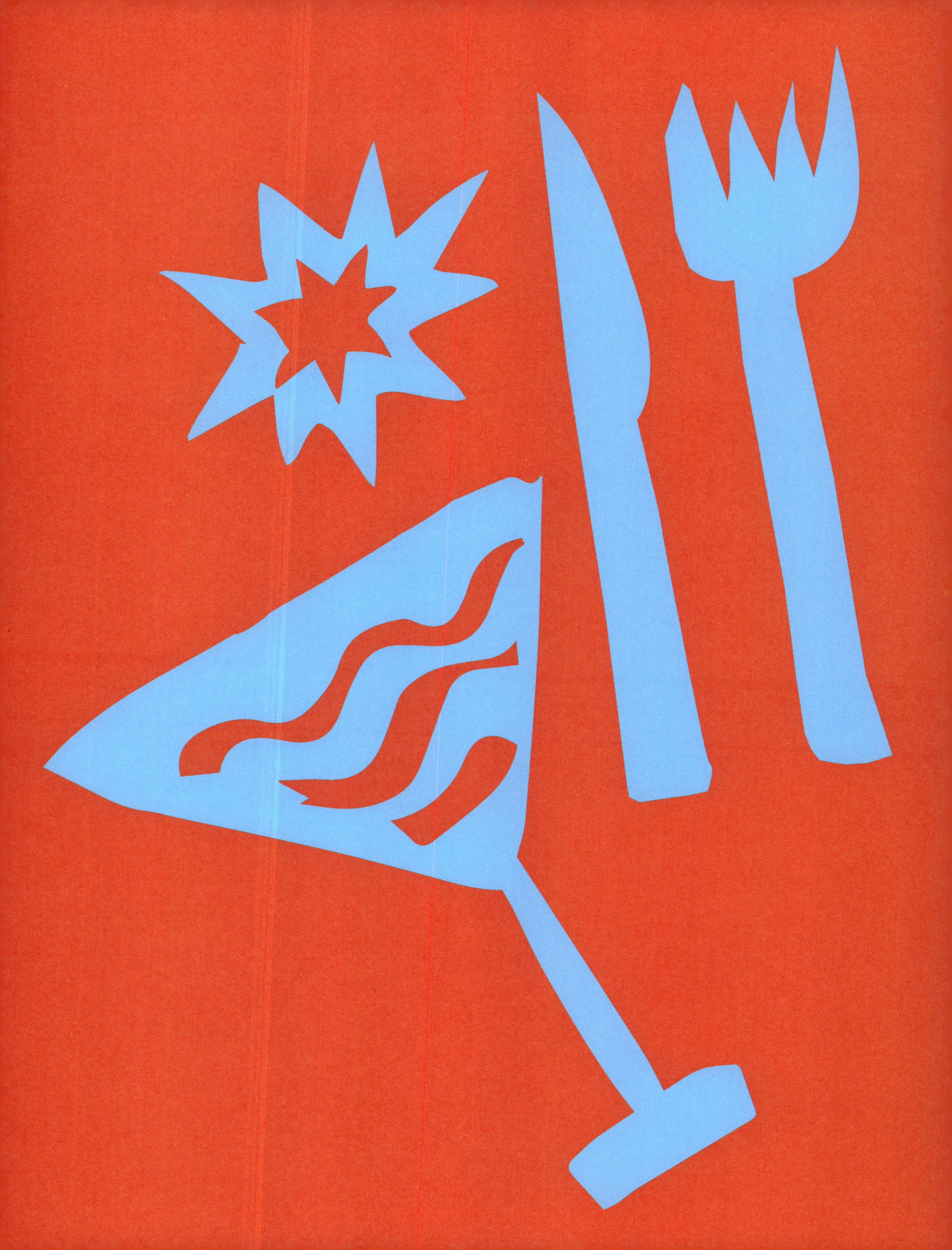

FOOD & DRINK

FOOD & DRINK

5	STRING CHEESE, CHORIZO, MEZCAL AND GRASSHOPPERS
6	SAMPLE THE WORLD'S BEST BAKLAVA
8	CRAFT BEER PILGRIMAGE TO BANGALORE
10	FINE DINING WITH FORAGED FOODS AND TRADITIONAL TECHNIQUE
15	HIGH TEA IN PARADISE
18	EXPLORING BOHEMIAN BEER HISTORY
20	SIP AND SAMPLE WITH LOCALS AT A *BÀCARO*
25	DUBLIN'S SIGNATURE SPICE BAGS
26	SAVOURING AMERICAN BARBECUE

"A round or two of *cicheti* equals a cheap lunch, and what might start as a pre-dinner aperitivo can easily morph into the evening's main event."

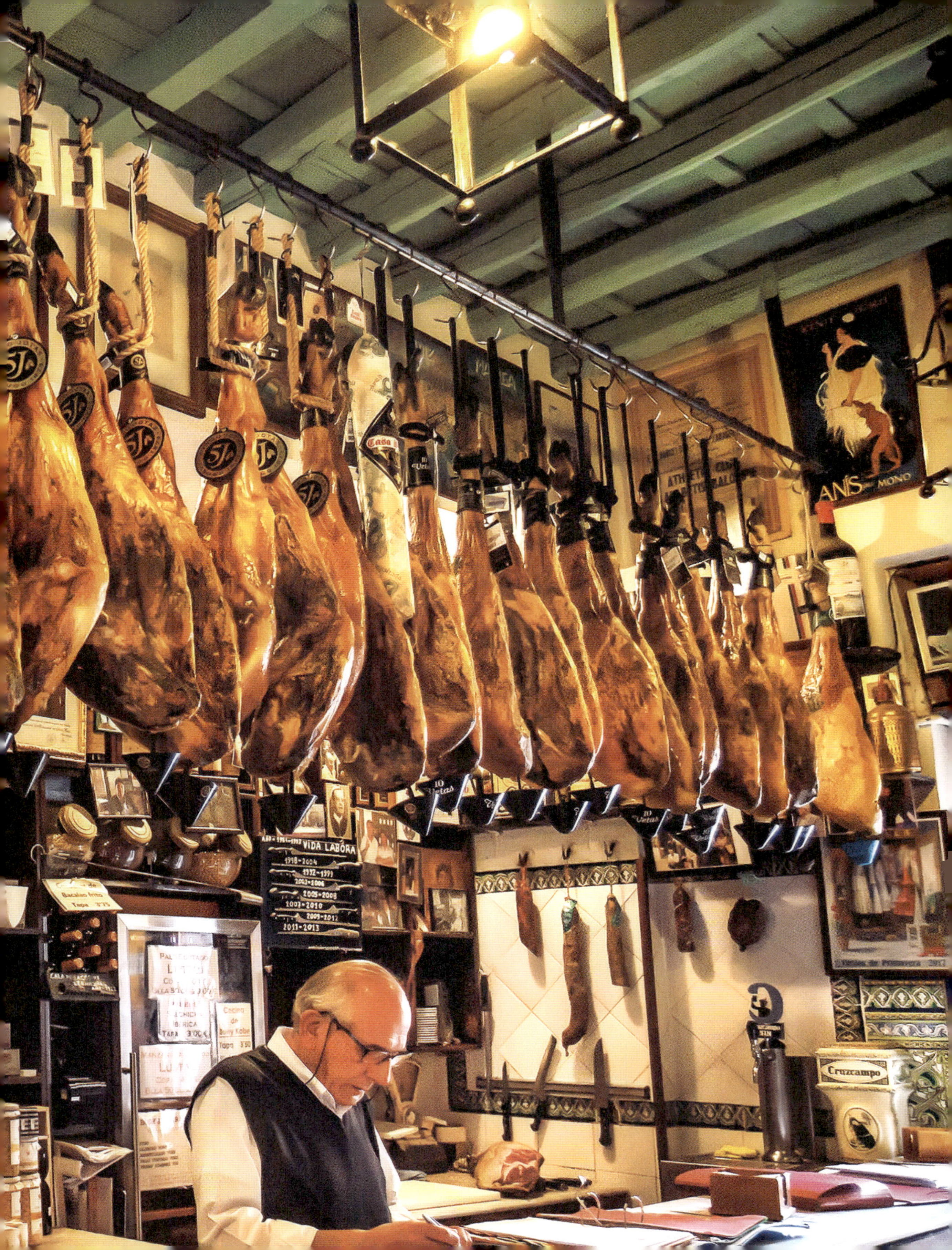
Cruzcampo

Mercado 20 de Noviembre has everything from grasshoppers to giant tortillas

CRISTINA ALONSO

STRING CHEESE, CHORIZO, MEZCAL AND GRASSHOPPERS

OAXACA MARKETS, MEXICO

Bustling, colourful, charming, sometimes a bit hectic and always delicious, the markets of Oaxaca encompass everything that makes this city so captivating. Exploring the aisles of the iconic Mercado 20 de Noviembre, located in the heart of the city, is much more than snagging a few cool souvenirs. Oaxaca's stunning crafts are true works of art, showcasing the talent of artisans who have inherited knowledge and skills accumulated over generations. Admire intricately woven wool rugs, beautiful pottery made with *barro negro* (black clay) and *alebrijes*, fantastic wooden creatures painted with excruciating detail.

And then, of course, there's the food. Look to your right and you'll spot mountains of freshly baked bread; to your left, there's *quesillo*, the state's incomparable string cheese. Keep walking, and you'll come across bottles and bottles of mezcal, Oaxaca's treasured agave spirit. See those baskets heaped with reddish insects? *Chapulines*. They're dried grasshoppers, and they are delicious.

You can sample all these delights and have a full breakfast or lunch at the market's many casual eateries or its legendary Pasillo de Humo. Smoke leads the way to the Pasillo de Humo, which translates to Smoke Hallway. A veritable heaven for meat lovers, this aisle is lined with stalls selling local specialties like *tasajo* (a thin cut of dried beef), *cecina* (salted, dried and sometimes spicy beef) and chorizo, fired up on the grill upon request. Once you have chosen the most tempting vendor, have a seat at one of the communal tables and place your order: a selection of meat plus sides like sliced avocado, grilled *nopales* (cactus paddles) and giant corn tortillas for DIY tacos.

BRETT ATKINSON

SAMPLE THE WORLD'S BEST BAKLAVA

GAZIANTEP, TÜRKIYE

Residents of Türkiye's biggest cities travel to Gaziantep just to eat. Flights back to İstanbul, Ankara and İzmir are full of travellers stuffing boxes of the world's best baklava – crammed with local *fistik* (pistachios) grown on the sunbaked plains of Mesopotamia – into the overhead lockers. The fragrant nuts are widely used in sweet and savoury dishes in the city, which combines the culinary influences of Türkiye and nearby Syria.

Due to an influx of migrants fleeing conflict – the Syrian city of Aleppo is 130km (81 miles) to the south – the influence of Gaziantep's close neighbour is strongly felt around the Irani bazaar neighbourhood. Before exploring Gaziantep's culinary highlights, a breakfast of Arabic coffee and flatbreads dipped in olive oil and the heady spice mix of za'atar is recommended.

Baklava from both Gulluoglu and Imam Cagdas is renowned across Türkiye and the Middle East, while Katmerci Murat's skilled bakers turn out gossamer-light *katmer* crepes layered with chopped pistachios, sugar, and *kaymak*, an unctuous Turkish spin on clotted cream.

A popular local dish at Imam Cagdas is *ali nazik*, smoked and spiced eggplant topped with sauteed lamb, while southeastern Anatolia's famous fat-tailed sheep are made into charcoal-grilled kebabs at smoky spots all around the honey-coloured old town.

Of course, a local variation incorporates the region's superb *fistik*. When the sun sets, wood-fired ovens dispense charred *lahmacun*, a pizza-like flatbread best enjoyed rolled up with fresh herbs and topped with lemon juice and a chilli hit from spicy Aleppo pepper.

SUPPORT LOCAL PRODUCERS AND COOK UP A STORM

Sylvia Athanasopoulou

Whenever I visit a new place, I love to explore the local food market. It's a great way to better understand the culture and everyday life of the local community. The best time to visit a neighbourhood food market is early morning to beat the crowds and interact with local farmers and vendors one-on-one. I usually wander around the stalls sampling regional delicacies and am always open to trying new and unfamiliar foods.

This is a wonderful chance to observe, smell and taste fresh fruits, cheeses, bread, honey and other specialties. And by buying from in-town farmers and producers, I can be sure that I am supporting the local economy.

Mouth-watering baklava on display

JULIAN TOMPKIN

CRAFT BEER PILGRIMAGE TO BANGALORE

BANGALORE, INDIA

Bangalore is known by many guises: the larger-than-life megacity; the traffic riddle; the cradle of cosmopolitan and culinary delights. But this futuristic metropolis – commonly cited as the Silicon Valley of India – has also emerged in recent years as the undisputed pub and craft beer capital of India. And in a nation of beer devotees, that is quite the achievement.

Craft beer's rise worldwide has been as staggering as it has been delicious, spearheaded by the resurgence of the India Pale Ale (IPA). While fashioned in the 1700s out of necessity – heavily hopped to help withstand the arduous journey from Britain to India by sea, as well as the heat – the style was 'rediscovered' in California in the 1980s. By the early 2000s the style had become the leading craft cult classic, setting the tone of the craft beer revolution to come.

Bangalore has been a natural inheritor of the craft beer renaissance in India: a vital trading centre with a huge professional population that lives at the coalface of contemporary Indian culture. Officially known as Bengaluru, the city is now India's third most populous and, with a year-round daily average temperature of around 25°C (77°F), it's blessed with perfect beer-drinking weather.

Depending on who you ask, Bangalore is home to around 80 craft breweries – ranging from hole-in-the-wall haunts and pubs with a house brew or two, right through to serious craft brewing bastions where everything on tap is brewed on site. What's certain is the once-ubiquitous reign of Kingfisher has been expelled for good here; in its place an artisan scene like no other in the country or region has emerged.

BANGALORE BREWING BRILLIANCE

* **Arbor Brewing Company:** The logical starting point for any craft beer pilgrimage in Bangalore is Magrath Rd, home to the storied Arbor Brewing Company. While billing itself as 'India's first American craft brewery', the beers on offer here marry the hallmarks of the American revival with the scintillating senses of India and the world beyond. A must-try tipple at the vanguard of flavour is the Smooth Criminal spiced ale, living up to its dapper moniker with a deceptive 8 per cent alcohol by volume (ABV) and accented with lavender, honey and the supple creaminess of oats.

* **Mannheim Brewery:** A short stroll down the street, the Mannheim Brewery perfectly articulates the heady olio (and sometimes apparent contradiction) that is contemporary Bangalore – a traditional German-style brewhouse situated in a modern Indian shopping mall. Under the somewhat irreverent motto of 'no crap on tap', the Tamarind Chilli Sour is a tangy twist on the Berliner Weisse style, with the telltale sweet/sour tang of tamarind, turbocharged with a tank full of red chillies.

* **The Toit:** For true acolytes of the IPA style, however, the Toit, in the discerning district of Indiranagar, is perhaps the most revered of all the paeans to the pint: an IPA made in the traditional British style of the 18th century, with generous lashings of hops, supple malt sweetness and the sort of low carbonation you would expect of an old British boozery. And while Toit treasures the past it also looks to the future with its Basmati rice blond pilsner that's a proud nod to the totemic flavours of the city that never sleeps.

Toit Brewpub in Indiranagar

BRETT ATKINSON

FINE DINING WITH FORAGED FOODS AND TRADITIONAL TECHNIQUE

LIMA, PERU

With four of the World's 50 Best Restaurants for 2023 – more than both Tokyo and New York – the Peruvian capital of Lima is an overachiever in global cuisine. Bold and experimental chefs are reinterpreting traditional Peruvian flavours; decades-old blends of cultures reinforce culinary fusions unique to Lima; and indigenous and seasonal ingredients foraged sustainably in the Andes and the Amazon are harnessed for thrillingly creative menus.

At Isolina's corner location in the raffish Barranco neighbourhood, chef José del Castillo's comfort food reinventions of traditional *comida criolla* (Creole cuisine) dishes blending indigenous Peruvian and Spanish influences are wildly popular with Limeño locals. There are usually queues on Saturdays and Sundays, so book ahead online or visit on a Monday or Tuesday. Isolina's rustic version of the traditional Peruvian dish ceviche is one of Lima's best, filling an overflowing bowl with citrus-cured fish, giant cobs of corn and sweet potato. Merging Peruvian and Cantonese influences in a hearty and spicy stir-fry, del Castillo's *lomo saltado* is a tribute to the simple Chifa restaurants he ate in when he was young. A short walk away in Barranco's historic 1870s Berninzon Mansion, Ayahuasca is a cocktail bar offering elevated tributes to authentic Peruvian flavours, including punchy pisco sour cocktails, shrimp empanadas and *anticuchos*, skewers of grilled beef heart traditionally served as a street snack.

Lima's food scene is a fusion of cultures and flavours

Top: Isolina is located in Lima's trendy Barranco neighbourhood

Bottom: *Causa a la limeña* is a typical Peruvian entrée of white meat encased in potato

FINE DINING WITH FORAGED FOODS AND TRADITIONAL TECHNIQUE

Lima's other culinary fusion is Nikkei cuisine, which blends Japanese influences with Pacific seafood and indigenous Peruvian ingredients like punchy *aji* chillies. Japanese migration to Peru began in the late 19th century, driven by work on sugar-cane plantations, and now Peru has the second-largest Japanese population in South America after Brazil. Developing from humble beginnings, Nikkei fusion is now a highlight of dining in Lima. Regarded as Lima's best Nikkei restaurant, Maido took the number four spot in the World's 50 Best Restaurants list for 2023, and chef Mitsuharu Tsumura's elegant 10- and 14-course tasting menus include surprises like *nigiris a lo pobre* (gossamer-thin Angus beef served with a quail egg injected with ponzu). Reservations can be difficult to secure, so a recommended backup is Fan, an approachable neighbourhood spot in leafy Miraflores. Shared plates include dumplings with truffle oil and parmesan chips, and tempura tacos topped with seared bonito tuna.

Judged the World's Best Restaurant in 2023, Lima's Central is masterminded by chef Virigilio Martinez. Twelve-course tasting menus covering Peru's diverse ecosystems harness seafood from the Pacific coast, foraged Amazonian forest herbs and tubers and root plants sourced sustainably high in the Andes. Kjolle, upstairs from Central, is more affordable and equally interesting, helmed by Martinez's wife, Pía León, and judged number 28 in the World's Top 50 in 2023.

To taste Lima's culinary future, secure a spot overlooking the open kitchen at Mérito where former Central chef Juan Luis Martínez (no relation) crafts surprising menus grounded in Peruvian ingredients and his Venezuelan roots. Seemingly simple but delivering complex flavours, his smoke-infused barbecued corn is served with a creamy dipping sauce laced with chilli.

Sipping on ceylon

JULIAN TOMPKIN

HIGH TEA IN PARADISE

NUWARA ELIYA, SRI LANKA

'You had better pack a scarf,' my Colombo host said with a mischievous grin. 'It gets chilly up there. Who knows, maybe this year you will get snow?' It was a comment that stayed with me as we began the five-hour drive east into the belly of Sri Lanka, and then upwards towards the knot of grey clouds that my guide informed me would only part for a perfectly brewed pot of tea.

While home to seven tea-growing districts, Nuwara Eliya is perhaps the most chimerical – a region that, for good or bad, has earned the colloquial moniker of 'Little England' due to its quaintness and affinity with the Brit's favourite beverage.

The first thing that strikes you on stepping out of the *tuk tuk* and into Pedro Tea Estate is the verdant growth – the tightly packed hedges of tea all glossy under a light rain. I picked a large and luscious leaf and crushed it between my fingers: its distinct aroma was immediate on the nose, albeit with a herbaceous hint of the tropics. As a lifelong tea drinker it felt more like a pilgrimage than a holiday, a chance to follow the prized bronze specks of my teapot back to the source, here high in the tablelands of one of the world's most fascinating countries.

Pedro Tea Estate is open to visitors year-round, offering tours of the factory and the plantations with a detailed tasting at the conclusion of the tour. Founded in 1885 and heralded by many as the 'champagne' of Sri Lankan tea, Pedro is also a place to get first-hand experience of tea harvesting, mingling with workers as they pluck leaves and place them neatly into cane baskets.

Green tea plantations blanket the rolling hills of Nuwara Eliya

Opposite: Tea factory tour in Katukitula

HIGH TEA IN PARADISE

Jumping back into the *tuk tuk*, we took the winding roads to Mackwoods Tea Estate, fabled for both its tea and its quaint museum, where afterwards you can enjoy the produce of the plantation on the terrace overlooking the verdant and undulating landscape.

As afternoon arrived and the plantations shut for some midday respite, we made our way back to the historic and fittingly named Grand Hotel, where high tea was the order of the day – replete with coconut prawn skewers, vegetable curry puffs and scant a scone or cucumber sandwich in sight. The dedicated tea sommelier approached the table with an encyclopaedic menu of Sri Lanka's finest, both natural and flavoured. 'Take your time,' he advised. 'Tea does not grow in a hurry.'

STEEPED IN HISTORY: THE STORY OF SRI LANKAN TEA

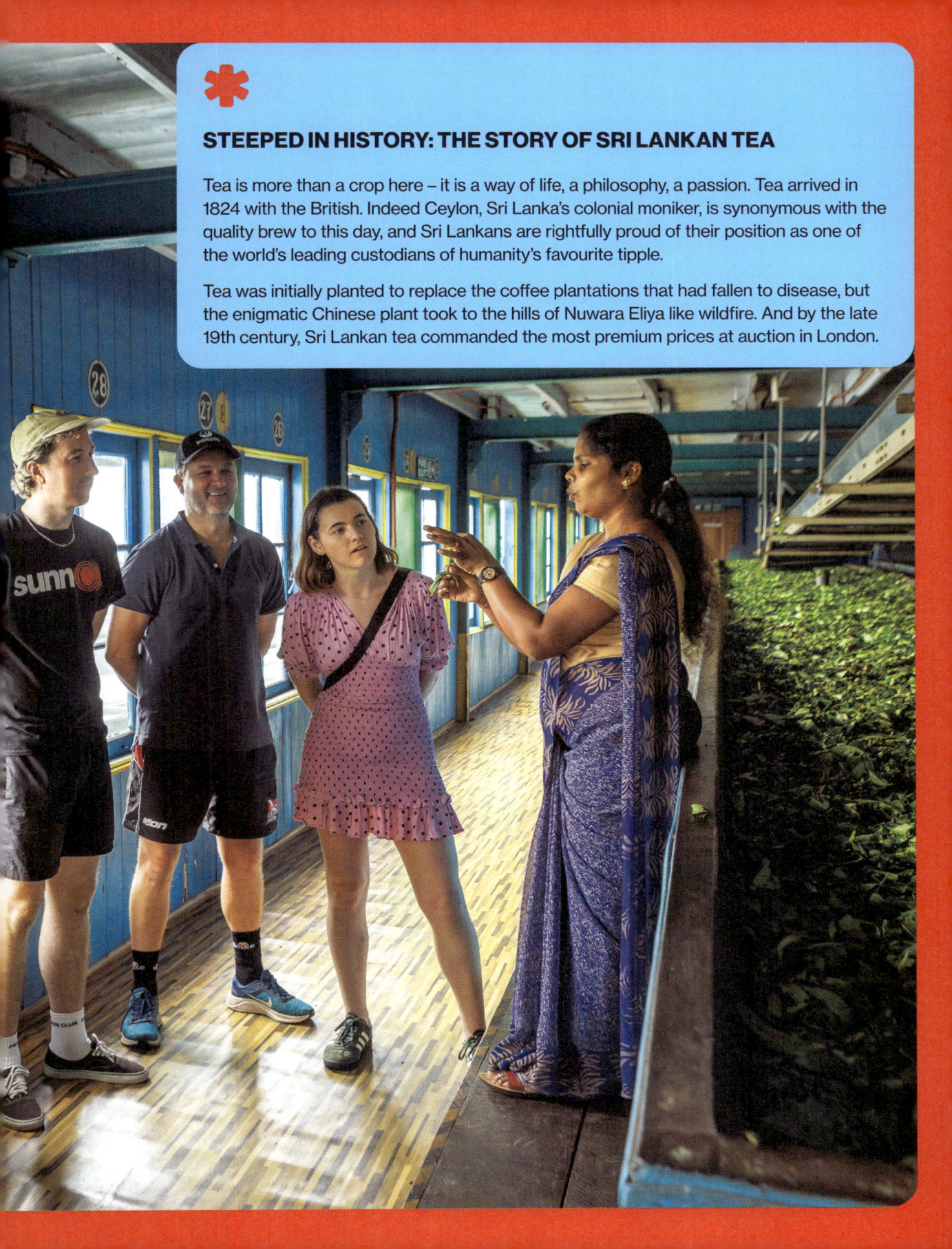

Tea is more than a crop here – it is a way of life, a philosophy, a passion. Tea arrived in 1824 with the British. Indeed Ceylon, Sri Lanka's colonial moniker, is synonymous with the quality brew to this day, and Sri Lankans are rightfully proud of their position as one of the world's leading custodians of humanity's favourite tipple.

Tea was initially planted to replace the coffee plantations that had fallen to disease, but the enigmatic Chinese plant took to the hills of Nuwara Eliya like wildfire. And by the late 19th century, Sri Lankan tea commanded the most premium prices at auction in London.

BRETT ATKINSON

EXPLORING BOHEMIAN BEER HISTORY

PLZEN AND CESKE BUDEJOVICE, CZECHIA

Enjoyed from Manhattan to Mongolia and Tokyo to Tashkent, golden-hued pilsners are the world's most popular beers. The style originated over 180 years ago in the Czech city of Plzen in 1842. Back then, Plzen was known as Pilsen and was a German-speaking city in the Kingdom of Bohemia in the Hapsburg-ruled Austrian Empire.

Before 1842, beer quality from scores of local breweries was inconsistent and mediocre, so the canny people of Pilsen pooled their experience and capital to establish a single municipal brewery, harnessing the latest in 19th-century brewing technology. The results were spectacular, and the crisp pale lager that Bavarian brewmaster Josef Groll created was dubbed Pilsner Urquell (Pilsen's Original Source). It's now one of the world's best and most imitated beers.

The brewery that put Pilsen on the map is still entered through an imposing stone gate dating from 1842. Guided tours of the brewery include a descent into underground tunnels hewn into western Bohemian rock. Here, the refreshing golden beverage is fermented and 'lagered' (stored at a cool temperature) in wooden barrels. After sampling delicious *netfiltrovany pivo* (unfiltered beer) served straight from the barrel, you can continue exploring a 500m (1640ft) section of Plzen's 11km (7 miles) subterranean labyrinth dating back to the 14th century. An alternative tour focusing more on Plzen's underground is also on offer.

From the brewery, it's a 900m (0.5-mile) walk south to Plzen's Brewery Museum. Check out centuries of brewing history, including the momentous occasion in 1838 when Pilsen's residents decided to pour all the city's inferior beer down the drain – right in front of Municipal Hall – and make the decision to fund a new brewery. Adjacent to the museum is Na Parkanu, a century-old beer hall where unfiltered and unpasteurised Pilsner Urquell is also served straight from the tank.

Historical brewery Pilsner Urquell, established in 1842

Over 180 years after the brewery's inception, Plzen is now home to contemporary craft breweries. Hoppy hotspots include the hip Pivovar Raven, while at the Purkmistr Brewery, there's the opportunity to take it easy in their onsite beer spa. Relaxing treatments include bathing in hop-laden waters and receiving massages infused with soothing hop oil.

From Plzen, it's 133km (83 miles) southeast to Ceske Budejovice, the second of Bohemia's famous beer cities. Named Budweis when it was a German-speaking region up until 1945, it's home to the original Budweiser beer. Immigrants to the United States co-opted the town's German name to launch Budweiser beer in the US in 1876. Still, the original brew using hops from the nearby Saaz region and Moravian malt is far superior. Ceske Budejovice's beers are now sold internationally under the Budvar label – ironically marketed as Czechvar in the US – and are best experienced on a brewery tour and in the city's popular Budvarka beer hall. Tours are not as historic as Pilsner Urquell, but tastings do include Budvar's Tmavy Lezak, a moreish dark lager brewed with roasted malts. It's a historic throwback to the time before 1842 when Bohemian beers were darker and more robust than Josef Groll's golden, world-dominating pilsner.

CRISTIAN BONETTO

SIP AND SAMPLE WITH LOCALS AT A *BÀCARO*

VENICE, ITALY

Venetians love a tipple. Even at 11am, with our market totes bulging with winter radicchio or blushing summer peaches, one of my cousins will invariably ask, *Ci fermiamo qui?* (Shall we stop here?). The 'here' in question is a *bàcaro* (plural: *bàcari*), Venice's version of the Spanish tapas bar. Scattered across the city, these convivial pit stops are usually packed with that most elusive of Venetian creatures: locals. Some sip a spritz, others an *ombra* (small glass of house wine).

I opted for a full glass of something nicer – perhaps a local Soave or Valpolicella. We all lined our stomachs with *cicheti*, Venetian-style tapas, for which the *bàcari* are famous. Scan the glass counter for the day's pickings: anything from toothpick-speared olive *ascolane* (deep-fried stuffed olives) to pancetta-wrapped local shrimps. Most have *crostini*, diminutive open sandwiches laden with fabulous combinations: burrata, fig and prosciutto crudo; ricotta and truffle honey; gorgonzola and anchovies. Seasonal produce commonly dictates the offerings, with year-round standards including *baccalà mantecato*, a local classic of whipped salted cod cooked for me by my nonna, Nori. A round or two of *cicheti* equals a cheap lunch, and what might start as a pre-dinner *aperitivo* can easily morph into the evening's main event. For me, this is often the case on Cannaregio's Fondamenta dei Ormesini, a canal-side street awash with *bàcari* and the vino-fuelled bonhomie of local students, artists and in-the-know travellers. Bar hop or find a favourite and settle in for banter and a *brindisi* (toast).

VENICE *BÀCARI* HITLIST

* **Cantine del Vino già Schiavi:** Canal-fronting bar famed for its highly creative crostini toppings.

* **All'Arco:** Top-quality cicheti made with produce from the nearby Rialto Market.

* **Osteria Al Cicheto:** Close to the train station, a snug wine bar obsessed with artisan produce and vino.

* **Vino Vero:** Hip Cannaregio wine bar serving natural wines and quality bites.

* **Cantina do Mori:** Time-warped tavern reputedly frequented by Giacomo Casanova.

Venetian *cicheti* delights

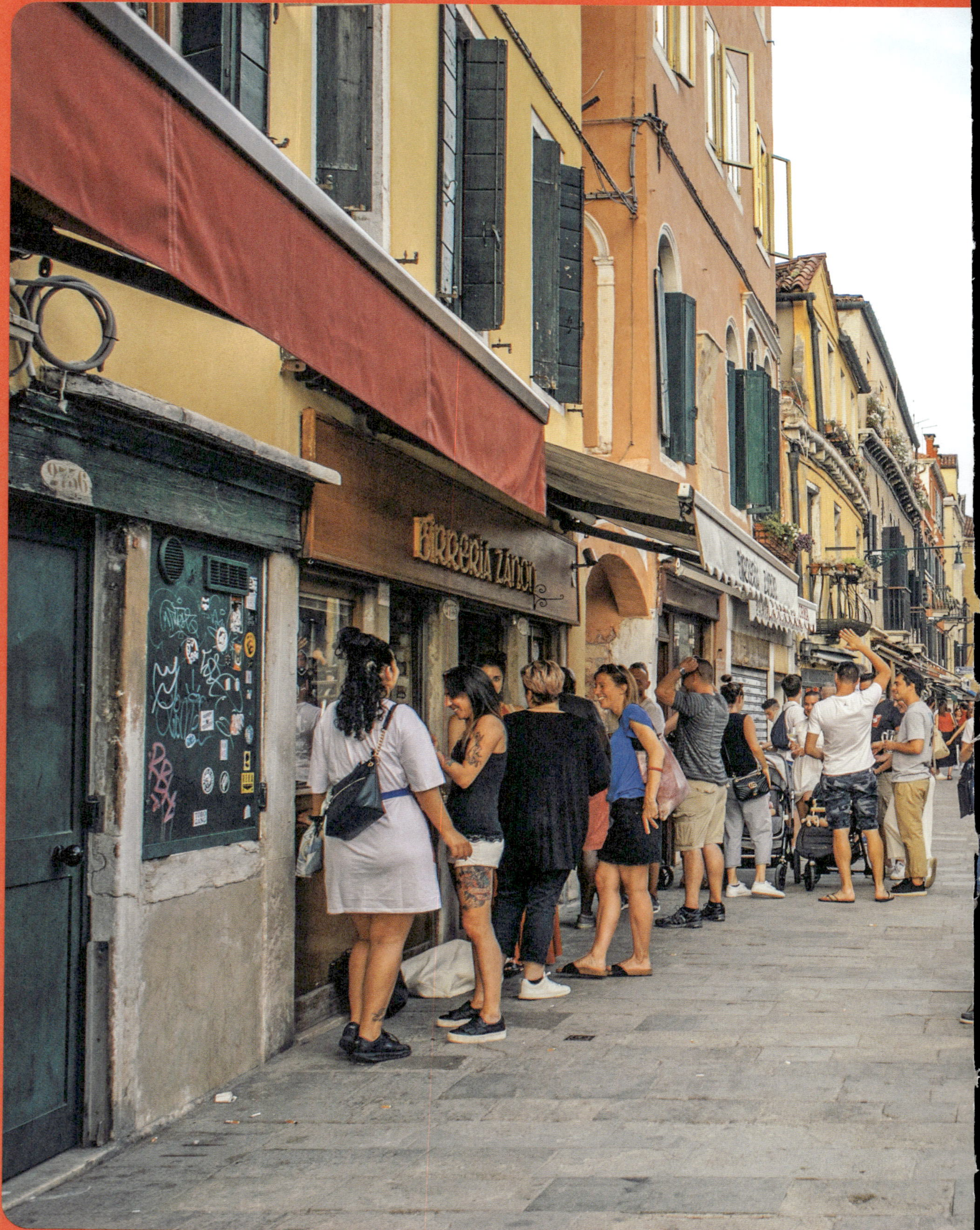
BIRRERIA ZANON

Venice canal dining

OTHER IRISH DELICACIES

Megan Cuthbert

- **Dublin Coddle:** Originating during a period of food shortages in the 1700s, when any available scraps and leftovers were thrown into a pot, Dublin coddle takes its name from the French term *caudle*, meaning to boil softly. Most Dublin families have their own unique recipe for coddle, but this rustic salty stew generally consists of pork sausages, rashers, potatoes, carrots, and onion. John Kavanagh – The Gravediggers (1 Prospect Sq, Dublin 9) serves up one of the best coddles you'll find in a Dublin pub, complete with slices of traditional Dublin batch loaf bread.

- **Barmbrack:** A sweet Halloween tradition, Barmbrack (*báirín breac* in Gaelic) is a rich, round tea loaf filled with plump raisins, sultanas, currants and other surprises. Typically, a gold ring wrapped in paper is baked into the brack. Legend has it, the person who finds the ring in their slice of brack will marry within a year or can look forward to other good luck. In the weeks leading up to 31 October, you'll find barmbrack on supermarket and bakery shelves all over Ireland. Happy hunting.

- **Soda Bread:** Slathered in butter, heaped with jam or dunked in Irish stew, soda bread is an Irish staple. Traditionally made using flour, buttermilk, bicarbonate of soda plus a pinch of sugar and salt, soda bread has a distinctive look (round with a deep cross cut through the centre – said to let the fairies out before baking and to bring good luck) and a unique flavour (light and slightly tangy).

- **Irish Coffee:** Reportedly invented by Joe Sheridan, a chef at Foynes Airport in Limerick on a chilly night in 1943 to welcome passengers from a cancelled New York flight, an Irish Coffee is a warm and comforting alcoholic drink that mixes coffee, Irish whiskey, sugar and cream. Enjoy after a meal, sip slowly by an open fire or for a twist on the original, pull up a seat at Bang Bang Bar in Teeling Whiskey Distillery (13-17 Newmarket, Dublin 8) where they serve a specially created 'Dublin Coffee'.

Spice bag from Xi'an Street Food, Dublin

FIONA HILLIARD

DUBLIN'S SIGNATURE SPICE BAGS

DUBLIN, IRELAND

A flavour-packed amalgamation of Dublin's best-loved takeaway dishes, the spice bag generally consists of chips, chillies, red and green peppers, onion and crispy chicken strips, all seasoned with a special mix of Chinese spices and heaped into a sturdy paper bag.

As typical Dublin delicacies go, the spice bag is a relatively recent newcomer, thought to have originated in 2010 as a signature speciality of Sunflower Chinese, a takeaway located in the Dublin suburb of Templeogue. When word got around about the spicy mash-up of chicken, chips and oriental flavours, other takeaways and restaurants across the city began creating their own variations. Since then, the dish has gone mainstream, appearing on just about every Chinese restaurant and takeaway menu in Dublin.

Each takeaway and restaurant puts its own unique spin on the original – some replace chopped onions with vibrant scallions, others favour sliced red and green chillies over chunky peppers, plus there are varying levels of actual spiciness (many lean more towards an aromatic Chinese Five Spice flavour).

For me, Xi'an Street Food on South Anne St serves one of the best versions in the city. Featuring shredded strips of chicken, chips, chillies and their own distinctive blend of chilli salt and pepper, it certainly delivers on its hot and spicy promise. The restaurant also offers a tasty vegan and vegetarian spice bag that mixes its spice-laden chips with deep-fried tofu and veggie balls. X'ian Street Food welcomes both eat-in and takeout diners.

ANDREW COLLINS

SAVOURING AMERICAN BARBECUE

TENNESSEE, MISSOURI AND TEXAS, USA

Americans have *feelings* about barbecue – about how it's smoked, which meats are used, what side dishes are offered and, above all else, the ingredients of sauces and seasonings. Three of the country's unofficial capitals of barbecue are Memphis, Kansas City and all of Texas.

As a longstanding culinary tradition, barbecue comes in countless variations, but it typically entails slow smoking over an indirect flame using fragrant fuels like hickory, cherry wood and applewood. Barbecue in the US can be traced directly to the Indigenous inhabitants of the Caribbean, who taught their techniques to European colonists. Some devotees argue that using any meat other than pork isn't truly barbecue at all. Less fundamentalist adherents use the word barbecue to describe any grilling – from turkey legs to portobello mushrooms – over an open flame (this is utter blasphemy to purists, however).

In Texas, barbecue tends to emphasise beef, especially dry-rubbed brisket and beef-pork sausages (or hot links), both of which reflect the state's prominent German heritage. The open-pit smoking is often over aromatic mesquite or pecan wood, and sauces are usually tomato-based in eastern Texas and molasses-based elsewhere. The famed Salt Lick BBQ in Driftwood boasts that its barbecue sauce, which traces back to the family settling in Texas in the 1860s, 'won't burn or become bitter' because it contains no tomatoes. German potato salad, mac and cheese and black-eyed peas are popular Texan sides.

'Everybody comes for the brisket and our giant beef ribs,' says Shawn Lindsey, of Black's Barbecue in Lockhart, which has been family-owned since 1932. 'But they also love our sausages – we hand-make them, using a very old technology called a water stuffer, which results in a looser, coarser grind.' Having devoured more than my share of thick, U-shaped sausages at Black's over the years, I recommend the jalapeño-cheddar variety. They're great with a side of Norma Jean's baked beans. 'She's my great aunt,' adds Lindsey. 'Norma Jean also came up with the recipes for our sauces.'

The ultimate destination for blues music, Memphis is a laid-back Tennessee city also known for smoked barbecue pork ribs, served either dry (coated in sweet-and-hot spice rub) or wet (slathered with a gooey molasses- or brown-sugar–infused tomato-based sauce). Order your ribs 'half and half' to try both versions. Central Barbecue is a standout for wet ribs, while Charlie Vergos's Rendezvous excels with the dry version. The founder of this 1948 institution based the dry rub seasoning on his dad's Greek chilli recipe. Kansas City embraces a somewhat similar approach to barbecue, but the regional specialty there is burnt ends, the fatty, smoked parts of brisket. Try this heady dish at Arthur Bryant's Barbeque or Gates BBQ, which is also the city's longest-running (since 1946) Black-owned restaurant.

Serving up at Charlie Vergos's Rendezvous in Memphis, Tennessee

Beale Street, Memphis

BLUES
HALL
Have a
Coke
I AM
MEMPHIS
MLK
50
A. Schwab
ESTABLISHED 1876
B B King Blvd
POLICE

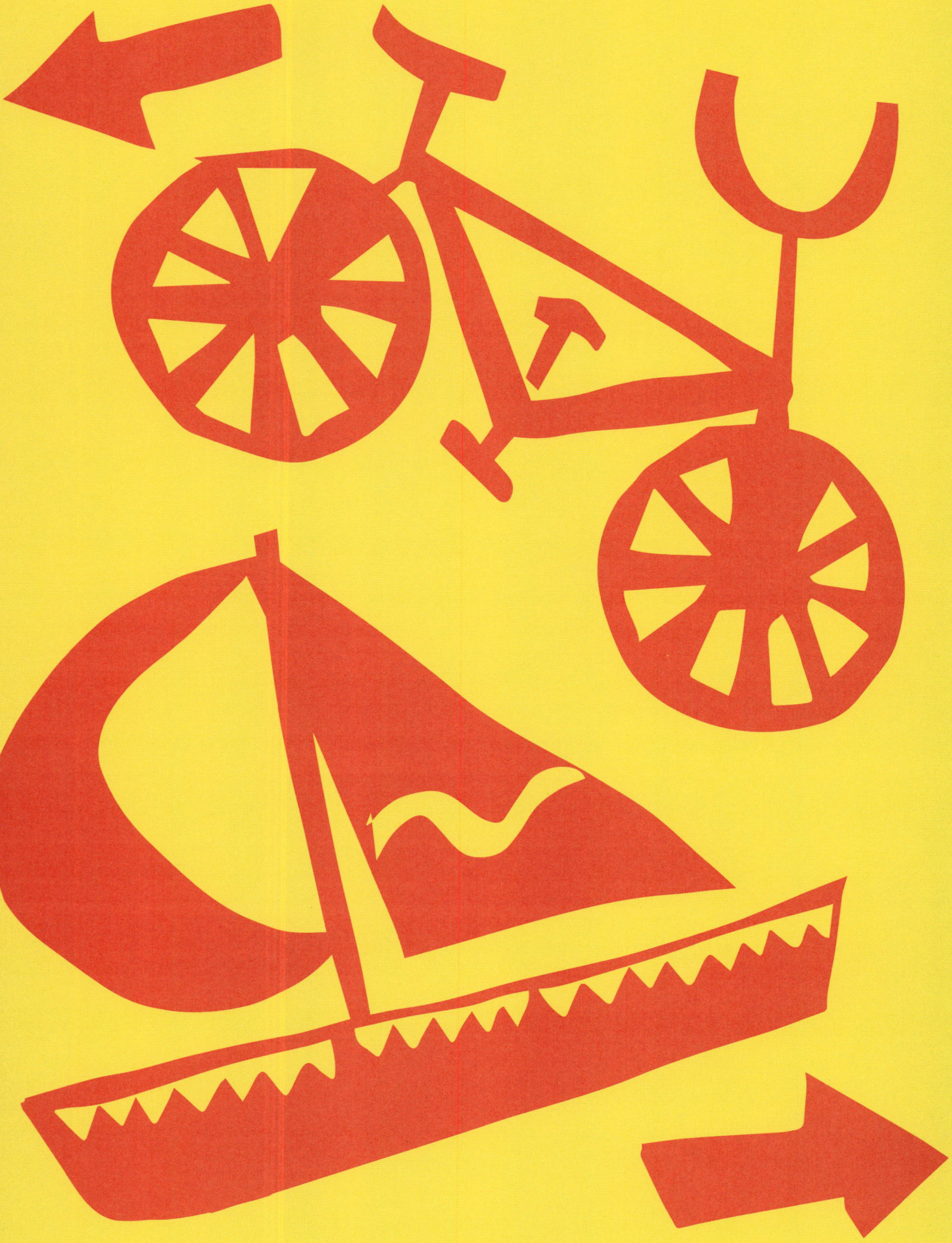

ACTIVITIES & SPORTS

ACTIVITIES & SPORTS

35   SEA SWIMMING AT FORTY FOOT
36   CANOEING THE LAHN RIVER
39   SOWETO BY BIKE
40   SAIL THE DALMATIAN ISLANDS
42   SNORKELLING IN REMOTE ISLANDS
46   WATCH A BASEBALL GAME
49   THE BIG WAVES OF NAZARÉ
50   WATCHING SUMO

"We were greeted in the small harbour by a man fanning the flames of an open fire with a sheet cut from an olive oil tin – the heady scent of sardine and swordfish grilling upon the twigs of cypress."

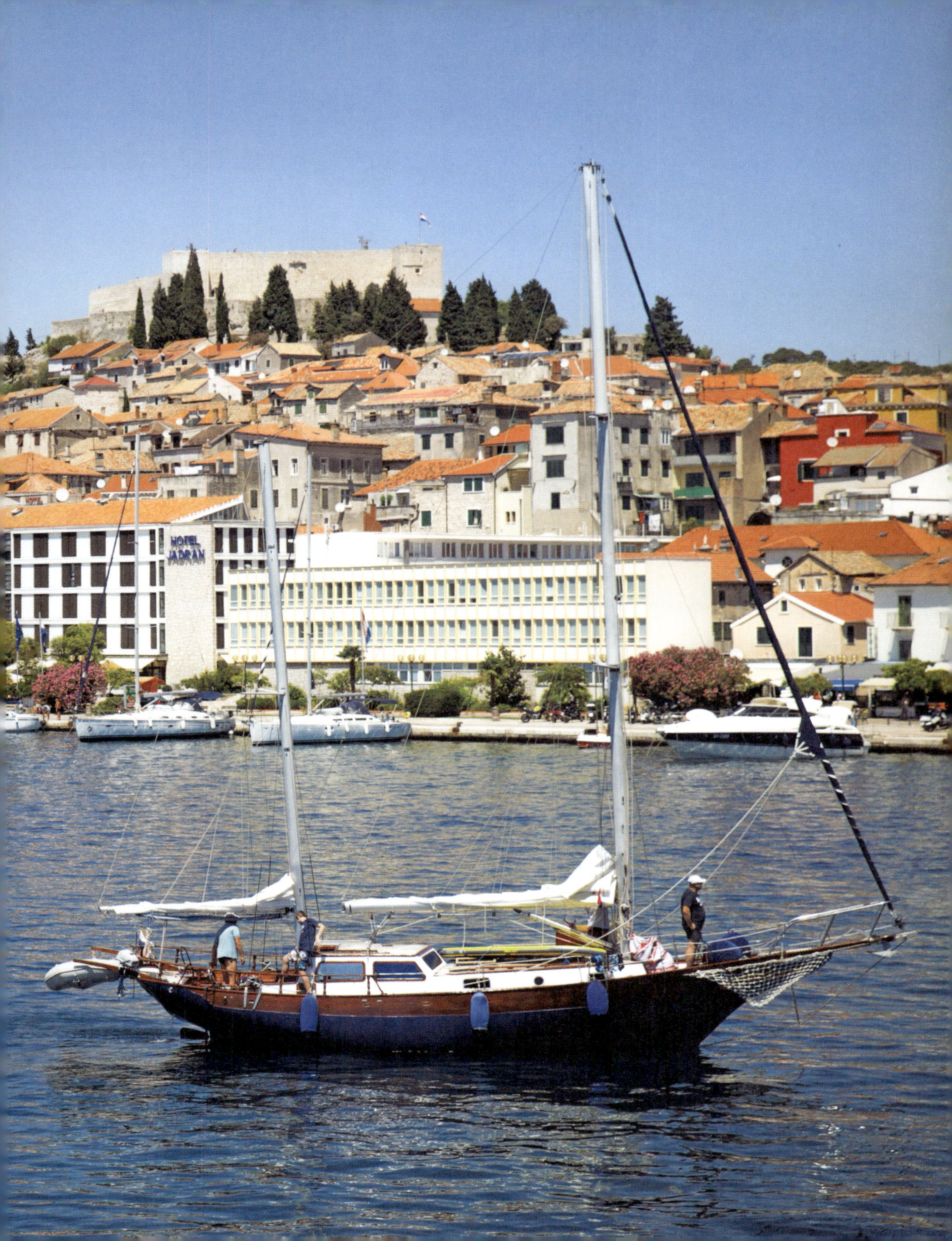
HOTEL
JADRAN

Join the locals and take the plunge at the Forty Foot in Sandycove

FIONA HILLIARD

SEA SWIMMING AT FORTY FOOT

DUBLIN, IRELAND

A 35-minute DART ride from Dublin takes you to the seaside village of Sandycove, where the Forty Foot bathing spot has been attracting sea swimmers for over 250 years.

Located next to Sandycove Beach, on the southern tip of Dublin Bay, and taking its name from the Fortieth Foot Regiment once stationed in the nearby battery, a dip in the Forty Foot is one of Dublin's most invigorating experiences, serving up craic ('good fun') and cold-water benefits in equal measure. Then, of course, there's the scenic view of Dublin Bay and its salty soup of seaweed-clad rocks, iconic Poolbeg Chimneys and even Howth on the opposite side of the bay – it really is unique.

Hardy locals and recent sea swimming converts take the plunge from sunrise to sunset all year round. The Christmas Day swim is a longstanding Dublin tradition, but the Irish Sea's teeth-chattering winter temperatures can be an acquired taste.

Back on dry land and just a two-minute stroll uphill is the James Joyce Tower and Museum, where you can find out how Joyce put the Forty Foot on the literary map with his novel *Ulysses* and learn more about the author through a series of self-guided exhibits and by chatting with friendly and knowledgeable local volunteers. Entrance to the museum is free, but donations are welcomed.

For hand-warming tea, coffee and something sweet nearby, I'd recommend Hatch Coffee in Glasthule or Sandycove Store and Yard – two easygoing spaces where you can sit in or order to go.

ROSANNA DUTSON

CANOEING THE LAHN RIVER

MARBURG, GERMANY

Travel by paddle – it's a popular pastime in Germany for both locals and tourists, especially since motorboats are not permitted on many of the country's rivers and lakes. It makes for a serene, slow journey through picturesque countryside.

Over six sunny August days, a friend and I travelled 160km (99 miles) down the Lahn River in a canoe. The route begins near Marburg, an hour's drive north of Frankfurt, but you can set off from any of the nine starting points along the river. A short induction from the tour operator ensures paddlers of all experiences are prepared, and then you're off.

For us, it was the ideal way to travel – everything was on our terms, with the ability to slow down and soak in the atmosphere or forge ahead. There are plenty of accommodation options along the river, the best of them (in our opinion) being the wallet-friendly riverside campgrounds, where you can pull up your canoe, pitch your tent and wander over to the nearest *Lokal* (pub) for a well-deserved beer.

The river carried us to charming towns we'd never heard of, and in the evenings we explored sites like historic Runkel Castle or the baroque town of Weilburg. The highlight, though, was the *Schleusen* (locks), which we needed to operate manually to move the water level up and down to move on to the next section. Built during the Industrial Revolution to maintain the river, nowadays they're mainly used for small trade and tourism and represent a series of checkpoints along the canoeing map.

Limburg Cathedral on the Lahn River

All skill levels are welcome on this cycling tour

MANDY ALDERSON

SOWETO BY BIKE

SOWETO, SOUTH AFRICA

Soweto, from the words 'South Western Township', is southwest of Johannesburg. This vibrant community holds stories and lessons best learned from its streets. One street in particular, Vilakazi St, was home to not one but two Nobel Peace Prize winners: Nelson Mandela and Bishop Desmond Tutu. There's no better way to get to the heart of Soweto than by bike. You'll find the welcome is warm, the community is strong and the past and present unite in the form of hope for the future.

There's something special about seeing the world from the seat of a bike. Even a non-cyclist like me can appreciate that. All skill levels are welcome, and with the help of the energetic and passionate team from Lebos Backpackers in Orlando West, you'll soon be cruising the backstreets, soaking up tastes, sights, sounds and history, learning from local guides who have grown up in these very neighbourhoods. And if cycling is not your thing, then colourful *tuk-tuks* (yep, in Soweto) are also on offer. You'll hear the stories of freedom fighters and visit the Hector Pieterson Memorial, built to commemorate the lives lost during the student uprisings in 1976. Learn about the proud defeat of the apartheid regime and the challenges still faced by the community today.

Don't miss sampling a South Africa favourite: *braai* (barbecue) and *potjiekos* (stew cooked in cast-iron pots over a fire in a traditional outdoor kitchen) accompanied by a post-cycle drink under the trees in Lebos Backpackers's community courtyard.

JULIAN TOMPKIN

SAIL THE DALMATIAN ISLANDS

DALMATIA, CROATIA

It was almost dark as the boat pulled into Jelsa, an alluring village on the northern coast of the island of Hvar. While the island's eponymous capital has inherited a reputation as the boutique enclave of the party set in recent years, Jelsa remains beguilingly rustic: the Croatia of yesteryear, undisturbed by the hundreds of thousands of tourists who flock to Dalmatia each and every year. We were greeted in the small harbour by a man fanning the flames of an open fire with a sheet cut from an olive oil tin – the heady scent of sardine and swordfish grilling upon the twigs of cypress. 'Now you're really in Hrvatska,' the man exclaimed, referencing the country's official name and offering up a mixed plate of fish, grilled pork and tomatoes kissed by the most generous sunlight. He raised a towering bottle of ice-cold Karlovačko beer: *'Živjeli!'* ('Cheers!').

A few doors down a woman sold sacks of green figs with kaleidoscopic purple flesh under lamplight, along with plastic bottles of homemade *plavac mali* – a red wine indigenous to this region. She offered a small bouquet of lavender with the purchase – a 'blessing from paradise,' she said with a smile – and we returned to the boat to set out once more into the enigmatic waters of the Adriatic, pockmarked with flickering embers of Dalmatia's 79 islands and over 500 islets.

✱ VOYAGE THROUGH TIME

Dalmatia is an aquatic paradise like few others – an archipelago speckled with little-known Venetian-era villages, secret coves and the sort of cerulean blue waters that remain in your dreams long after you have left. And to truly uncover its treasures it is best explored by boat, with a range of offerings – from budget to boutique, public to private – operating from Split and Dubrovnik.

Banje Beach, Dubrovnik

The next day our boat – skippered by a Frenchman named Eric and accommodating 10 people – set its bow for the island of Korčula: its graceful old town rising like an apparition in the early morning light. Along with the locals enjoying breakfast in the cafes, we had the town to ourselves to wander. After taking lunch in a traditional *konoba* (tavern) we set sail for the enchanted blue water caves of Biševo, only accessible by boat – the refracted light within giving a sense that we were swimming towards the very heart of the earth.

The boat took sanctuary in Vis for the night and some of us decided to sleep on deck to enjoy its charmed harbour, shaped like an amphitheatre and fringed with traditional houses and fragrant pine trees. The morning was met with a swim at the secluded Stiniva Bay, which – save for one fisherman casting his net – we had entirely to ourselves.

Following a lunch of fresh-grilled squid on the boat, Eric took a poll: the island of Brač or Mljet? With its verdant hinterland, untouched lakes and ancient Benedictine monastery, Mljet won out and we set our course south-east, following the ancient trail of Odysseus – who, lore tells us, was entrapped unto the island's spell for seven years. On tasting the fabled olives, wine and traditional goat cheese in the village of Pomena, it all makes sense – an island of complete quietude, where the scent of cypress is omnipotent, and the small boats patter a hypnotic rhythm in the harbour. 'Where to next?' someone queried as the day made way for the stillest of nights. 'Anywhere,' Eric offered. 'You cannot make a wrong turn in Dalmatia.'

JULIAN TOMPKIN

SNORKELLING IN REMOTE ISLANDS

COCOS KEELING, AUSTRALIA

The plane landed at Christmas Island and the majority of passengers disembarked. While this is a stunning island replete with dream-state beaches and otherworldly fauna (none more iconic than the red crab, fabled for its mass migration), a few of us remained aboard. Then came the announcement: buckle up, next stop Cocos Keeling Islands.

Cocos Keeling is the sort of place that appears in the exclusive realm of the imagination – a coconut-palm-fringed South East Asian utopia that is actually part of Australia. Two postcard atolls composted of coral islets and home to two settlements, Home Island and West Island.

Predominately home to ethnic Malays with a population of around 600, West Island is the kernel of most island activity, with a range of eateries and simple but charming accommodation options. It is the island's southernmost point, however, that is the focus for most people – a stunning and dreamy lagoon where angelfish, dugongs and turtles frolic in the warm tropical waters amid the kaleidoscopic gallery of coral. The snorkelling here is easy and accessible and never disappointing.

UNDERWATER PARADISE

With its closest neighbour being Indonesia (the island of Sumatra is around 1000km (621 miles) away), Cocos Keeling sits roughly midway between Australia and Sri Lanka. It is home to one of the most expansive and protected marine sanctuaries on earth: nearly 500,000 sq km (193,000 sq mi) of unsullied waters, animated with life and awaiting exploration.

Over 500 species of sea critters call the sanctuary home, including manta rays, pygmy angelfish and dolphins.

Discover the *Catalina* wreck by snorkel

For the more intrepid explorer, however, Direction Island remains a once-in-a-lifetime destination – remote and staggeringly beautiful, with a few makeshift beach shacks being the only signs of civilisation. Ferries travel here twice per week – Thursdays and Saturdays – and visitors need to come prepared with supplies of food and water. Stepping into the sapphire-blue waters feels as though you are crossing into another realm – a prismatic explosion of hues. It is an unforgettable experience, albeit one that needs a decent level of fitness to navigate the strong currents.

As well as self-guided snorkelling, the island offers several scuba experiences for those wanting to descend deeper into this enigmatic underwater jungle. As we returned to shore, a member of the crew tended a small fire in one of the public barbecues that speckle the beach. While we were swimming he caught some endemic wahoo fish, and was now grilling them on kindling of palm and fern. It was a truly heady scent, and we enjoyed it straight from the fire with our hands – washed down with freshly harvested coconut water. Beyond the shore, the marine sanctuary was absolutely still – never betraying the majesty that lies beneath.

As the boat made its way back to West Island one of the crew offered up a plate of locally grown fruit, including pawpaw. 'I often feel jealous that we are not so popular as Bali or Phuket,' he said. 'But then I realise, this is a blessing. Cocos is a secret – Australia's very own heaven on earth.'

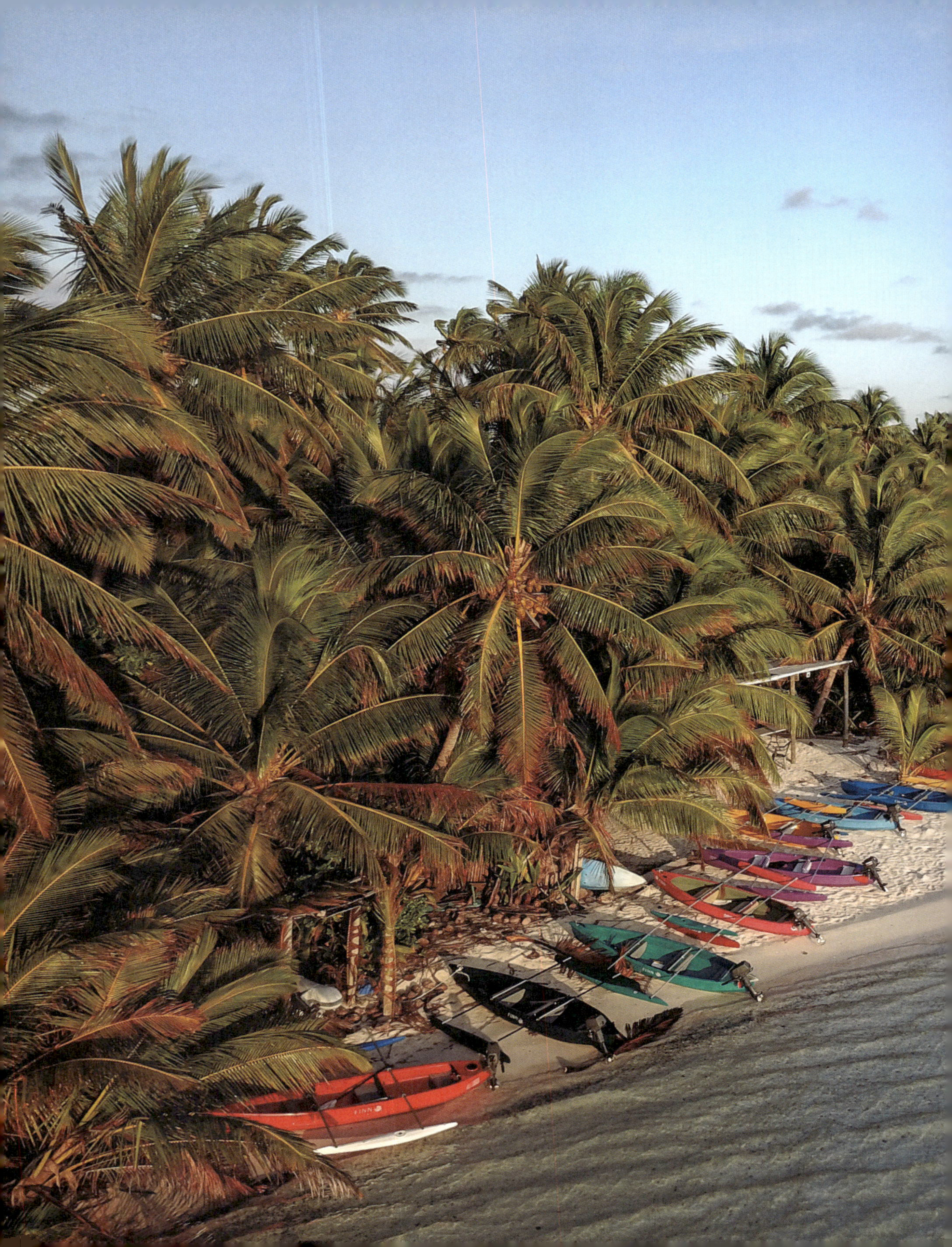

The Cocos Keeling Islands are the picture of paradise

ANDREW COLLINS

WATCH A BASEBALL GAME

FENWAY PARK (BOSTON) AND WRIGLEY FIELD (CHICAGO), USA

If baseball is America's national pastime, Fenway Park and Wrigley Field are its two greatest shrines. The only remaining stadiums from the game's early era, these beloved buildings exude history and are beloved for their unusual designs. Home of the Boston Red Sox since 1912, Fenway Park is famous for its hulking 11m-high (37ft-high) left-field wall, known as the Green Monster, which features an original scoreboard manually operated at its base. In the rare event that a player hits a ball that passes through a hole in the scoreboard while a worker is changing the numbers, he's automatically awarded a ground-rule double. Fenways's offence-friendly confines greatly abetted legendary Red Sox hitters like Ted Williams and Wade Boggs.

Built in 1914, handsome Wrigley Field anchors a lively north-side Chicago neighbourhood and is surrounded by residential buildings whose owners run profitable side gigs by charging fans to watch games from their rooftops. Wrigley's brick outfield walls have been famously covered in climbing ivy since 1937. Fielders occasionally lose track of a ball while wrestling with these unruly vines. Games at this boisterous ballfield are also famous for the observance of the seventh-inning stretch, during which fans are led, often by a visiting celebrity like Eddie Vedder or Bill Murray, in a rousing singalong of 'Take Me Out to the Ball Game'. Pro tip: while you watch the game, order a classic Chicago-style hot dog from Hot Doug's concession.

When watching games in these iconic spaces, be prepared for their design quirks. My first time seeing a Sox game at Fenway, my view of the field was partially obstructed by one of the many support pillars in the centerfield grandstand. Yet surrounded by boisterous fans and delighted to be seated in this iconic stadium, I still had an amazing time at the ballpark.

Top: Baseball park bleachers
Bottom: Fenway Park, home of the Boston Red Sox

A massive wave breaks beyond the Fort of Nazaré Lighthouse

DANIELLE DOMINGUEZ

THE BIG WAVES OF NAZARÉ

NAZARÉ, PORTUGAL

Nazaré had long enchanted my son's father, a Milanese surfer-wannabe who watched endless clips of giant, beastly waves gobbling up tiny humans who dared to scale their veiny, grey underbellies. On a family trip to Portugal, upon learning that our trip coincided with the Big Wave Challenge, we abandoned our post in Lisbon and we made straight for Praia do Norte, the northern beach of Nazaré. Huge waves occur largely due to the underwater Nazaré Canyon at the Sitio headland that juts out dramatically and separates the north from the much calmer southern beach, Praia da Nazaré. During storms and times of large swells, this deep canyon can boost the size of waves coming through to 30m (98ft).

Arriving at Praia do Norte, I was surprised at how nondescript it all seemed. It was peak big wave season and yet there was no entry fee or fanfare, but for a few motorhomes and roaming tourists and locals. I was beginning to question our decision to come, but when the roaring sea came into view, I was stunned into silence. It was majestic and ominous, a sea of hurtling force and froth like no other I had witnessed.

The two of us ventured across the foam-covered shore and over craggy rocks towards the headland. There were no barricades or safety measures – nature was as undisturbed as a quiet beach – yet it was far more treacherous. I was desperate then to see what we had come for, despite my fear of falling off a rock. We were not disappointed.

The size of the waves became apparent when jet skis began to tow surfers out to sea. They were mere flecks in an expanse of murky grey and frothy white, waves colliding, gathering and swirling into a powerful and relentless moving mass that was altogether terrifying. Each surfer leapt from the jet ski and into the angry sea as a wave began to form. After this perilous plunge, they skirted the inner wall of a wave, racing against the monster that would soon close in on them. Knowing surfers die in those waves and the folly of it all – surfer versus Mother Nature at her grandest – had me simultaneously shaking my head and barely blinking so as not to miss a moment. One surfer on this very day almost didn't make it.

Later, over a seafood lunch in town, we marvelled at what we had seen. Big wave surfing was officially off the table for this surfer. His biggest concern was the barista who wouldn't make him a cappuccino because only black coffee was acceptable in the afternoon. Milan lore in Nazaré.

BRETT ATKINSON

WATCHING SUMO

TOKYO, JAPAN

Sitting high in the stands at Tokyo's 11,000-seat Ryogōku Kokugikan stadium, I watched a United Nations of surprisingly agile men-mountains from Mongolia, Egypt and Georgia all go toe-to-toe with the best of Japan's sumo practitioners.

I was there for the year's most prestigious basho (sumo tournament), an exciting event enlivened by the passionate support of Tokyo locals cheering on their fan favourites. Banners with the names of Endō Shōta (Japanese) and Kirishima Tetsuo (Mongolian) were unfurled, while businessmen arrived after work for a few beers and the last two hours of action.

Ringside seats around doyhō (sumo ring) were reserved for sponsors, but even from my elevated seating near an increasingly busy beer concession, it was easy to observe the action. Support bouts featuring junior wrestlers kicked off at 8am, and at 4pm it was time for the sport's elite Makuuchi division to make their theatrical entrance. Before each bout began, the wrestlers threw salt into the ring in a purification ritual.

Yet sport trumped tradition and the action was rapid, intense and compellingly physical. Winning wrestlers crashed out of the ring milliseconds after their defeated opponents, and when some match-ups became stalemates, the gyōji (referee) restarted the bout by re-positioning the wrestlers like giant action figures. Patrolling the perimeter, five judges could harness video replays if they thought the referee had made the wrong call. In a country known more for its Zen-inspired calm, it was a surprisingly raucous night watching the action way down below in the doyhō.

Top: Two sumo wrestlers at the Tokyo Grand Sumo Tournament

Bottom: Fans crowd this sumo wrestling arena in Tokyo

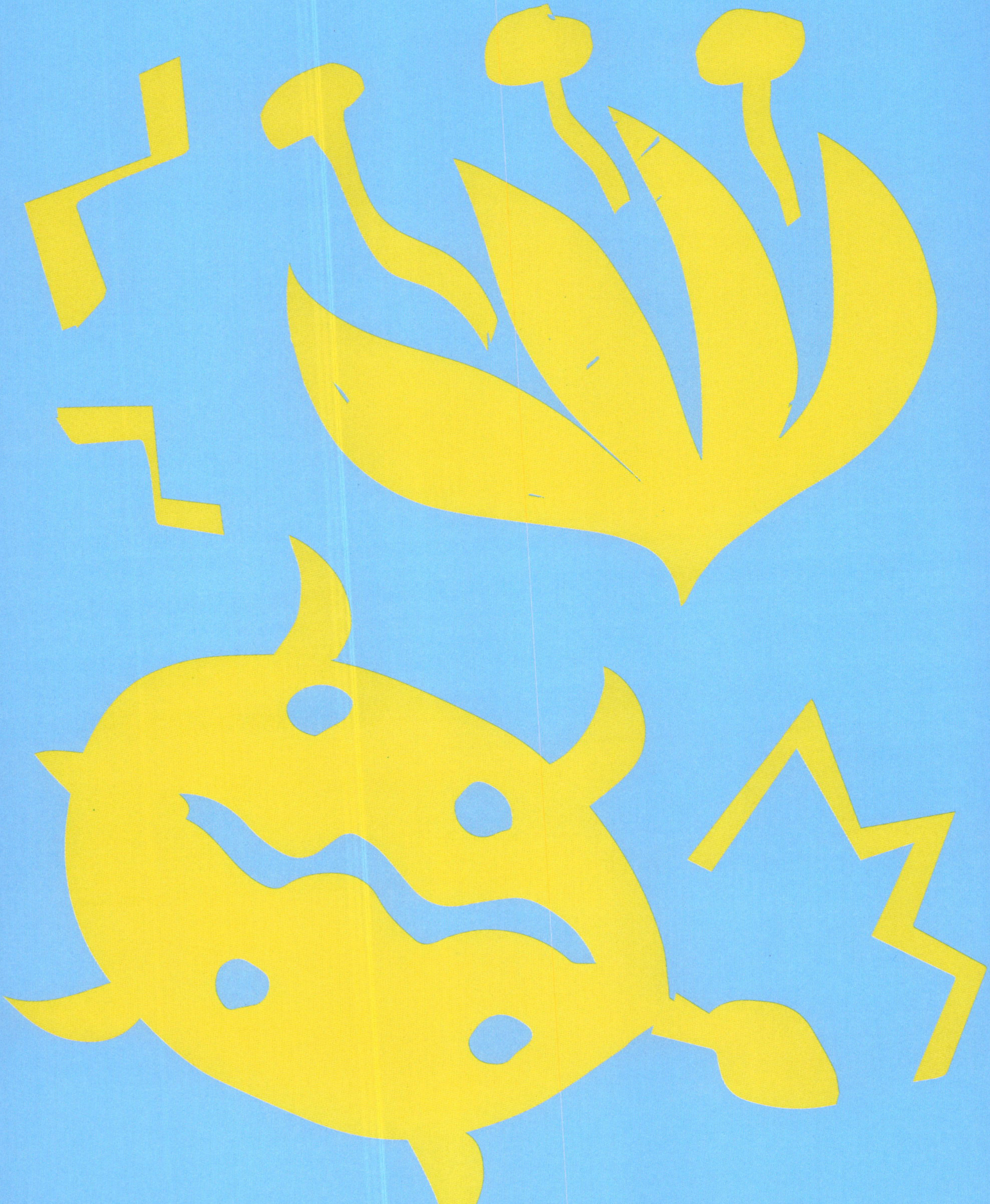

WILDLIFE

WILDLIFE

56	ADVENTURE CRUISING IN THE AMAZON
59	KAYAKING AMONG KILLERS
63	CAMP IN THE DEPTHS OF THE JUNGLE
65	GET YOUR TWITCH ON IN ANOTHER JUNGLE
66	BEAR VIEWING IN ALASKA
69	CLOSE ENCOUNTERS WITH HOLY CROCODILES
70	A KICKER-ASS SNORKEL
75	WILDLIFE WATCHING AT A FORMER PENAL COLONY
76	OBSERVE ELEPHANTS FROM A *MOKORO*
81	A BEACH WITH BITE
82	SWIMMING WITH HUMPBACK WHALES
84	FLOODED FOREST IN THE AMAZON

"Pinnacle Rock forms a dramatic backdrop to swims among sea lions, turtles and – star above stars – Galápagos penguins from the island's small breeding colony."

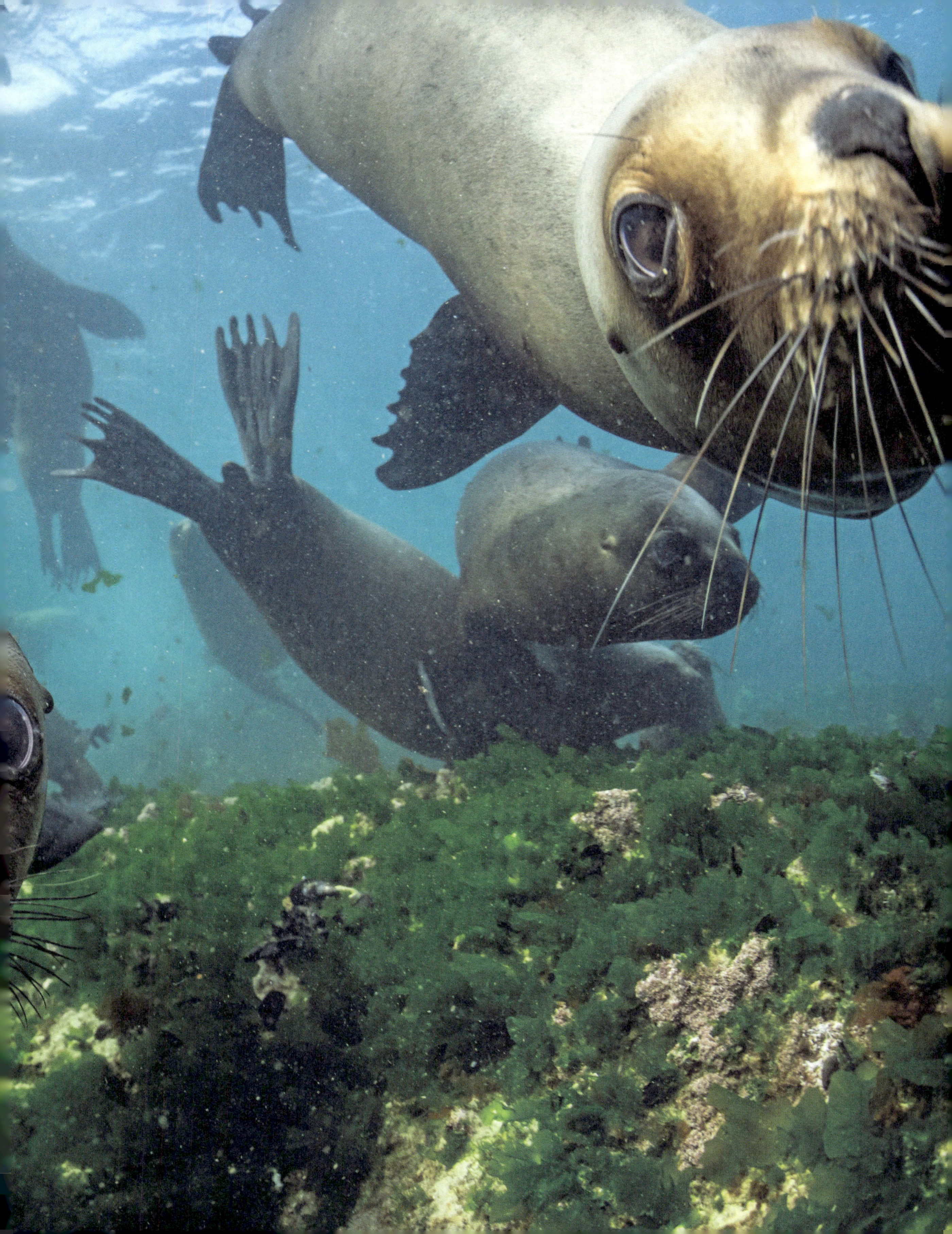

BRETT ATKINSON

ADVENTURE CRUISING IN THE AMAZON

NAUTA, PERU

'Quick! Before it runs away!' joked wildlife guide Ericson Pinedo Salas. I was warned Amazonian wildlife can be hard to spot, but it was already a two-sloth kind of day on my first morning on the *Delfin III*. Separated by a few branches, both examples of nature's most purposeful creature moved painstakingly slowly and looked blissfully down at our skiff with a stoner's grin.

A journey on the *Delfin III* begins at Nauta, a riverine town near the sprawling city of Iquitos, formerly a 19th-century rubber boomtown and now a place on the edge of most maps. Travelling at the end of the wet season, the high waters of Peru's Pacaya Samira Reserve made it easier to venture up sinuous blackwater creeks in the boat's agile skiffs. Morning and afternoon excursions off the boat revealed pink and grey river dolphins circling in calm, tannin-infused waters. At the same time, vibrant flashes high in the forest canopy were identified as scarlet macaws. On board, the boat's talented chefs incorporated traditional Amazonian ingredients into elevated versions of South American culinary classics like ceviche, and sundowner pisco sour cocktails in the boat's bar were the preferred option for most guests after a day's exploring.

Zipping through an area dubbed El Bosque Reflejado (the Mirrored Forest), there was one final and spectacular chance to refute the Amazon's (undeserved) reputation for wildlife being hard to see. Scores of snowy white egrets quickly became hundreds, taking off in unison and filling the horizon with a vibrant HDTV experience lifted from Sir David Attenborough's highlights reel.

Top: Cruising in the Amazon
Bottom: A sloth sighting

An orca surfaces on Johnstone Strait

ANDREW BAIN

KAYAKING AMONG KILLERS

JOHNSTONE STRAIT, CANADA

In summer, the narrow Johnstone Strait separating northern Vancouver Island from the Canadian mainland doubles as a marine wildlife highway. As narrow as 3km (1.8 miles) in parts, it serves as a funnel for salmon heading to the Fraser River, the world's largest spawning river. Behind them (cue *Jaws* theme music now) come up to 150 hungry orcas, creating a feeding frenzy and one of the world's great wildlife spectacles for lucky kayakers.

Guided trips include spending nights camped on the shores of Vancouver Island, typically near the edge of the Robson Bight (Michael Bigg) Ecological Reserve, the only place in the world where orcas are known to cruise almost ashore to rub their skin on the smooth pebbles (kayaks and other boats are banned from actually entering the reserve).

By day, you can kayak out from the shores, casually paddling among the salmon and the feasting killer whales – the former leaping from the water in the chase (sometimes clattering into the kayaks and even the kayaker), the latter elegantly surfacing behind them. Regulations demand that you paddle at least 100m (330ft) from the orcas, but the reality is that orcas can't read the rules. When I paddled here, they occasionally surfaced just a few metres from my kayak, their dorsal fins, which are up to 2m (6.5ft) in height, rising above my head. It was as humbling and thrilling a wildlife encounter as I've ever experienced.

And take heart – Johnstone Strait's killer whales are resident orcas (rather than transient), which only eat fish. You're only on the water, not the menu.

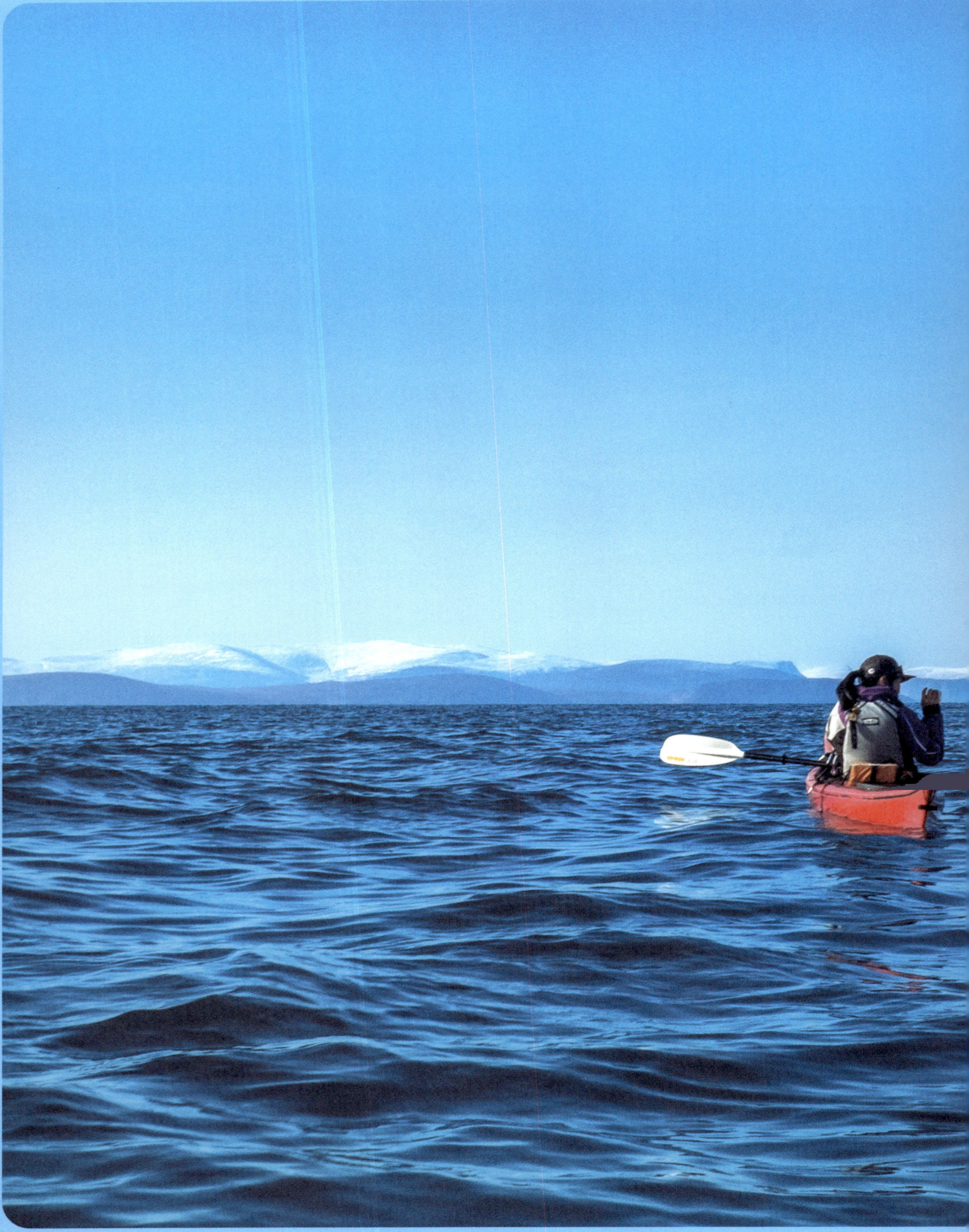

Paddling Johnstone Strait

An orangutan swings through the treetops above
Opposite: Traditional Indonesian eats served up at the small campsite deep in Gunung Leuser National Park

DANIELLE MCDONALD

CAMP IN THE DEPTHS OF THE JUNGLE

SUMATRA, INDONESIA

By 2pm, we'd spotted more orangutans than I could count on two hands.

Gunung Leuser National Park is found on the Indonesian island of Sumatra. This place is one of the most biodiverse forests on the planet – home to Sumatran tigers, rhinoceroses and elephants – and it's one of the only places on earth where orangutans still thrive in the wild. We spent six hours trekking through the steamy wilderness en route to our makeshift campsite for the evening. Along the way, with the help of our guides and leader, we saw 14 wild orangutans swinging about in the treetops above. Not to mention the peacocks, macaques and monkeys that appeared. There is nothing quite like seeing animals doing what they do best – hanging out in the wild while hanging in the wild yourself.

This wasn't like anywhere else I'd trekked before. There were no well-worn paths and signposts along the way. This was wild and remote and certainly required an experienced guide. The campsite where we spent the night and ate our picnic meals was basic, but that's kind of the point, right? It might not have been five-star accommodation, but I give this experience an 11 out of 10 rating.

Top: Observing the peaceful life of birds in the biosphere reserve of Prek Toal
Bottom: Pelicans gather in a tree in Prek Toal Bird Sanctuary, Siem Reap

SAMNANG MAO NICK

GET YOUR TWITCH ON IN ANOTHER JUNGLE

PREK TOAL BIRD SANCTUARY, CAMBODIA

Cambodia's Prek Toal Bird Sanctuary covers 21,342 ha (57,737 acres), making it the second-largest sanctuary in Southeast Asia. The birdlife here is incredible, with cormorants, little egrets, great egrets, giant ibises, greater adjutant storks and many other rare species. Birdwatching at Prek Toal is a very aesthetic experience, as the 3000-tree forest is flooded with water.

A permanent population of birds enjoy the rich fish stocks in the sanctuary, though unfortunately they are facing increasing threats. Deforestation, illegal hunting, plastic pollution, poaching and overfishing all put pressure on the food supply. Significant funds are required to protect the sanctuary, so the authorities have introduced a ticketing system for foreign visitors to help protect the birds. It's a small price to pay to catch a glimpse of these beautiful creatures.

Birdwatchers should aim to visit from October to February, the prime breeding season, to catch glimpses of baby birds. From March to May, the sanctuary dries up and low water levels make it too difficult to travel by boat. The best viewings are early in the morning, around 7.45am, as most birds will move to find shade later in the day and become harder to see.

Facilities in the sanctuary are limited, so make sure you use the bathroom before you go, and bring along food, sunscreen and a hat.

BRETT ATKINSON

BEAR VIEWING IN ALASKA

LAKE HOOD, USA

Fuelled by coffee and enjoying the brisk temperature and dewy freshness of an Alaskan morning, my day of bear viewing began at Anchorage's Lake Hood seaplane base. A busy flotilla of seaplanes was taking off to all parts of Alaska, with my 8am departure with Rust's Flying Service scheduled for a 45-minute journey south-west to the Big River Lakes region. Flying at an altitude of just 3000m (9840ft), Alaska's extreme patchwork of glaciers, snowcapped mountains and braided rivers unfurled below our bright red Cessna before we arrived at Redoubt Bay Lodge on remote Cook Inlet. Framed by the Chigmit Mountains, the lodge – 'rustic and wild … in the heart of bear country' according to their website – is renowned as one of Alaska's best spots to see bears.

Further energised by a second coffee in the lodge's relaxed lounge, I boarded a flat-bottomed pontoon to cross Cook Inlet and parked up at Wolverine Creek. At this sheltered inlet, a few early risers in aluminium dinghies were trying their luck at catching sockeye salmon at the base of a meandering and rocky brook. We soon learned that bear viewing, like most wildlife watching, is a waiting game and spent the first hour spotting bald eagles circling above the bay before making their way back to nests secreted in the towering pine trees framing Cook Inlet. Without

BEAR BASICS

Olivia Brown

Bear watching can be a beautiful experience for travellers (as long as it's a planned visit). But when coming nose-to-snout with a bear, there is key bear-watching etiquette to 'bear' in mind.

Most importantly, remember that you are in their home and should respect bear country. Bears are typically afraid of humans and will only attack when threatened. Keep all food in a closed container to avoid attracting bears too close to your location and never feed a bear. Maintain a safe distance at all times and never attempt to get close to the animal – no selfie is worth risking your life.

A mother brown bear and her three cubs

warning, a shiny black nose emerged cautiously from the scrubby undergrowth, and a massive 300kg (660lb) brown bear negotiated a steep trail down to the water's edge. Floating nearby, the beer-drinking crew of fishermen wound in their reels, also keen to take in the Animal Planet magic unfolding before us.

Three cubs around the size of a labrador followed their mother down the bank, scrapping and wrestling at the water's edge like boisterous teenagers. Suddenly, the largest bear dived into a school of salmon, just metres from the prime viewing location of the fishermen's dinghy. It was enough to make them choke on their rapidly warming Bud Lights.

It was an unsuccessful first attempt though, and the mama bear encouraged her cubs to follow her further around the cove. For the next 30 minutes, the ursine quartet explored the cove both on land and in the water, nabbing a few unlucky salmon, but generally having a frustrating time securing breakfast. The cubs' still-growing legs needed to be fully extended to awkwardly traverse the creek's tangle of boughs, and they looked up regularly to check on Mum's location before hastily catching up. Rambunctious play-fights inevitably meant a couple of the cubs were always running late.

At the cove's eastern edge, another bear with three cubs also emerged from the thicket. Both adult bears became aware of each other, and for a few minutes, an Alaskan standoff developed. There was no real chance of aggression though, and it's apparently not unknown for cubs to play together and then follow the wrong mother for a few days.

As the morning's laid-back family interaction unfolded, my early start from Anchorage made perfect sense.

HOLY ANIMALS

Olivia Brown

In Edinburgh, Scotland, there resides another revered animal – Sir Nils Olav. As the world's only knighted king penguin and official mascot of the Norwegian King's Guard, Sir Nils Olav has earned worldwide notoriety – millions have flocked to the Edinburgh Zoo to catch a glimpse of this famed penguin. Since arriving at the zoo in 1972, he has climbed the military hierarchy and been rewarded with promotions such as Corporal (1982), Sergeant (1987), Regimental Sergeant Major (1993), Colonel-in-Chief (2005), Knighthood (2008) and Major General (2023). The current distinguished title is held by Sir Nils III, maintaining the rich lineage and history of Sir Nils Olav I.

Top: Local devotees channel their ancestors by dancing during a spiritual ritual in Manghopir

Bottom: A devotee presents offerings for a holy crocodile, Karachi, Pakistan

SAHAR AMAN

CLOSE ENCOUNTERS WITH HOLY CROCODILES

MANGHOPIR, PAKISTAN

There are few places in the world where you can walk up to a pond full of crocodiles and live to tell the story. Manghopir might be the only place on earth where it's considered a sacred experience.

One of the oldest parts of Karachi, this rural area is home to mugger crocodiles, the shrine of Sufi saint Pir Mangho and sulphur spring waters believed to have healing properties. On visits to Sindh's capital city, my family and I packed into a clattering old Suzuki van to navigate the bumpy road from Federal B Area to Manghopir and visit the crocodiles. It was something of a ritual.

According to an old local folk tale, Pir Mangho's peaceful relationship with the mugger crocodiles transformed them into an incarnation of the saint. Natural science explains that floods created Manghopir Lake and brought the creatures to the area eons ago, where they collected at the pond. Archaeological investigations suggest the existence of a Bronze Age settlement that worshipped crocodiles.

To this day, Manghopir remains a deeply spiritual place. I've experienced many shrines across Sindh, but at Pir Mangho you come face-to-face with faith and nature. Visitors and devotees flock to Manghopir to pay their respects at the shrine every year. They gather at the pond to see hundreds of crocodiles and to feed and adorn them with flowers.

While my family and I aren't devotees, we are regulars. For us, Manghopir is an adventure that captures spiritual exploration, nature's wonders and the mysteries of the world.

ANDREW BAIN

A KICKER-ASS SNORKEL

GALÁPAGOS ISLANDS, ECUADOR

Any visit to the Galápagos Islands is a likely compendium of wildlife experiences – giant tortoises lumbering across Isla Santa Cruz, sea lions sprawled along the main street of Puerto Baquerizo Moreno or reef sharks sleeping in shallow channels at Las Tintoreras – but many of the best things in the archipelago happen at sea.

Roll overboard at any dive or snorkel site in the birthplace of the theory of evolution, and it's as though you're suddenly an extra in the animations of *Finding Nemo*. Rays stir up sandstorms on the ocean floor, turtles glide nonchalantly past and sea lions turn cartwheels, almost childlike in their demand for your attention.

There are myriad sites to snorkel in the equatorial island group, but when I recall watery moments here, it's always Kicker Rock that first comes to mind. In this wildlife wonderland, Kicker Rock's Spanish name, Leon Dormido, is suitably descriptive – the 'Sleeping Lion', named for its likeness to the figure of a sleeping sea lion. (The name 'Kicker Rock' comes from another of the rock's perceived resemblances: a shoe.)

Five kilometres (3 miles) off the coast of Isla San Cristobal, Kicker Rock rises sheer from the ocean in cliffs that stand almost 150m (492ft) high. It's imposing and impenetrable, but slicing through its south-eastern tip is a channel that separates it from another tall rock. It's inside this channel that some of the Galápagos's best snorkelling can be found.

The moment I entered the water from my cruise ship's *panga* (zodiac), I had company – a sea turtle swimming past, seemingly welcoming me into the ocean like an attendant at a wedding. A school of yellow-tailed surgeon fish briefly surrounded me, sardines flickered almost psychedelically in the light and away in the distance a manta ray leapt from the water like popcorn.

In the middle of the channel, the sea is around 20m (66ft) deep – about as deep as the channel is wide – and it's here that things turned memorable. Through the blue, nothing beneath me, I could discern the shape of sharks. Hammerheads are sometimes sighted around Kicker Rock, most often by divers, but these were the sleeker figures of Galápagos sharks. Soon, instead of swirling beneath me, one was shooting towards me – a 2m (6.5ft) torpedo, menacing in shape but not in intent. It came within a couple of metres, then turned and swam away. Soon, another shark followed, their movements seemingly choreographed to frighten and fascinate simultaneously. I could have floated and watched this marine show forever.

The Galápagos offers abundantly colourful marine life

Spectacular sites are easily reached by snorkel

MORE GALÁPAGOS SNORKELLING SITES

Andrew Bain

The well-named Devil's Crown is an encirclement of rocks just offshore from the popular Punta Cormoran on Isla Floreana. The fish life is a swatch of colours, but the Crown is best known for its hammerhead sharks.

As the name on the tin says, Los Tuneles is a place of submerged lava tunnels on the south coast of seahorse-shaped Isla Isabela. Fittingly, it's the best place in the Galápagos to snorkel among seahorses.

Spearing out of a headland on Isla Bartolome's western end, Pinnacle Rock forms a dramatic backdrop to swims among sea lions, turtles and – star above stars – Galápagos penguins from the island's small breeding colony.

Top: Buildings from the former penal colony still remain
Bottom: A wombat grazes on the hillside

BRETT ATKINSON

WILDLIFE WATCHING AT A FORMER PENAL COLONY

MARIA ISLAND, AUSTRALIA

Getting to Maria Island from Tasmania's east coast involves a ferry journey from the coastal hamlet of Triabunna across the Mercury Passage. Views on arrival include the remains of the Darlington Probation Station – Maria Island was one of Australia's first convict settlements from 1825 to 1832 – but uniquely Australian wildlife also attracts travellers to this rugged destination that's both a national park and a UNESCO World Heritage–listed site.

Most visitors have their first animal encounter around historic Darlington. Wombats graze on the grass, and from October to November, wombat joeys are usually seen. Cape Barren geese mooch around near Ruby Hunt's Cottage, the former residence of the island's long-term radio operator.

Maria Island is car-free, so rent a mountain bike and explore south to the Painted Cliffs. Forester kangaroos, wallabies and pademelons, reintroduced in the 1960s after Maria Island's farming era, are seen along coastal paths and in scrubby bushlands, while the island's band of Tasmanian devils – released as a disease-free population of around 20 in 2012 – has now grown to a community of around 100. Largely nocturnal, they're more likely to be seen around the island's campsites after dark. For birdwatchers, avian species include the rare and endangered forty-spotted pardalote.

A daytrip with Encounter Maria Island or Maria Island Cruise & Walk is most popular, but it's also possible to camp or overnight in bunk rooms in Darlington's former penitentiary. The Maria Island Walk is a guided four-day hike exploring all around the island.

ROWAN WATERS

OBSERVE ELEPHANTS FROM A *MOKORO*

OKAVANGO DELTA, BOTSWANA

Have you ever been on a *mokoro* in the Okavango Delta? A *mokoro* is a fibreglass canoe – they're no longer carved from wood for sustainability reasons – propelled by a 'poler' who generates speed by pushing off the bottom of the narrow channel.

We went out on the *mokoro* on our last morning in the delta. We saw a crocodile from only a few feet away, mouth wide open, posing dead still for a selfie. We disembarked for a walk and watched hippopotamuses run, snort and challenge each other in the shallows. Then we headed back to our *mokoros*, ready to make the leisurely float back to camp before we were due to fly out from the dirt runway.

Walking slowly and chatting quietly we spotted a herd of impala on the edge of the tree line. Something was off, they were more skittish than normal. An elephant emerged from the trees, then another elephant, and another. Approximately 30 elephants were now walking the plains, heading straight for the water in front of our *mokoros*. We looked at each other with amazement, smiling and giggling like schoolchildren.

'Behind me now!' our usually smiley guide urged in a stern, quiet voice as we realised the seriousness of the situation. He advised us to quicken our pace as he took a small device from his pocket that could emit a loud bang imitating a gunshot – it was our only protection. With the elephants walking to the water and that water channel being our ticket home, we needed to get there before they did.

To my adventurous delight, the elephants won the foot race, and we were forced to wait in the *mokoros* as they drank from the water in front of us. At our low height, inches above the waterline, the elephants were huge as they drank and cooled off. We were close enough to see the flies on their backs.

While we watched in amazement, another elephant came out from the tree line – a male bull with ivory white tusks, walking in a nonchalant slow rhythm. I quietly chuckled in excitement from my vantage point on the *mokoro*.

An elephant crossing a channel in the Okavango Delta

OBSERVE ELEPHANTS FROM A *MOKORO*

Our guides shifted into protector mode, banging the wooden poles against the fibreglass boats and shouting towards the herd to move it along. The male approached the herd and forced a river crossing right in front of us so he could have the water to himself. Thirty majestic elephants walked across the small channel, metres in front of us, trunks in the air above the water, flapping their ears dry as they emerged.

WHAT IS THE OKAVANGO DELTA?

Megan Cuthbert

Found in northern Botswana, the Okavango Delta is a rare oasis of wetlands surrounded by dry climates. Well-known by animal lovers and conservationists around the world, this internal wetland system owes its existence to the Okavango River. Seasonal floods provide necessary habitat and feeding grounds for a variety of endangered animal and bird species, including the cheetah, rhinoceros and lion. As recognition of the importance of this unique ecosystem, the Okavango Delta was inscribed as a UNESCO World Heritage Site in 2014.

Aerial view of the Okavango Delta
Opposite: *Mokoros* **gliding easily through the waters**

An orca beaching to catch a South American sea lion, Punta Norte

WE ALL NEED TO EAT

Megan Cuthbert

An orca buffet may not be to everyone's viewing taste. Those who wish to witness a slightly more vegetarian-friendly feeding ground should head to Zambia's Kasanka National Park. Every year around October, when the fruits of a local tree ripen, millions of straw-coloured fruit bats descend on the park, ready to gorge themselves. The bat population surges in November, but the numbers dwindle through the end of the year, the bats having picked the trees clean. Importantly, their buffet feast will result in spreading the tree seeds over distances of up to 75km (47 miles). This seasonal experience is not only a show of impressive migration – one of the largest in the world – but also vegetarian-friendly and an example of the replenishing nature of the circle of life.

ANDREW BAIN

A BEACH WITH BITE

PUNTA NORTE, ARGENTINA

There's a chilling scene (at least if you're a sea lion) in David Attenborough's *Trials of Life* series in which hunting orcas burst from the shallows of the Atlantic Ocean, riding up onto a beach to snatch sea lion pups as ocean snacks. This hunting behaviour is unique to a single beach – Punta Norte on Argentina's Peninsula Valdés.

This World Heritage–listed Patagonian peninsula is no stranger to wildlife wonders. It's home to the planet's only continental colony of the enormous southern elephant seal and the world's largest breeding population of southern right whales. But it's the orcas that steal the show, at least from February to May, when southern sea lion pups born on Punta Norte are first discovering the sea. It's then that orcas lurk offshore, waiting to ambush them in surprise attacks that typically leave the killer whales beached. To return to the sea, they wriggle back down the beach by thrashing their bodies from side to side.

Visitors aren't allowed onto the beach, but the El Mirador walkway atop the dunes behind the beach peers directly down onto the action. Like all wildlife encounters, sightings aren't guaranteed – I spent several days here and saw little activity beyond playful pups – but chances are best around high tide (the orcas need high water to get over the offshore reefs) and on days with low waves. It's also worth monitoring the Facebook and Instagram pages for the Punta Norte Orca Research station, which track sightings.

BRETT ATKINSON

SWIMMING WITH HUMPBACK WHALES

NIUE

Remotely located in Polynesia, around 2500km (1550 miles) northeast of New Zealand, tiny Niue is the world's smallest self-governing island nation. Many Niueans call Auckland or Sydney home – just 1700 people live on the compact island known as the 'Rock of Polynesia' – and from July to October they're joined by cetacean visitors travelling all the way north from the nutrient-rich and frigid waters of the Southern Ocean.

Leviathan humpback whales are inspired to make the journey to give birth and nurse their calves in warmer South Pacific waters. Because of Niue's unique geography, they're often spotted just a few hundred metres off the island's coastline of sea caves and craggy cliffs. Established in 2020 and spanning 130,000 sq km (50,000 sq miles), Niue's Moana Marine Protected Area surrounds the island and is a Pacific sanctuary for visiting humpback whales.

Scanning the near horizon for spouts, tail flukes and the occasional excitement of a breaching whale is popular along Niue's sea cliffs, but the best way to experience the migratory visitors travelling along Niue's humpback highway is on a boat trip with experienced local operator Niue Blue. On offer from mid-July to September, whale tours run according to a strict code of conduct to ensure the protection and wellbeing of the whales. Boat skippers must adhere to a minimum distance from the whales of 20m (65ft), no more than six swimmers are allowed in the water at any one time and swimmers are not allowed to physically move towards the whales. These essential guidelines in no way impinge on the enjoyment of tours, and by following the directions of Niue Blue's snorkelling guides, getting up close and personal with the whales is very straightforward. Simply ease gently off one of Niue Blue's inflatable Zodiacs, float quietly on top of the water and Niue's clear waters and superb visibility make it easy to spot whales and their calves even up to 30m (98ft) away. The whales are usually content just to bask in Niue's tropical sunshine, but often swimmers also enjoy the spectacular sight of them effortlessly swimming away with calm and languid flicks of their powerful tail flukes. Whale tours with Niue Blue often also include interacting with the island's resident pod of spinner dolphins – always the sign of a great day.

A humpback whale and calf, South Pacific Ocean

NIUE'S UNIQUE GEOGRAPHY

The island of Niue is the tip of an ancient volcano, and the ocean offshore gets very deep, very quickly. According to locals, a handy rule of thumb is the depth of the water will be roughly equivalent to the distance from the island. That equates to a depth of 200m (650ft), just a couple of hundred metres offshore.

Game fish, including wahoo, tuna and mahi mahi, are all caught with ease, and as the world's largest raised coral atoll, there are no rivers or runoff from the land. Niue's gin-clear waters offer underwater visibility up to 80m (260ft), making the submarine caves and canyons around the island's coastline popular with snorkellers and divers.

MONIQUE CHOY

FLOODED FOREST IN THE AMAZON

CUYABENO NATIONAL PARK, ECUADOR

Ecuador is a nation divided by the great spine of the Andes. To the west, banana plantations spread down to the Pacific, while to the east, the foothills disappear into the great Amazon jungle. Here, the rivers of the spectacular Cuyabeno National Park, the country's second-largest nature reserve, swell and flood every year, drowning the forest and making many of the Siona, Secoya and Cofan Indigenous villages in the reserve inaccessible by road.

Deep in the park, on the Laguna Grande and the twisting river that accesses it, a number of eco-lodges introduce visitors to the astounding diversity of the forest here. To reach it, we had to travel to the frontier oil town of Lago Agrio, then make the final 100km (62-mile) journey into the jungle by canoe.

The wildlife experience began almost the minute we stepped into the boat. Squirrel and titi monkeys leapt through the trees, while macaws and anis, woodpeckers and toucans cut through the air. By the time we reached the lodge we were eager to meet our naturalist guide to hear the story of the jungle. Each day we took a boat along the waterways, sometimes nosing into the undergrowth to spot otters, pink dolphins, microbats and sloths.

On a night tour we trudged around the perimeter of our lodge to discover we were surrounded by 3m (10ft) caimans, tarantulas, anacondas and other creatures our thatch-roofed cottages seemed unlikely to keep out. In the evenings we climbed the lodge's tower into the canopy to watch the pink sunset reflect off the water surrounding us.

And we woke each morning to the sound of oropendola birds that had colonised a tree opposite our cottage. These incredible birds build hanging nests that look something like a tennis ball in a stocking. They will fill a tree with them – some are cosy nests to hide their babies from predators and some operate as decoys. The dawn is full of their fascinating song, which sound something like large bubbles rising to the surface from deep underwater. By the end of our stay, we were absolutely enchanted by this place that is incredibly remote, yet teeming with life.

Glide between trees in the flooded Amazonian forest

A small town is reflected in the Yanayacu River, Peru

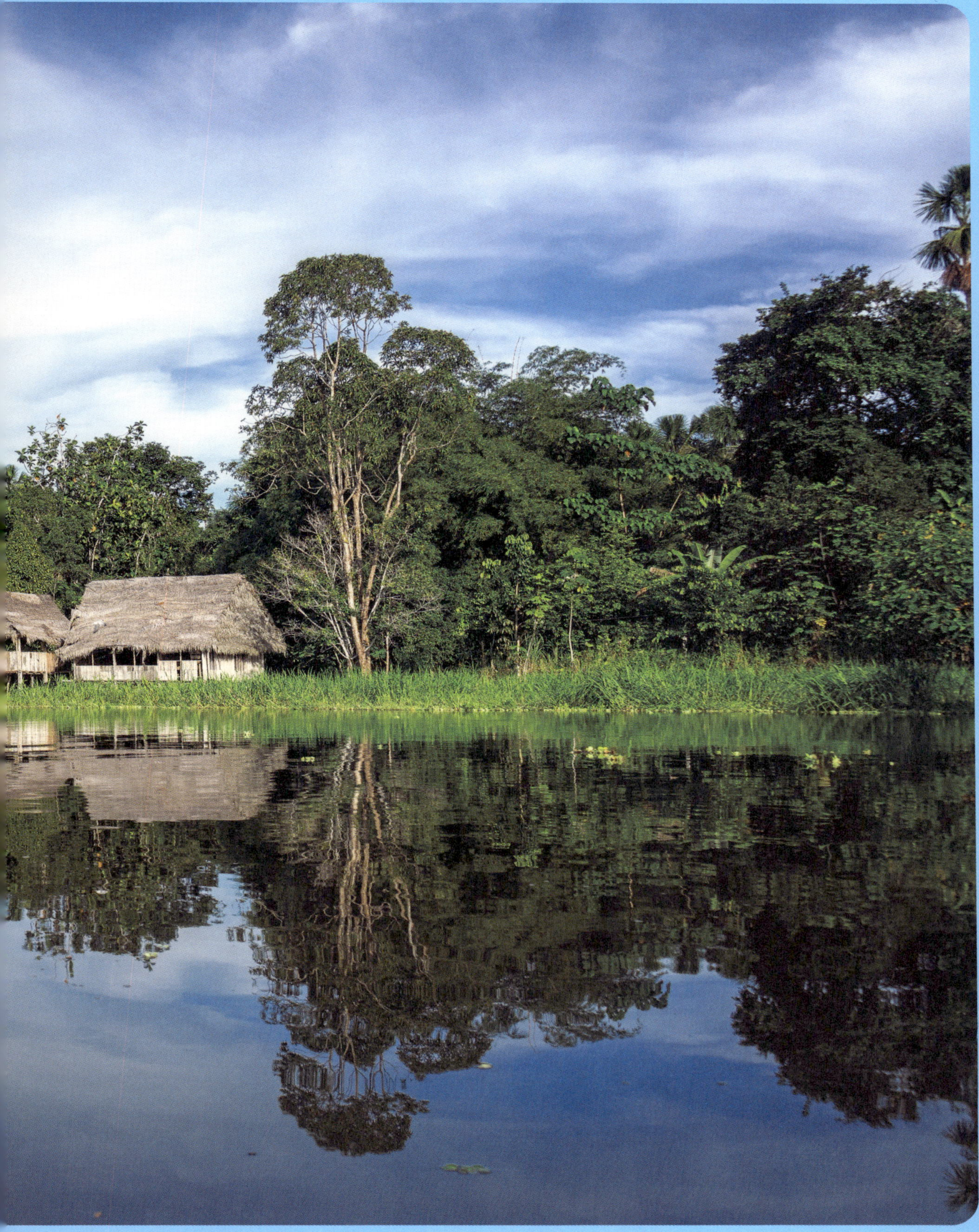

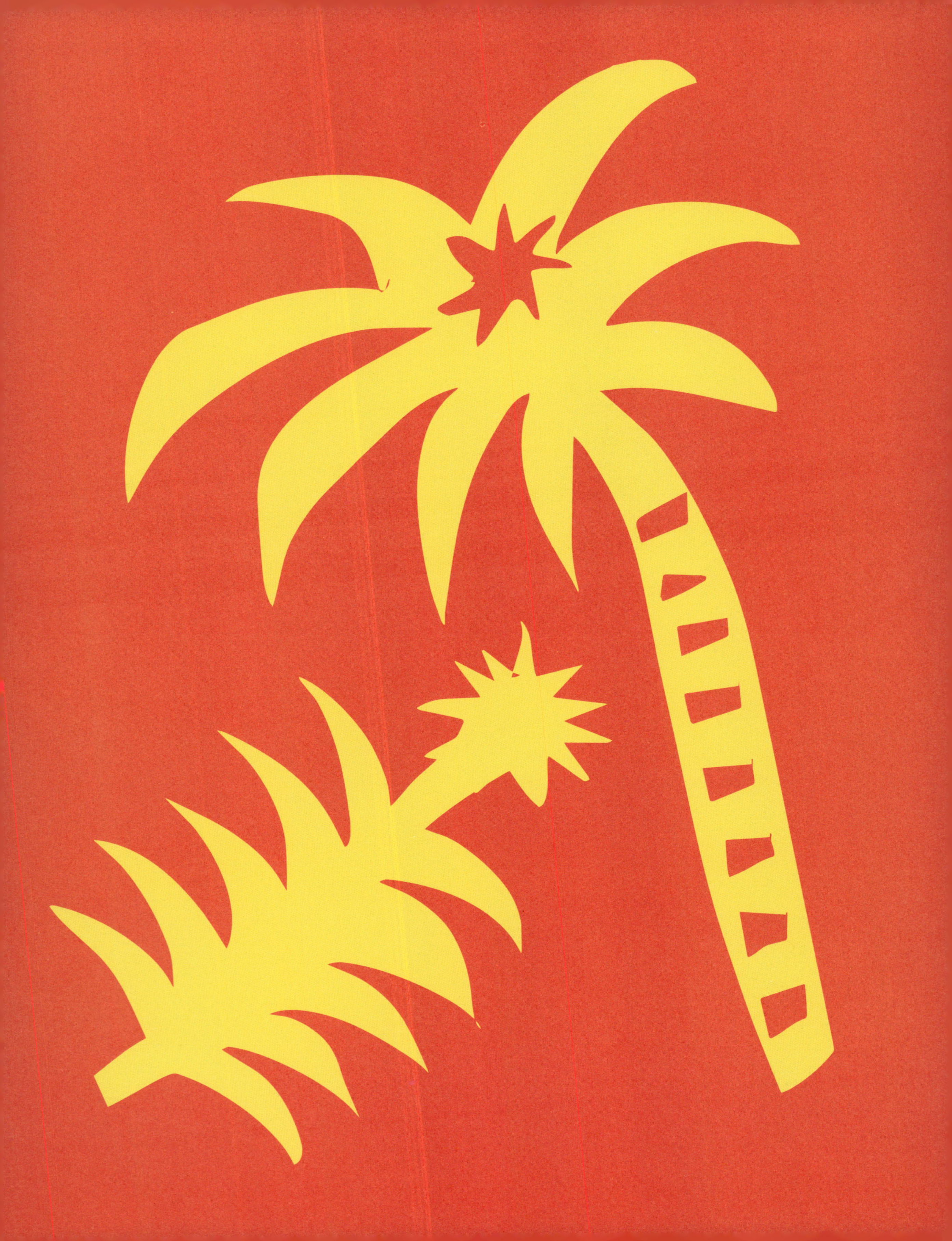

NATURE

NATURE

92	SEE THREE COUNTRIES FROM THE TOP OF A VOLCANO
94	SOUTHERN HEMISPHERE DARK SKY EXPERIENCES
98	AFRICAN LANDSCAPES AND WILD WALKING
100	UNIQUE GEOLOGY OF SOUTHWEST USA
104	FEELING THE HEAT IN THE LAVA SHOW
108	GOING UNDERGROUND IN THE WORLD'S LARGEST CAVE
110	LEAVE THE BUZZ OF BUENOS AIRES FOR LEAFY CANALS
113	COME ALIVE AT THE DEAD SEA
114	THE SIMPLEST OF THE SEVEN SUMMITS
117	GO OFF-GRID IN MOALBOAL
118	SWIM THE BLUE HOLES
119	A DIP IN ANCIENT SINKHOLES
122	SLEEP UNDER THE MILKY WAY
124	WATCH NEW ENGLAND'S BRILLIANT FALL FOLIAGE
127	ENDURE EXTREME TEMPERATURES IN THE NAME OF GOOD HEALTH
128	CAMPING ON ISLA DEL PESCADO
131	TAKE IT EASIER TO EVEREST!

"It was as if we'd arrived on another planet. We were camped on a desert island, enveloped in a motionless white sea and surrounded by hundreds of slender cacti."

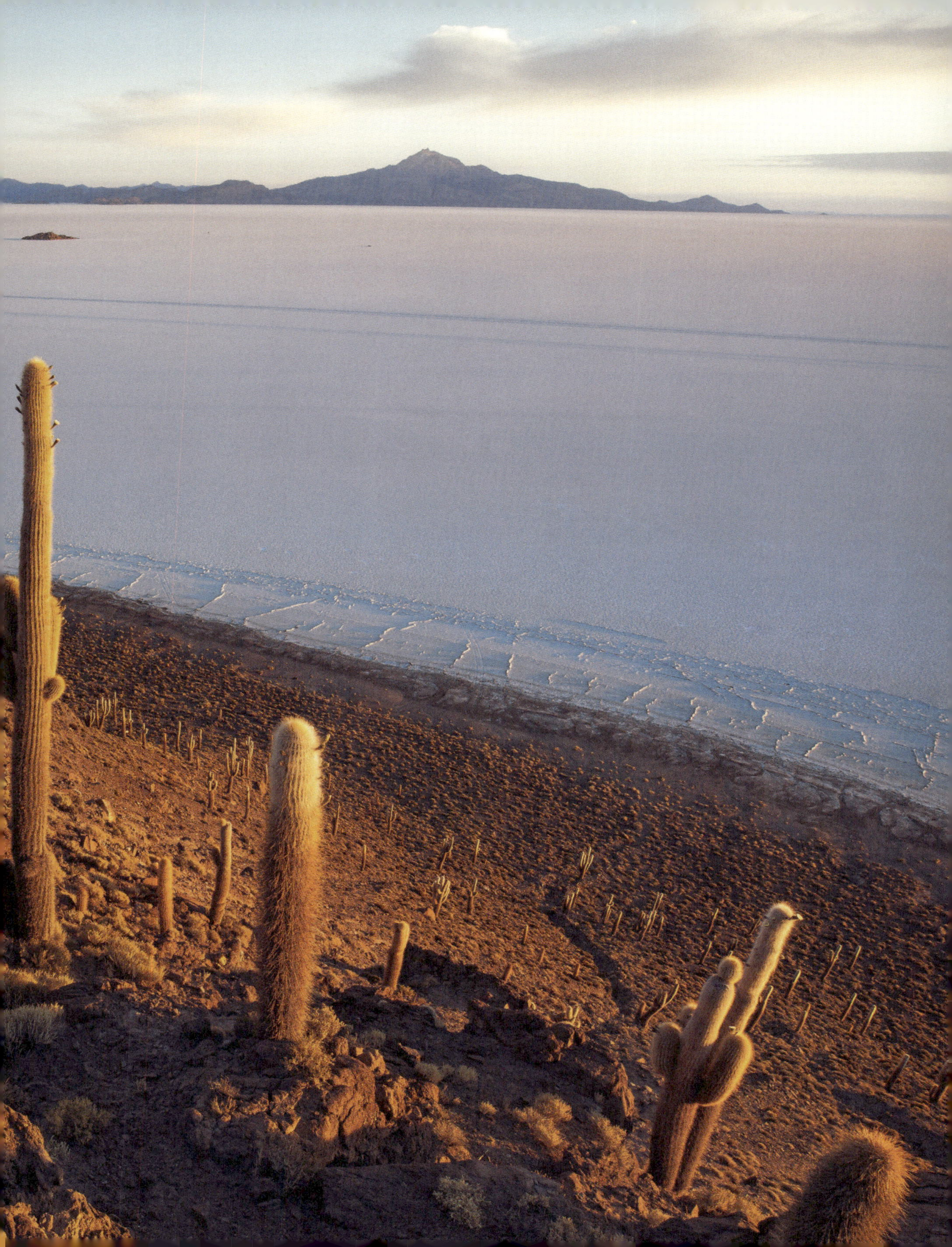

CLIFF BIELAWSKI

SEE THREE COUNTRIES FROM THE TOP OF A VOLCANO

COSIGÜINA, NICARAGUA

According to *National Geographic*, Nicaragua has 19 volcanoes – though some sources say it has more than 50. In a country with this many volcanoes, you can usually see one no matter where you are.

While living and working at a surf camp in a remote beach town outside Chinandega I could see at least three every day, including San Cristóbal – Nicaragua's largest volcano.

So the first time I saw Cosigüina, I didn't think much of it. When I looked north up the coast from the surf camp, it barely rose above the horizon and lacked the triangular shape you expect to see from a volcano. That's because in 1835, the top was blown off by the biggest eruption in recent Nicaraguan history. It wasn't until I climbed the 859m (2800ft) summit that I realised what makes Cosigüina special. From the top, I could see a 500m (1640ft) deep crater lake overlooking the Gulf of Fonseca with amazing views of Honduras, El Salvador and, of course, Nicaragua. Several more volcanoes dotted the horizon.

The hike to the top can be easy or difficult depending on the season and the path you take, but either way, I recommend a guide because the volcano is very isolated. The north-western part of Nicaragua doesn't get many visitors, but those who do visit quickly learn what a special place it is.

The 1745m (5725ft) summit of San Cristóbal (left) and Casita (right) volcanoes, Chinandega, Nicaragua

BRETT ATKINSON

SOUTHERN HEMISPHERE DARK SKY EXPERIENCES

AOTEA/GREAT BARRIER ISLAND, AOTEAROA/NEW ZEALAND

Just 45 minutes by plane from New Zealand's biggest city, Great Barrier Island is officially part of the overwhelmingly urban Auckland Central electorate, but in reality the remote island known to Māori as Aotea ('Cloud') is a laid-back destination of sweeping beaches, good fishing and forested bush walks. And with minimal light pollution from a resourceful and resilient population of around 1000, it's also a brilliant place to observe the night sky. There is no mains electricity or street lights – all island residents use either solar power or batteries – and Aotea's 90km (56-mile) separation from Auckland means there's no impact from the 'light dome' emanating from the Big Smoke. For these reasons, the International Dark Sky Association designated Great Barrier Island a Dark Sky Sanctuary in 2017, just the third Dark Sky Sanctuary in a global list that now includes almost 20 different locations.

The most popular way to experience Great Barrier Island's southern hemisphere celestial surprises is with Good Heavens, a local stargazing operator established by island residents Hilde Hoven and Deborah Kilgallon. Both are now keen and authoritative guides – aka fully trained 'Dark Sky Ambassadors' – for visitors wishing to explore the pollution-free night skies of their adopted island home.

After dark, Hilde and Deborah set up their powerful telescope amid sheltered sand dunes on the edge of Medlands Beach, an arcing bay that's one of the island's most popular beaches. It's not uncommon for dolphins to visit Medlands, surfing in on the waves and subtly illuminated by the soft moonlight. Comfortable 'moon chairs', blankets, warming mugs of hot chocolate and quite possibly New Zealand's best chocolate brownies make stargazing Great Barrier–style an easygoing and relaxed affair, but there's no trade-off in the experience on offer. Depending on the progression of the astronomical year, highlights of guided Look Up & Get Lost experiences with Good Heavens could include sightings of Jupiter, Saturn (and the planet's rings) and shimmering displays of the Milky Way and the Magellanic Clouds. Stargazing experiences last around two hours and are a treat for visitors from the Northern Hemisphere, as many of the sights are unique to southern skies. For around one week per month, Good Heavens also offers Moon Walk experiences combining stargazing with a sandy stroll on a deserted, moonlit beach.

Hilde and Deborah also share celestial knowledge from a Māori perspective, including Maramataka, the traditional Māori lunar calendar, and the importance of Matariki, the Māori New Year celebrating the rising of the Pleiades star cluster in late June or early July. The celebration of Matariki is becoming an important part of New Zealand culture and society, and in 2022 it was recognised as an official public holiday.

Booking ahead with Good Heavens for your first night on the island is recommended to allow maximum flexibility with weather conditions. Another Aotea dark sky option is the Kaitoke Hot Springs Twilight Trek with StarTreks, combining stargazing with a relaxing sunset soak in natural hot springs.

Dark sky stargazing

The ultimate Milky Way–viewing experience

SPACE TRAVEL

Olivia Brown/Megan Cuthbert

Why confine your travel to the Earth when there's plenty of opportunity for a little space travel for your next trip?

Witness the beauty of the night sky at the Pic du Midi Observatory in France. Perched above the clouds, the Pic du Midi Observatory can be accessed by taking a cable car from La Mongie. The observatory dome is also home to a telescope that allows visitors to directly view the sun.

The Natural Bridge Monument in Utah, USA, provides visitors with a unique visual experience: The River of Light phenomenon. The natural placement of the Owachomo Bridge frames the night sky when the Milky Way rises over the rock formation, leaving thousands of dazzling stars visible to the naked eye.

Zselic Starry Sky Park in Hungary is more than 9000 hectares (22,000 acres) of protected parkland with clear dark night skies, perfect for stargazing. On a clear night, you can see the Triangulum Galaxy with the naked eye. Zselic is part of DarkSky International, which aims to protect environments from light pollution and the resultant harmful effects on communities and nature. You can find many more protected DarkSky areas on their website, darksky.org.

ANDREW BAIN

AFRICAN LANDSCAPES AND WILD WALKING

SIMIEN MOUNTAINS, ETHIOPIA

From the high cliff edge of the Simien Mountains, the plains of northern Ethiopia seem to stretch forever. In the foreground, angular peaks rise like giant chess pieces, and behind you, the plateau seems alive with gelada baboons and wandering walia ibex.

For days, this clifftop has been the guiding line for trekkers marching towards Ras Dashen, the 4550m (15,000ft) mountain that is the tallest in Ethiopia and among the highest peaks in Africa. However, it's more than just a high mountain. Ras Dashen crowns the Simien Mountains, a range that was among the first 12 sites inscribed on UNESCO's World Heritage list in 1978. It was selected for its dramatic landscapes and rare animals, such as gelada baboons, the world's only grass-eating primates, and walia ibex, a mountain goat endemic to the range. To wander through this living nature documentary as you ascend into Ras Dashen's thin air is a mountain climb like no other.

Beginning near Debark village, the trek to and from the mountain takes around eight days, walking much of the way atop a line of cliffs that tumble up to 1km (3280ft) into the plains. It's precipitous enough to have drawn comparisons to the Grand Canyon, especially at popular lookout points such as Imit Gogo, reached on the third day of walking.

Any trek in the Simien Mountains has the compulsory requirement of an armed scout (though as village children run happily about waving and calling out greetings, it's not often clear what they're protecting you from). Most trekkers come with a tour operator to ease the logistics of acquiring permits and hiring guides and scouts.

A valley cuts through the Simien Mountains
Opposite: Gelada baboon

ANDREW COLLINS

UNIQUE GEOLOGY OF SOUTHWEST USA

SOUTHERN UTAH, USA

Soaring red-rock buttes and natural stone arches immediately leap to mind when you envision the national parks of southern Utah. This expansive section of the Southwest's storied Four Corners region abounds with awesome geologic formations that you can explore within the borders of five national parks – Arches, Bryce Canyon, Canyonlands, Capitol Reef and Zion – along with one enormous national monument, Grand Staircase–Escalante.

The region's unique geology is like nothing else on the planet. Delicate arches and crooked spires rise over the carpet of pinyon and juniper in Arches National Park, basking in shades of crimson and orange, especially when the rising or setting sun reflects against them. And then there are the thousands of otherworldly pointed hoodoos that dominate the landscape of Bryce Canyon and the towering red-rock cliffs and peaks you can hike among at Capitol Reef. To get a sense of what southern Utah's parks offer, allow seven to ten days for an unforgettable road trip. Keep in mind that you can easily tack on visits to many other nearby incredible natural wonders including the Grand Canyon, Monument Valley and Mesa Verde.

But there's even more to this breathtaking tract of high desert and craggy mountain peaks than those brilliant red rocks. At Zion, for example, arguably the park's most famous and fascinating hike is the wet-and-wild trek through a riverbed gorge called The Narrows, framed by 300m (1000ft) sheer cliffs. The rustic and historic national park lodges at Zion and Bryce Canyon are among the Southwest's most impressive human-made sights, while Capitol Reef is famous for its prolific orchards, where visitors have been invited to pick peaches and apples for generations. The Green River carves a dramatic course at Canyonlands National Park, and you're treated to dazzling views of the confluence of two mighty rivers, the Green and the Colorado. The parks' gateway communities – including Moab, Springdale and fast-growing St George – are magnets for myriad recreational activities, from mountain biking to river rafting.

Top: Bryce Canyon National Park
Bottom: Paddleboarding in Arches National Park

Sunlight turns Bryce Canyon National Park to gold

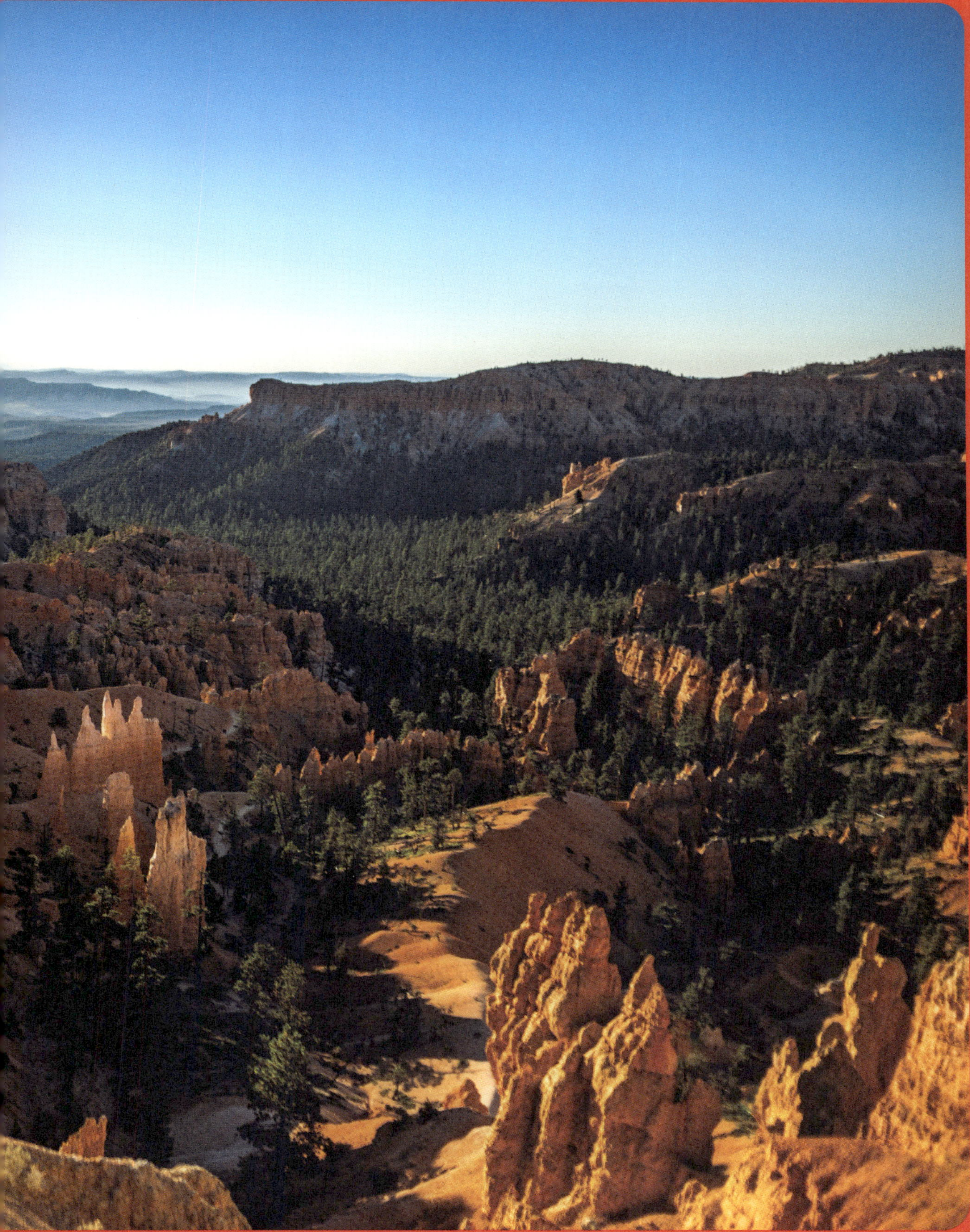

JAMES TAYLOR

FEELING THE HEAT IN THE LAVA SHOW

VIK AND REYKJAVIK, ICELAND

Iceland is truly a dream destination for amateur volcanologists. And aren't we all exactly that? The spectacle of an eruption is awe-inspiring, a vivid reminder of nature's power. In Iceland, that experience is up close and personal; this is a country with a smouldering core, where magma pulses beneath the craggy landscapes and ice caps, spewing forth from rifts and fissures, sculpting new terrain. It's an unparalleled destination for volcano enthusiasts.

And now, there's a place in Iceland to witness molten lava up close: the Lava Show. 'We had the idea to show off lava in a controlled environment after witnessing the largest lava fall in recorded history, when there was an eruption at Fimmvörðuháls in 2010,' said Ragga, who, along with her husband Júlíus, has masterminded the Lava Show, which has daily demonstrations in both Reykjavík and Vík.

That 2010 eruption sent lava oozing over a mountain ridge, plummeting about 200m (650ft) off the cliff to the ground below. 'It was an indescribable experience for us, looking at this towering flow of lava. We thought to ourselves, how can we capture this feeling and share it with the rest of the world?'

Their answer to that question is the Lava Show, where an advanced furnace heats up lava rocks until they liquefy back into their molten state. That lava is then poured down a chute into a room full of amazed onlookers, watching in awe as a presenter endures the sweltering heat to manipulate the lava with a long metal rod – lifting, overturning and eventually breaking it open when it cools to show the glowing, fiery core. 'We think of it as edutainment – part education, part entertainment. People are often shocked when the lava first comes out. I remember when we first began, people didn't believe it was real,' said Ragga.

It's one of the more obvious volcanic tourism experiences in a country brimming with explosive spectacle. Iceland's primordial landscapes have hypnotised tourists since the 2010 Eyjafjallajökull eruption, which unleashed a colossal ash cloud leading to the most extensive air-traffic shutdown since World War II. Major eruptions are behind most of what makes Iceland so tempting, pooling into dark fields of lava, scoring mountains with red, orange and yellow hues, and eroding into black-sand beaches on the coast and wind-whipped deserts in the interior. Beneath the ice caps, volcanic activity triggers monumental glacial floods, surging forth to carve out canyons and give rise to thunderous waterfalls.

And it's not just the aftermath of eruptions that spark interest, but eruptions themselves. Thanks to a handful of visitor-friendly eruptions occurring on the Reykjanes Peninsula, just a short drive from Reykjavik, seeing molten lava spew forth from a fissure has become a reality for many. Scientists predict this volcanic zone is entering an era of heightened activity, but that's a cause for concern. This is Iceland's most populated corner, meaning there's a significant risk to homes and livelihoods if an eruption threatens towns or critical infrastructure. 'Eruptions can be amazingly beautiful but also devastating,' said Ragga.

Whether it's a real-life volcanic eruption, watching lava in the controlled environment of the Lava Show or exploring the volcanically sculpted terrain, Iceland presents an opportunity to experience the fascinating – and frightening – power of volcanoes.

Witness molten lava up close at the Lava Show

FIVE MORE VOLCANIC ACTIVITIES IN ICELAND

James Taylor

* **The Thríhnúkagígur Lava Chamber (Capital Area):** This is the only place on Earth where you can descend into a dormant volcano and explore its giant lava chamber. Usually, lava solidifies after an eruption, but here it's like someone pulled the plug instead. It's likely that the lava seeped back down towards the Earth's core, leaving behind the gigantic chamber, which could fit the Statue of Liberty inside with room to spare.

* **Krafla, Leirhnjúkur and Hverir (North Iceland):** In North Iceland, the area around Lake Mývatn is home to a collection of fascinating volcanic phenomena. There's the Krafla volcanic crater filled with milky-blue water and the still-steaming Leirhnjúkur lava field. The geothermal power of the place is also on full display at Hverir, an area of Mars-like landscapes, belching mud pots and steam gushing from vents in the earth.

* **Hike the Fimmvörðuháls Pass (South Iceland):** Location of the lava fall that inspired Ragga and Júlíus, the Fimmvörðuháls Pass is a popular day trek between the waterfall Skógafoss and the Thórsmörk Nature Reserve. It can also be added on to the longer Laugavegur Trek, Iceland's most famous multi-day hike between Landmannalaugar and Thórsmörk.

* **Snæfellsjökull National Park (West Iceland):** One of the few cone-shaped volcanoes in Iceland, the Snæfellsjökull ice cap and volcano sits at the very tip of the Snæfellsnes Peninsula at the heart of its own national park. Here, there are lava fields that spill into the ocean, twisted coastal cliffs, giant volcanic craters and windswept black-sand beaches.

* **Askja Volcanic Caldera (Highlands):** A far-flung corner of Iceland's wilderness, located north of Vatnajökull, is the Askja Volcanic Caldera. The landscape here bears the scars of the nation's most violent eruptions, with huge craters, battered lava fields and Víti, a crater lake filled with chalky water warm enough for a dip.

Lava Fields at Krafla volcano

BRETT ATKINSON

GOING UNDERGROUND IN THE WORLD'S LARGEST CAVE

PHONG NHA-KE BANG NATIONAL PARK, VIETNAM

What a difference a decade makes. Guided access to Hang Son Doong, the world's largest cave, was only approved by the Vietnamese government in 2013, but now the sleepy riverside village of Son Trach is an essential stop for intrepid travellers exploring the southeast Asian country. Other subterranean cave systems punctuating the region's karst limestone landscapes are also popular, providing more affordable and more easily booked alternative experiences to Son Doong's world-beating grandeur and thrills.

In deep forest close to the Vietnam–Laos border, Son Doong was discovered by accident by local hunter Ho Khanh in the early 1990s, but its gargantuan dimensions – more than 5km (3 miles) long, 200m (650ft) high, and in some places, 150m (500ft) wide – were only confirmed when British cave experts returned with Khanh in 2009.

Expeditions exploring Son Doong can only be booked with Son Trach–based Oxalis Adventure Tours and, with a maximum of 1000 visitors per year, they always sell out quickly. Be prepared to book at least a year out from travel for a physically challenging five-day/four-night adventure, including camping deep within the cave. Also, be prepared to stump out around USD$3000. Highlights include soaring stalagmites up to 80m (260ft) high, massive cave pearls 10m (32ft) in diameter and the considerable challenge of climbing the 'Great Wall of Vietnam', a massive 90m-high (300ft-high) calcite overhang. Fully guided adventures run during the region's dry season from February to August.

MORE CAVES TO EXPLORE

❋ **Hang En:** Discovered in 1994, Hang En is part of the full Son Doong experience, but can also be visited on a two-day/one-night adventure.

❋ **Hang Va:** Underground river passages discovered in 2012 and opened to visitors in 2015.

❋ **Paradise Cave:** Accessed by wooden staircases coursing through darkness to a giant space resembling a cathedral.

❋ **Phong Nha Cave:** Includes a boat trip through a cavern incongruously illuminated by colourful lights.

Entry to Hang Son Doong, the world's largest cave

MANDY ALDERSON

LEAVE THE BUZZ OF BUENOS AIRES FOR LEAFY CANALS

DELTA EL TIGRE, ARGENTINA

Stay in the thick of Buenos Aires's buzzing neighbourhoods sizzling with steak, soccer and smooth tango moves, and you'll be plenty content. But did you know there's a whole other world no more than an hour from the city that flows to a very different rhythm?

Escape the tango beats and colourful streets of Buenos Aires and head for an easier, breezier way of life in Delta el Tigre. Don't be fooled by the name; there are no tigers here (or jaguars as there were once). Here, where five rivers converge, you'll find the third-largest river delta in the world, made up of over 3000 islands and dotted with local life and private jetties leading to basic wooden shacks, imposing mansions, BnBs, local homes and everything in between.

Ease onto delta time in the town of Tigre with a stop for supplies at Puerto de Frutos, a fruit-turned-craft market, then stroll along the river to admire the Tigre Art Museum before a laid-back boat journey through the nearby backwaters and canals.

A daytrip will give you a chance to kick back with a delicious lunch and refreshing drink or two, perhaps at a biodynamic riverside eatery, with options to kayak, swim or simply watch the world drift by from a well-positioned riverside hammock. To get a real feel for river life, seek out one of the many lodges or BnBs and stay a while longer as the Porteños do when hoping to escape the city heat. I kicked back in the Senador Dupont Hotel & Restaurant, the perfect place to rest and refuel with delicious food and generous cocktails.

Boats docked along a lush Tigre Delta canal

Therapeutic relaxation 45 minutes from the capital

JULIAN TOMPKIN

COME ALIVE AT THE DEAD SEA

DEAD SEA, JORDAN

As night descends the ochre red hills simmer down towards darkness. The stillness, however, is broken by the sudden call to prayer contrasting the silent and oscillating lights of the small Israeli villages on the opposite banks of the Dead Sea. The stars emerge like a giant puzzle, keeping watch over this beguiling and complex land. I stand on the shoreline and feel the enormity of this deeply consequential place.

While the Israeli shore is today home to an array of bustling tourist resorts promising a compelling cocktail of health and hedonism, the Jordanian fringe of this enigmatic lake retains a more measured and nourishing pace – a tranquil oasis in a land of sand and stone, where you will find solitude and sustenance in its healing waters and circadian rhythms.

Renowned for its therapeutic properties, this most saline of water bodies – 427m (1400ft) below sea level and packed with as many minerals as ancient myth and lore – is in easy reach of the cosmopolitan Jordanian capital of Amman. The city is a mere 45-minute drive away, with accommodation options ranging from the folkish to the perfectly opulent. Away from the main resorts, the northern banks of the inland sea are home to Mount Nebo and the ancient mosaic city of Madaba – both must-visits, with historic treasures and panoramic views across the storied waters.

Despite its uninspired moniker, the Amman Tourist Beach is the most popular with locals – connected by bus directly from the city and well-resourced with amenities. Families laugh, frolic and float weightlessly as if in space. For those in search of a decidedly more lavish experience, the Kempinski Ishtar is unrivalled, its Babylonian architecture rising like an apparition from the desert sands. I join the locals for an unforgettable float in the buoyant Dead Sea waters, followed by a therapeutic 'scrub and wrap', where the body is cleansed with salt and minerals then cosseted in mud, courtesy of the Dead Sea.

ANDREW BAIN

THE SIMPLEST OF THE SEVEN SUMMITS

KILIMANJARO NATIONAL PARK, TANZANIA

Mountaineers the world over aspire to climb the Seven Summits, the highest peaks on each of the seven continents. Most, such as Everest, Denali and Carstenz Pyramid, are committed mountaineering expeditions, but then there's Mount Kilimanjaro.

The simplest and most straightforward of the Seven Summits, Africa's highest mountain (5895m/19,000ft), rises beside the equator along Tanzania's northern border with Kenya. To reach its summit, you need only a good level of fitness, a guide (a compulsory regulation on the mountain) and a little luck or planning with altitude.

There are seven routes to the summit, all converging on the slopes or crater rim of the dormant volcano. The Marangu Route – the so-called Coca Cola Route for its popularity – might be the fastest and most famous ascent, but it's the lingering approach on the Lemosho Route that is my favourite. This seven- to eight-day trek (compared to the five-day rush of Marangu) brings one of the highest summit success rates on Kili, but there's more to its beauty than summit fever.

I woke each morning to views across the tops of clouds packed into the plains below. Only Mount Kilimanjaro and the neighbouring Mount Meru rose above them like islands, and the desert-like slopes through which I trekked bristle with the mountain's Dr Seuss-like giant groundsels.

Summit day began – as it always does – around midnight from Barafu camp, 1200m (4000ft) below the summit, and I set out in a line of headtorches, moving at glacial speed towards this summit dotted with its own glaciers. They are curious and fragile remnants – residue blocks of equatorial ice like no other glaciers I'd ever seen. They were fine company for the final steps onto the summit, poised above the rim of the crater, which I reached moments after sunrise, the day's first rays hitting me and the mountain like a celebratory spotlight.

Top: Grinning at the summit
Bottom: The climb ahead

Top: Idyllic life in Moalboal
Bottom: A school of sardines

ALISIA BUFANO

GO OFF-GRID IN MOALBOAL

PANAGSAMA BEACH, PHILIPPINES

For me, the thrill of travelling to unusual places is not just in the destination itself, but also in the joy of explaining my peculiar choices and relishing the inevitable question, 'Why there?'. This was the reaction I received when I set my sights on Panagsama Beach in Moalboal, far north-west of Cebu Island, Philippines. So, why here? In a nutshell, this small haven revolves around marine life.

While Panagsama Beach isn't a hidden gem, its charm attracts a specific kind of traveller: domestic tourists and dedicated divers, who often become repeat visitors. It's common to meet marine enthusiasts who will ask what dive spots you've been to and what marine life you've seen before they ask your name.

Catering to everyone, from novice snorkellers to seasoned divers, Panagsama Beach offers unforgettable experiences like sunrise snorkelling with sea turtles or the opportunity to experience a sardine run in the wild. Pescador Island beckons divers with its marine life and calm, warm water. It's frequented by whale and thresher sharks, as well as white-tip sharks.

Beyond its aquatic wonders, Panagsama Beach surprises the senses with traditional barbecue joints and sunset views.

Panagsama Beach, a delightful fusion of marine wonders and gastronomic bliss, ensures an unforgettable sojourn off the beaten path.

ANNETTE SHARP

SWIM THE BLUE HOLES

SANTO, VANUATU

Enjoying one of Vanuatu's blue holes

The water in the blue holes on the east coast of Vanuatu's largest island, Santo, is so blue you think you are about to dive into blue jelly, but really it's the fresh water streams from the volcanic mountains and underground limestone caves. It is a deep, pure blue, so clear you can see the rocks at the bottom.

There are three blue holes to choose from on Santo, all magical and all less famous than the shipwreck diving the island is known for. They are relatively remote, each tucked at the end of a river, so you might be sharing the water with local kids or no one at all. The owners have built diving platforms, rope swings and ladders, but if you don't want to channel your inner Tarzan, it is perfectly peaceful just listening to the birds calling to each other in the lush forest surrounding you as you swim.

Getting to a blue hole is part of the adventure – why go by car when you can canoe? The tidal rivers are gentle, clean and quiet. It's an easy 30-minute paddle inland to the largest, Matevulu Blue Hole. Take a snorkel, your lunch and a book, and you are ready for a simple but special day.

EMMA GLENCORSE

A DIP IN ANCIENT SINKHOLES

YUCATAN, MEXICO

The crystalline water of a cenote is a welcome and refreshing respite from the Mexican heat. There's nothing quite like the humbling feeling you get as you float in a sunken oasis that has existed for more than 66 million years.

Protected by UNESCO, the estimated 10,000 cenotes across the Yucatan have something for everyone – whether you're interested in culture, geology, history or a combination of all three. Each cenote is unique. Some have very bare-bones setups on local farmland where the entry fee simply goes to the upkeep of the cenote, such as Cenote Noh-Mozon, which I had the privilege of visiting in 2019. Others have dedicated eco-parks built around them, offering experiences tailored towards families and children where you can expect to pay a slightly higher entry fee.

Before heading to your nearest cenote, take a wide-brimmed hat and clothing to protect your skin from the sun. You can't wear regular sunscreen or insect repellent to ensure the water remains unpolluted (organic or reef-friendly sunscreens and repellents are A-OK).

Some even branch out into underground river systems that you can explore with a local guide – no scuba gear required! Wandering among the stalactites and stalagmites lit only by torch or swimming from section to section alongside my guide Pakoloa, it's easy to see why the cenotes were held sacred by the Indigenous Maya as portals to Xibalba (the underworld).

A cenote in Yucatan

SINK OR SWIM

Olivia Brown

There are many sinkholes around the world that are safe and open to the public – you just need to know where to look! Many require a level of mobility to get into and out of the water, and can involve a walk to and from the locations, so accessibility can be difficult!

The Bimmah Sinkhole in Oman is found 130km (80 miles) from the capital of Muscat. This large natural swimming hole has golden limestone walls and azure waters and a handy set of stairs to help you descend into this swimming utopia.

Found on a sheep farm in Australia, the Kilsby Sinkhole welcomes snorkellers, free divers and open water–certified scuba divers to explore its enticing depths. Booking a guided tour is a necessity for this memorable aquatic experience.

On a trip to Iceland, you can dive between two tectonic plates, the only place in the world you can do so! At Silfra fissure in Thingvellir National Park, the North American and Eurasian tectonic plates have cracked open, so divers and snorkellers brave enough to plunge into these chilly glacier waters can marvel at Mother Nature.

MANDY ALDERSON

SLEEP UNDER THE MILKY WAY

WHITE DESERT, EGYPT

If anyone can play a strong desert game, it's Egypt. With around 95 per cent of its landscape divided into the Eastern and Western Deserts, encompassing parts of the Libyan, Sahara, Sinai and Great Sand Sea deserts, should we be surprised that somewhere past Bahariya Oasis, beyond the volcanic-shaped mounds of the Black Desert is a magical moonscape like no other; the White Desert? Of all my middle-of-nowhere desert experiences, this one night under the stars has been etched on my mind for life.

All going well, a five-hour road trip south-west of Cairo will bring you to the heart of the White Desert. Driving off the road, deep into the landscape, the limestone cliffs and chalk-like sculptures carved by the desert winds appear to have grown up from the white sand beneath them. In reality, this is an ancient seabed, still lingering in the form of limestone, quartz and calcium, covering 300 sq km (115 sq miles) of the Farafra Depression. You won't bump into many people out here, but don't be surprised if some curious desert wildlife comes to check you out.

With zero light or sound pollution (aside from the glow and crackle of the campfire) and only a sleeping bag and mat between you and the universe, sunset to sunrise feels like an ever-changing, multi-dimensional, technicolour adventure in a front-row seat to the Milky Way, complete with falling stars, delicious mint tea and traditional meals served by your Bedouin guides who will also ensure that you, eventually, make it back to reality.

Driving through the White Desert
Opposite: Clear views of the Milky Way

ANDREW COLLINS

WATCH NEW ENGLAND'S BRILLIANT FALL FOLIAGE

NEW ENGLAND, USA

Every autumn, New England's millions of deciduous trees put on one of the most spectacular shows on earth. Watching the leaves turn throughout this six-state region, abundant with soaring mountainsides, winding country roads, historic covered bridges and postcard-perfect hamlets is a beloved rite.

The most dramatic leaf-peeping occurs in the region's mountainous interior, where the Appalachian Range snakes from ridge to summit, stretching from western Connecticut and Massachusetts up through central Vermont and New Hampshire and ending in interior Maine. In these rugged woods, you'll find the tree species that produce the most riotously colourful displays: sugar maple, oak, ash, beech and birch among them. These cooler interior areas hit their peak colour early, starting around the very beginning of October.

Anywhere you go in New England this time of year, you'll see shimmering leaves carpeting the countryside. For the most enjoyable exploring, stick with slower roads that have plenty of turnouts for hopping out to snap photos. US Hwy 7, from the Litchfield Hills of northwestern Connecticut up through the Berkshires of western Massachusetts and the west side of Vermont is a stunning route. When you get to the dapper college town of Burlington, the view west across rippling Lake Champlain frames yet more stunning foliage in upstate New York's Adirondack Mountains. In New Hampshire, I also recommend driving completely around ravishing Lake Winnipesaukee, and then continuing north into the White Mountains – the tallest range in the north-eastern United States. A favourite scenic road in this area is the Kancamagus Scenic Byway, aka 'The Kanc'. Across the border in western Maine, the brilliant colours continue as you drive east through the Rangeley Lakes area and up to Moosehead Lake.

Many farms and orchards host family-friendly events during this season. Treworgy Family Orchards in Bangor, Maine, has an amazing corn maze whose design changes every year, while Autumn Hills Orchard in Groton, Massachusetts, is a lovely place to pick apples and admire the changing leaves. There are also annual gatherings with music, food and art to enjoy amid the changing leaves, such as the Newfane Heritage Festival in southern Vermont and the Warner Fall Foliage Festival in central New Hampshire.

Beautiful fall foliage across the White Mountains, New Hampshire

And even though New England's interior gets more attention, don't overlook the stunning coastline, which still packs plenty of fall colour, especially over the last two weeks of October. Beachcombing in Acadia National Park or Cape Cod National Seashore against a backdrop of shimmering crimson, orange, yellow and bronze leaves makes for a truly alluring spectacle.

A CORNISH LEAF-PEEPING ITINERARY

As a part-time resident of New Hampshire's Lake Sunapee region, the beginning of October is my favourite time of year for country drives and scenic hikes. My partner and I love walking among the pastoral grounds of the Saint-Gaudens National Historical Park in Cornish, then driving through nearby Cornish-Windsor Covered Bridge – a landmark since 1866 – to cross the Connecticut River into Vermont. From there we like to meander up US Hwy 5 for a hike in the breathtaking 50m-deep (165ft-deep) Quechee Gorge and then end the day amid the gracious homes, inviting galleries and restaurants in the centre of Woodstock, with its classic tree-shaded village green.

SAUNA FAVOURITES

- **Saunas of Sammuntupa:** Sauna and ice-dipping place in Lapland.
- **Sompasauna:** Volunteer, community-run sauna in Helsinki.
- **Oslo Fjord Sauna by Fjord CleanUP:** In my experience, this is the most affordable public floating sauna in Oslo, Norway. Profits go to supporting a good cause: volunteer-run fjord clean-up projects.
- **Tromsø:** This is another one of my favourite public saunas with cold-dipping opportunities in Norway.

Enduring the icy dip, northern Finland

KATI PANKKA

ENDURE EXTREME TEMPERATURES IN THE NAME OF GOOD HEALTH

FINLAND AND NORWAY

The combination of a hot sauna and ice dipping is my favourite way of rejuvenating the mind and the body. I understand it sounds intimidating. Shocking even! You're probably thinking: why on earth would anyone voluntarily plunge themselves in ice-cold water or roast themselves inside a steaming hot room?

And well ... shock is actually what you should expect. Your body first goes through a natural shock reaction when you're stepping down the ladder and immersing yourself in the numbing cold water. But trust me. If you remember my advice, and keep breathing calmly, you can push through it. Your body will endure and your mind will adapt. And once you've done it, you'll feel so proud of yourself. Exhilarated and relaxed. It's a thrilling feeling when your heart beats faster and your blood is rushing through your veins.

This hot-cold combo can be experienced in many different settings. One of my favourites is along a frozen river – a traditional Finnish sauna, which is rented privately to groups. But if you travel solo, you can also score authentic bathing experiences. Public saunas are the most budget-friendly options and you can find them in many cities in the Nordic countries.

Some of my favourites are community-run places like Helsinki's Sompasauna and Oslo Fjord CleanUP Sauna. Both of these places are also conscious of the environment and focus on recycling and cleaning their surroundings.

MARK WATSON

CAMPING ON ISLA DEL PESCADO

SALAR DE UYUNI, BOLIVIA

Our surroundings were unfamiliar, it was as if we'd arrived on another planet. We were camped on a desert island, enveloped in a motionless white sea and surrounded by hundreds of slender cacti.

The sun had broken the distant horizon, rising into a cloudless sky. Our island cast a shadow that reached across the salt that surrounded us, reaching into infinity. The salt around us was off-white, dead flat and so hard you couldn't push a tent peg into it. The skyline was occasionally interrupted with faraway mountains and cones of volcanoes, which shimmered above the salar like mirages. The only man-made objects I could see were our bicycles and tent, pitched below near the edge of the island.

We were on Isla del Pescado, a lump of volcanic rock deep in Bolivia's Salar de Uyuni. Spanning over 10,500 sq km (4000 sq miles), it's not only the biggest salt flat on earth; it's the biggest flat place, and one of the most remarkable natural wonders of the world.

Yesterday we cycled here from a village on the 'shore', 30 km (18 miles) away. For a couple of hours, our universe became the hypnotic crunch of the salt crust beneath our tyres, our breathing and the deep blue dome of the sky overhead. Scale and distance became impossible to guess, disorienting us.

In this era of elusive solitude, it was special to feel so small and remote and alone.

Top: Sunrise illuminates cacti on Isla del Pescado
Bottom: Mysterious salt formations on the surface of the Salar de Uyuni

EVEREST IN THE NEWS

Megan Cuthbert

Everest has been making the news for different kind of extremes. The stark images of long queues of people waiting to reach the summit and the records of garbage being left on the mountain are reminders of the effects travel can have on natural environments. Now, more than ever, how we go is just as important as where we go when travelling.

Spectacular views from a road less-travelled

SAJIYA SHAH

TAKE IT EASIER TO EVEREST!

LUKLA, NEPAL

My journey to the Everest region was one of the most thrilling experiences of my life. It started with the flight to Lukla. Arriving at Tenzing Hillary Airport at 2840m (9000ft), with mountains and hills surrounding the tiny runway, was exhilarating yet horrifying. From here, the trek began. Every day's walk was a new challenge. The terrain was an amalgamation of flat, uphill and downhill, through beautiful forests and past big and small sacred stones, always watched over by the breathtaking Himalayas. The Dudhkoshi River was a great companion, and we crossed several suspension bridges.

We made a two-night stop at Namche Bazaar, the main city of the Everest region. This is the first point of acclimatisation. The vibrant city has its own charm, offering last-minute shopping for the trek, money exchange, food and the chance to enjoy some beers at an Irish pub at an altitude of 3450m (11,000ft). Plus, it has the best running hot showers available in the Everest region.

The acclimatisation hike to Everest View Hotel offered gorgeous vistas of Everest, Ama Dablam, Lhotse, Nuptse and other peaks, which are visible from here. From here, the walk became more strenuous, and I was challenged not only by the trail but also by the elevation gain.

A highlight was reaching Dingboche (4410m/14,000ft), the second stop for acclimatisation. Here, you discover if your body is coping with the high altitude and whether you are ready for a 5000m (16,000ft) ascent. The view of Mount Ama Dablam is mesmerising, and I was even more awestruck when I reached Kalapatthar (5545m/18,000ft), where I had the most unforgettable encounter with the almighty Mount Everest. This was the moment I realised why it is on the top of the list for travellers worldwide.

Mount Everest as seen from Namche Bazaar

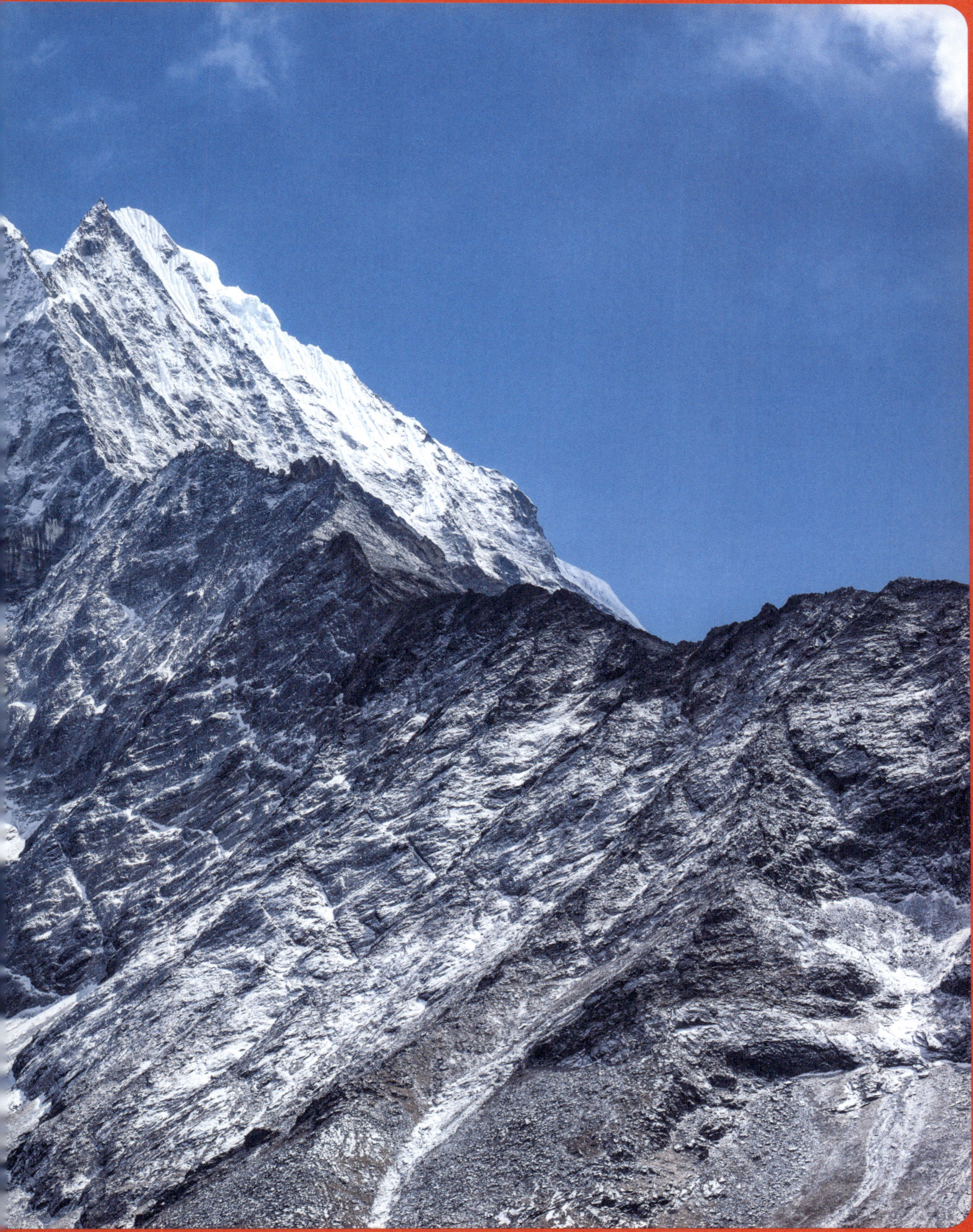

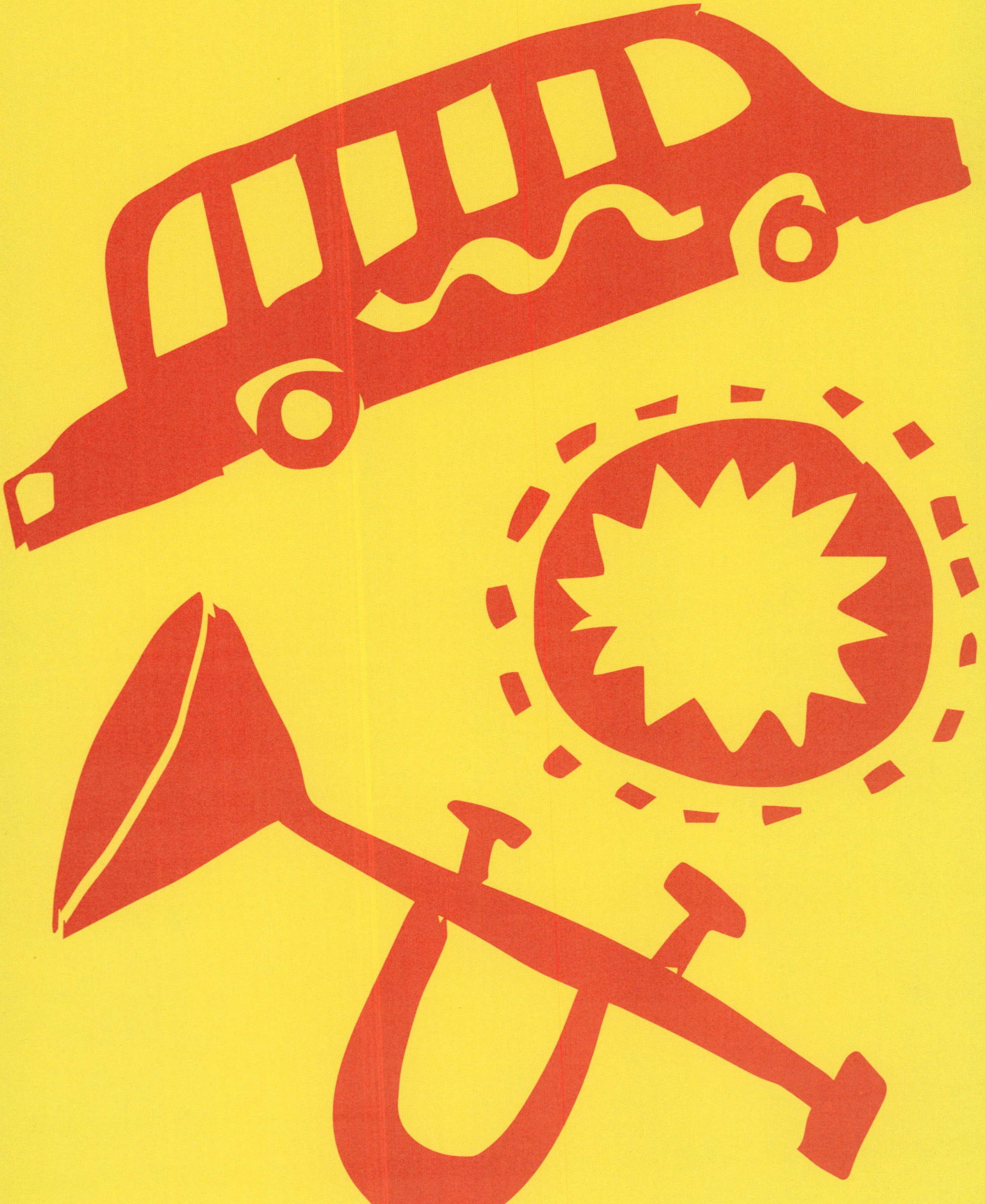

ART & CULTURE

ART & CULTURE

139	FEED YOUR SOUL WITH TRADITIONAL MUSIC
140	JAMES TURRELL'S RODEN CRATER
143	LIFE IN POLYPHONIC
144	RIO'S STREET ART
147	ART, ARCHITECTURE AND ARTISANS
148	FIND YOUR VOICE AMONG NEW FRIENDS
150	ARTS AND CRAFTS IN A SECRET PARADISE
152	FOREST OF FUTURE BOOKS
155	UNDULATING COLOUR IN A DREAMSCAPE
156	DUENDE IN SEVILLE
159	RELIVE THE '60S AT A KOREAN RECORD BAR
162	WHERE MAYAN AND CATHOLIC RITUALS COLLIDE
165	CELEBRATE LGBTQIA+ CULTURE IN CASTRO
166	DANCING A 65,000-YEAR-OLD TRADITION
170	GET A GLIMPSE OF NOMADIC LIFE
173	AN ENCOUNTER WITH THE ANCESTORS
174	EXPERIENCE THE DEEP RESONANCE OF INUIT THROAT SINGING

"What better way to break the ice than to sing your heart out in front of a group of people you've just met?"

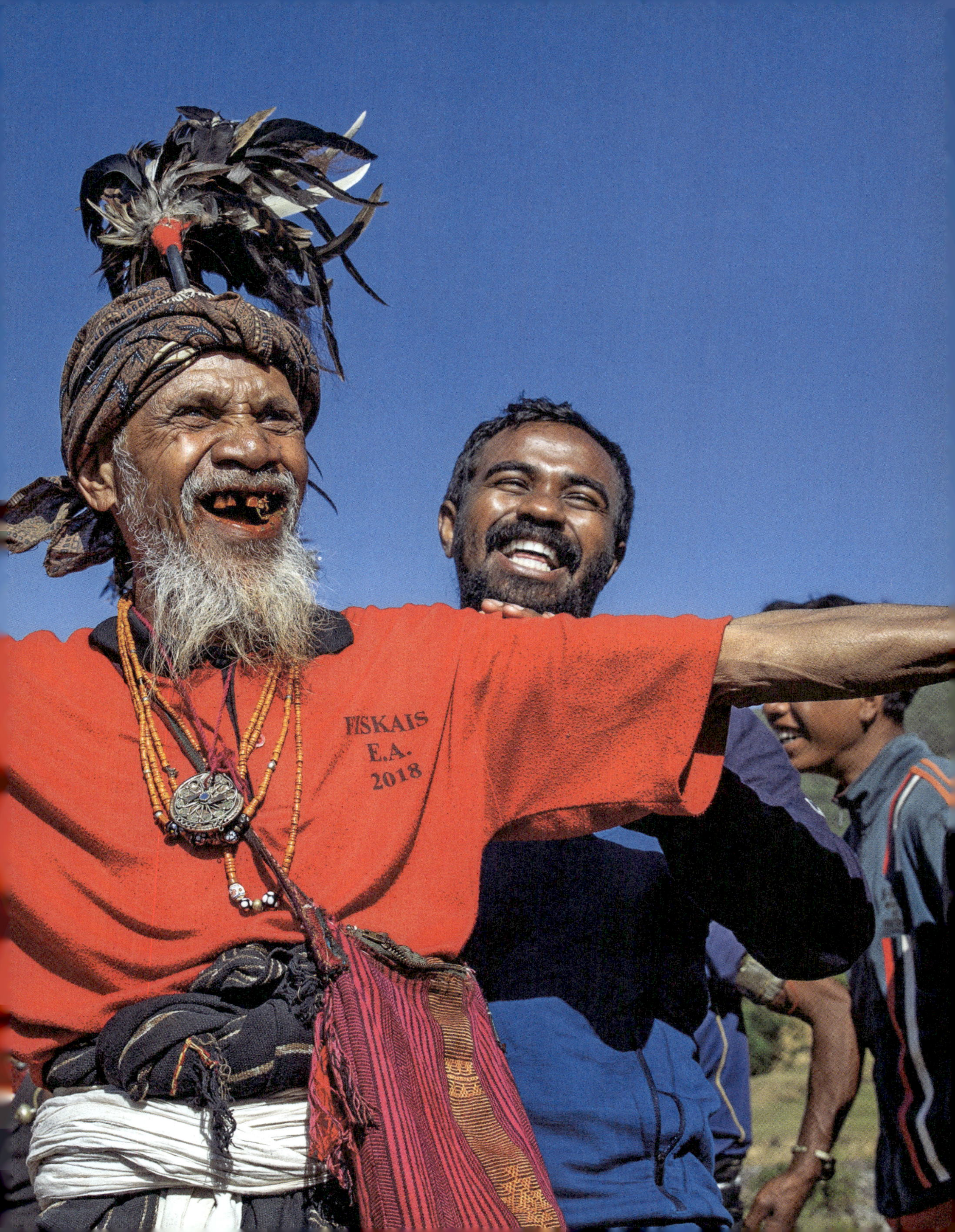
FISKAIS
E.A.
2018

The leader of the Houariyates troupe brings the group to their feet through song and dance in Marrakech

RACHEL MILLER

FEED YOUR SOUL WITH TRADITIONAL MUSIC

MARRAKECH, MOROCCO

It was a sticky, humid night when I found myself in a back alley in the medina in Marrakech, standing before a door camouflaged into the red-clay shell of the city. Behind the door, a traditional Moroccan performance by the Houariyates awaited our group – an experience that would change my perspective on art, music and feminism forever.

We took our seats and enjoyed a feast of sizzling tagines before being ushered to the front of an intimate living room to enjoy a lively dance filled with percussion and passion. The Houariyates are an all-female band with an infectious energy. They sing about desire and sensuality with unabashed emotion and enthusiasm.

Their performances are typically exclusive to female audiences, so we all chuckled when our trip leader translated the lyrics being chanted towards the only male in our group: 'F*** off Stephen'! But it was all in jest; the women had us up on the tables – Stephen included – swinging our hips and joining in song despite not knowing a word of their local dialect.

It was simple fun to us, but it was so much more for the troupe: a legacy and, above all, a succession. They told us they were proud to be Houariyates and were preparing their daughters to perpetuate their art and traditions. This symbolises the strength of their voices in a society that has historically silenced them. As we said our goodbyes and headed back into the bustle of the medina, I left with a new outlook on the power of music to change the way we all see the world.

ANDREA BLACK

JAMES TURRELL'S RODEN CRATER

PAINTED DESERT, USA

The work of renowned light and space artist James Turrell can be found in 30 countries, from Australia to Norway, but his magnum opus, 47 years in the making, will be his greatest legacy. Roden Crater in the Painted Desert region of northern Arizona is finally set to open in 2025. Described as an unprecedented, large-scale artwork – a series of tunnels and chambers created within a volcanic cinder cone – this much-anticipated immersive work is designed to be seen under moonlight. Since 1977, when he acquired the land, Turrell has been working on the crater. He chose Roden Crater for its remote location, far from artificial distractions, and its high altitude, offering unlimited sightlines of the vast sky.

The crater is 176m (580ft) tall and nearly 3km (2 miles) wide. While minimally invasive to the external natural landscape, internally the red-and-black cinder has been transformed into specially engineered spaces, creating a gateway to the contemplation of light, time and landscape. It has taken a huge amount of time and resources – Kanye West notably kicked in USD$10 million after a private tour by Turrell. He reportedly said, 'His lights turn you into a Zen state.'

So why, after all these years, could 2025 be the date we begin to see the light? The 80-year-old artist knows that every 18.61 years, the moon reaches its northernmost and southernmost maximums, an event known as a Major Lunar Standstill. Turrell's work is built to align most perfectly during a Major Lunar Standstill. It's next occurrence? April 2025.

Roden Crater, Arizona

Top: Musicians in traditional costume in Tbilisi, Georgia

Bottom: Traditional polyphonic folk music singers performing at Bagrati Cathedral, Kutaisi, Georgia

JULIAN TOMPKIN

LIFE IN POLYPHONIC

TBILISI, GEORGIA

The sound descends as though it is being transmitted from the heavens. It is a physical sensation, the rich intonations wrapping around the stone church and the people lucky enough to be seated inside the tiny chamber. The polyphonic music of Georgia is one of the world's great and most enigmatic musical traditions, recognised by UNESCO as Intangible Cultural Heritage of Humanity. Georgia is a country at the visceral intersection of history and global culture – perched between Asia, the Middle East and Europe. It is as ancient as it is contemporary, with a distinct character that can be found in its wine, architecture and song.

While the polyphonic musical form predates Christianity's arrival to Georgia, Tbilisi's oldest church – the Anchiskhati Basilica, constructed in 522 CE – is today the custodian of this mystical and ancient tradition. It is home to the universally lauded Anchiskhati Choir, whose performances are as transcendent as they are popular.

This small ensemble of musical mystics has been performing since 1987 and continues to be the preeminent exponent of this folk tradition: a hypnotic chant scafolded around a tonal drone that is augmented by dissonant harmonies. The group performs in the church sporadically throughout the year – most notably Sunday morning mass in various guises – but the annual Christmas night liturgy remains the most iconic of them all, and a true rite for any intrepid cultural traveller.

While this is a sacred place of worship, the parishioners welcomed us in on a cold spring morning – the medieval stone basilica was misty with incense and candlelight. And suddenly there it was: the primordial chorale of voices washing over the room, otherworldly and sensorial beyond sound. The sky responded with the first snows of spring.

BRETT ATKINSON

RIO'S STREET ART

RIO DE JANEIRO, BRAZIL

According to Nina Gani, my guide to the ever-changing street art scene of Rio de Janeiro, the megacity's municipal workers are the best guides to new urban canvases forever popping up around town.

Nina is a passionate Carioca (born and bred Rio local) who is both a graphic artist and a friend of the city's most celebrated street artists. I met her at the Mural das Etnias, a massive 3000 sq m (32,000 sq ft) artwork completed for the 2016 Olympics and jointly funded by Instagram, the International Olympic Committee and Rio de Janeiro's city council. Sao Paolo artist Eduardo Cobra's 170m-long (550ft-long) artwork reflecting representatives of all of humanity is now slightly faded, but its transformation of Rio's once unsafe port district remains tangible.

On the edge of the port area, abandoned warehouses are also being repurposed into offices and apartments. Following the officially sanctioned art of Rio 2016, Nina explained that the street art scene has now evolved to be ephemeral and dynamic. Her deep knowledge and personal connections helped me learn about Rio's roaming band of artists, many of whom are also active in community projects in the hillside favela neighbourhoods framing the city. Tags from @warkrocinha and @rafamon, both renowned Rio artists, become familiar, and Nina explained their wall-covering works often reference social justice, LGBTQIA+ issues and women's rights.

On a city block undergoing transformation, Rio's hardworking cleaners have probably already noticed colourful new works of art on a wall awaiting demolition and subsequent renewal.

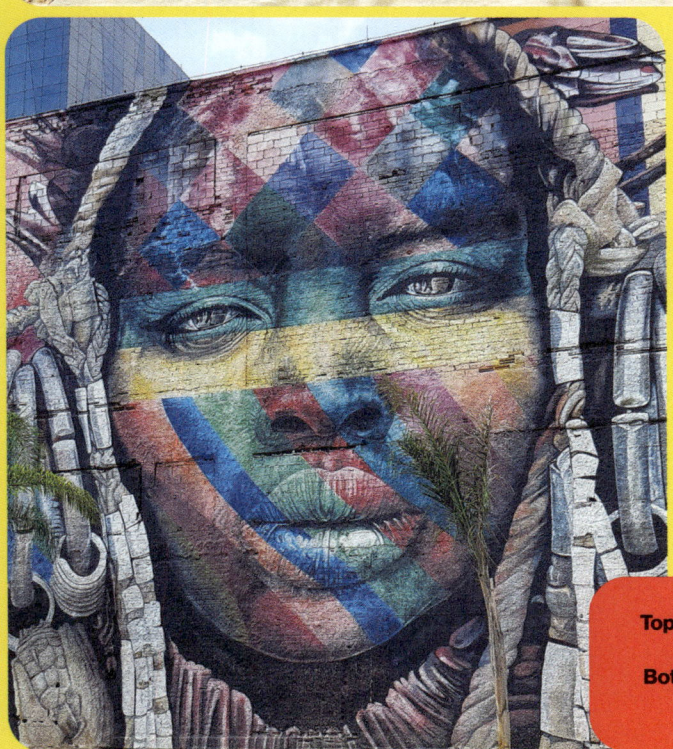

Top: Escadaria Selarón is adorned with multicoloured tiles

Bottom: Mural das Etnias is the largest street art in the world

Top: *Containbow*
Bottom: Fremantle Markets

✱
FREO FREQUENTS

The sprawling **Fremantle Prison** (1852) in the East End is a protected World Heritage Site, with artesian tunnels to explore and regular concerts in the courtyard.

A favourite for any visitor, the **Fremantle Markets** house stalls peddling artisan produce and wares, tourist trinkets and street food.

The little sibling of Fremantle Arts Centre, the **Moores Building** very much holds its own on Freo's creative landscape. The art gallery hosts regular exhibitions and concerts.

As well as housing numerous studio spaces for practising artists, **PS Art Space** on Packenham Street is Freo's most progressive artistic enclave, open daily with regular exhibitions and events.

The best-preserved heritage precinct in WA, the **West End** defines the goldrush grandeur of 19th-century WA, and is lined with gracious merchant buildings converted into art spaces (including Japingka Aboriginal Art), and restaurants.

JULIAN TOMPKIN

ART, ARCHITECTURE AND ARTISANS

FREMANTLE, AUSTRALIA

Fremantle is a place of consequence. The greater Fremantle area, known as Walyalup, has been a deeply important meeting point for Traditional Owners – the Whadjuk Noongar People – for tens of thousands of years. Post colonisation, it has been the primary port of Western Australia (WA) – a place of arrival, connection and exchange.

It is this frontier status that has sculpted Fremantle's unrivalled position as WA's capital of culture – home to a deeply progressive and creative community, fashioned by many cultures and creeds. It is here that the Swan River spills into the Indian Ocean – a deeply sacred place for Noongar people, where the creation tales of the Wagyl rainbow serpent forever resonate.

Here you will find the WA Maritime Museum, featuring walls etched with the names of thousands of immigrants who have arrived at this very spot to build new lives. Fremantle's immigrant foundations are as compelling as they are ubiquitous – from the quaint Italian eateries to the sculptures of Greek and Portuguese fishermen in the still-working fishing boat harbour, where today tourists congregate to enjoy produce freshly unloaded from trawlers.

Here, you will also find a bronzed homage to Freo's most notorious rapscallion, AC/DC singer Bon Scott. Music runs deep beneath this limestone bedrock – home ground to global icons Tame Impala and WA's most important music venues, Mojo's included.

Once an asylum, today the splendorous gothic manor at the city's eastern end houses the Fremantle Arts Centre, which houses the state's finest contemporary art and cultural program, including the annual Revealed, a First Nations art celebration. After visiting, you can get snapped beneath the city's most photographed public artwork, the *Containbow*. Set your creativity free ... in Freo.

VANESSA ONDRADE

FIND YOUR VOICE AMONG NEW FRIENDS

HIROSHIMA, JAPAN

What better way to break the ice than to sing your heart out in front of a group of people you've just met? There is none, in my opinion. If you ever find yourself among the bustling streets of Japan, you must put karaoke on your to-do list. There are many karaoke bars, but my group ended up at Big Echo in Hiroshima, which had plenty of private rooms and offered all-you-can-drink (yes, alcohol) for less than USD$30 per person. We had pretty low expectations going into the experience, but everyone was blown away when we entered our room. It had disco lights, a mini stage, and an extensive list of song choices in various languages, which was perfect for channelling your inner superstar. We were all a bit shy at first, but as the night went on and we had a little more liquid courage in us, we were all fighting for a chance with the microphone.

There's something about screaming at the top of your lungs to an ABBA song that automatically brings people closer together.

Sing your heart out at a Japanese karaoke bar

JULIAN TOMPKIN

ARTS AND CRAFTS IN A SECRET PARADISE

HYDRA, GREECE

Hydra quite literally takes you by surprise. The ferry skirts the barren rock, 70km (43 miles) south of Athens, before suddenly taking a sharp left to reveal an ancient whitewashed town etched like a watercolour print. It is an arresting sight that has compelled many to immortalise it in paint, words, acetate and song – among them Henry Miller and Leonard Cohen, Sophia Loren and Giorgos Seferis.

Hydra is an island that pushes the frontiers of both the imagination and the thighs. Indeed, as well as being a cultural ganglion, it is notoriously vehicle-free. While a visit to any other Mediterranean isle demands fatalistic games of chicken with kamikaze mopeds, Hydra's absolute tranquillity is wholly unique – the only audible sounds are the chorus of cicadas and the introspective din of the vesper bells.

CRAFTY HABITS

- **Hydra Archives:** Set upon the gracious agora, this prominent building is home to the Hydra museum and also hosts regular art exhibitions, book launches and cultural events, all open to the public. The Hydra School Projects building next door holds an annual summer exhibition.

- **Prophet Elias Monastery:** A transcendent hour-long hike up Mount Eros (600m/1970ft), this remote monastery continues its ancient tradition of fashioning artisan wares and produce, many on offer for a donation – including religious ephemera, essential oils and on site-produced honey.

- **DESTE Foundation for Contemporary Art:** Once home to the island's slaughterhouse, today this cliffside building is home to an annual program curated by the DESTE Foundation, based in Geneva. The golden Apollo Wind Spinner sculpture by Jeff Koons – visible on arrival to Hydra harbour by ferry – has become a true cultural icon of the island since its installation in 2022.

- **Hydrama Theatre:** Set in an ancient stone amphitheatre in the small village of Vlychos, Hydrama Theatre hosts a program of classic Greek theatre – most often with a contemporary twist – each summer beneath a resplendent canopy of stars, with the lights of the Peloponnese flickering in the distance. Entry and boat transfer from Hydra harbour are free.

The township is cut into a mountainside, which means walking ... lots of walking. However, the charmed donkeys in the amphitheatre-shaped harbour are on hand to transport luggage to your accommodation.

Today, Hydra remains a sanctuary for the artistically inclined. On any given day, you're likely to bump into David Gilmour of Pink Floyd – who keeps a house here – or Jeff Koons, who visits most summers in his impossible-to-miss yacht (painted with an enthusiastic nod to Cubism). Join in the melee with animated dinners at Dousko's Tavern and sunset drinks at the Pirate Bar upon the agora, where the words of Cohen's fabled canticle to the island, 'Bird on a Wire', remain ever prescient: 'I have tried in my way to be free.'

The view from Hydra

ANDREW BAIN

FOREST OF FUTURE BOOKS

OSLO, NORWAY

In the forests above Oslo, a remarkable library is growing. Planted in 2014, the copse of 1000 trees will stand for 100 years, at which point they'll be felled, pulped and used to print 100 previously unpublished manuscripts from some of the world's top authors.

Each year until then, a new manuscript is written and held in trust in the specially designed Silent Room of Oslo's Deichman Bjørvika public library, with works from writers as prominent as Margaret Atwood, David Mitchell and Karl Ove Knausgård already in the collection.

The manuscripts can be glimpsed – but not read – in handmade glass drawers inside the top-floor Silent Room, which faces the Future Library's forest and is lined with wood from the trees that were cleared to plant the new forest.

The most tangible way to experience this anthology-in-waiting is to visit the forest. Head to Frognerseteren, a hillside station at the end of Oslo's subway system looking down onto the city and Oslo Fjord. It's about a 20-minute walk along wintertime ski tracks or through summertime forest with carpets of blueberries, following signs to Framtidsbiblioteket (Future Library).

There's no formality or hype (or even signs) when you arrive, just indistinct trails wandering into and through the young stand of spruce trees. There's a tangible sense of greatness, however, and when I was here, I found myself laying hands on the trees, wondering if this one was a Knausgård novel or that one a Tsitsi Dangarembga story. Only time – lots of it – will tell.

The walls of the Silent Room in Oslo's Deichman Bjørvika public library house manuscripts that will not be read until 2114

More than 100,000 globes illuminate the Sensorio Field of Light, Paso Robles

BRETT ATKINSON

UNDULATING COLOUR IN A DREAMSCAPE

PASO ROBLES, CALIFORNIA, USA

Opened in May 2019 and originally envisaged as a temporary art installation, *Sensorio: Field of Lights* near the Californian town of Paso Robles celebrated its fifth anniversary in May 2024. It's now a permanent attraction and a popular drawcard for visitors venturing to the rural heart of Paso Robles wine country.

Spanning more than 6 ha (15 acres) of rolling hills, *Sensorio* is one of a series of ground-breaking light installations developed by English/Australian visual artist Bruce Munro in outdoor locations around the world. Other Fields of Light enliven Uluru in Australia and New York's Freedom Plaza, but *Sensorio* is the largest and arguably the most spectacular. Around 100,000 stemmed globes lit by fibre optics slowly change hue, gently morphing to encompass delicate shades of purple, blue, green, red and yellow. The colours undulate in unison across *Sensorio's* natural contours, and visitors walk through the site immersed in a colourful and ever-evolving dreamscape.

The transition from twilight to darkness is special – the spheres resemble vibrant blooms of flowers gradually growing in intensity and luminosity. In 2021, Munro added the *Light Towers*, an array of 69 towers composed of 17,000 wine bottles, accompanied by a spirited and choreographed musical score. Munro added *Gone Fishing* and *Fireflies*, two additional solar-powered light installations, in 2023; these also invite visitors to engage with the environment around them. Booking ahead is recommended for *Sensorio*, especially during summer in California.

JULIAN TOMPKIN

DUENDE IN SEVILLE

SEVILLE, SPAIN

Duende is more a feeling than a word. It's a heightened state of consciousness, where the body and the soul elevate into a harmonious realm of euphoria, as the music and rhythm take hold. But this most profound of artforms has suffered in recent years, as Seville has emerged as one of the world's most popular tourist destinations – unable to avoid the breakneck commercialisation of the city's cultural touchstones.

Leaving the throngs of travellers in Santa Cruz – home to the city's blockbuster landmarks – we crossed the Río Guadalquivir to Triana, the district at the very epicentre of Seville's flamenco subculture. The district – a traditional gypsy quarter, with its winding roads and traditional tapas bars – has become increasingly popular in recent years, but it remains the heart and soul of the city's flamenco tradition: and none more so than Simpecao (Calle Castilla 82).

While most flamenco shows are polite ticketed affairs today, Simpecao is as traditional as *jamón Ibérico de Bellota* (cured pork from a pig fattened exclusively on chestnuts). Pull up a stool, order a drink and some tapas (mandatory if you're staying for the show – albeit with plenty of budget options) and let the experience transport you to another plane of consciousness.

Unlike the more commercial flamenco shows that have flooded the city, haunts such as Simpecao allow for the innate spontaneity of the form, where the performers and audience are whipped to a cathartic crescendo – best tempered with a cold glass of local sherry. After the show, and approaching 1am, we spilled onto the street arm-in-arm in a state of euphoria and headed along the river walk towards Lo Nuestro (Calle Betis 31) – another surviving bastion of the artform. A pair of hands clapped. A guitar struck a clarion chord. And once again we were off on a journey to a place beyond the realm of imagination.

Top: Traditional Moorish arches frame a restaurant courtyard in Seville, Spain
Bottom: A flamenco dancer

Top: You'll find bartenders with great taste in drinks and music in Seoul
Bottom: Nighttime bustle of Hongdae Street market

ANDREA BLACK

RELIVE THE '60S AT A KOREAN RECORD BAR

SEOUL, SOUTH KOREA

In the evening, atop Seoul's bland-looking office blocks and down its basement stairwells, passionate bar owners cue up their favourite vinyl records. Like Japan, the capital of South Korea is full of LP bars hidden in plain sight; you just need to know where to look. These aren't the usual DJs who haul their records around town to different gigs. These are record collectors who run bars just so they can play their prized albums and 45s every night. They work the turntables in front of shelves of records while serving *soju* (a clear spirit) and Hite lager. These bars feel like an extension of a friend's comfortable lounge room. It might be Seochon Blues in Jongno-gu, Woodstock in Gangham or – the best – Cream in Hongdae, where the owner Choi Byung-ik specialises in '60s psyche, blues, rock, folk and oldies.

At the wooden bar, there's a block of white paper and pencils to write down your requests, which can encompass any genre. Mr Choi encourages guests to get creative. Over in the far corner of the room is an art wall featuring drawn requests: Liam Gallagher in the realism style, a strident Axl Rose, a tousle-haired Robert Plant and even a forlorn-looking Eric Carmen as seen on the cover of the self-titled album featuring 'All by Myself'.

When we visited, Mr Choi refreshed our drinks and offered plates of pretzels and nuts. He was up for the request challenge, and we were keen to be schooled in Korean music from the '60s and '70s. For every Neil Young, Ike and Tina Turner or Beatles song, he'd play us Korean cover versions from the post-war Korean 'group sounds' era carefully pulled from his collection. Over this sound system, 'Heart of Gold' by Tempest and 'Hey Jude' by the Key Boys might have been the best cover versions I've ever heard. It could have been because Mr Choi stood there, handing us the record sleeves to peruse, looking enthusiastic. His English was way better than our Korean, but right then, we were all captivated by the incredible sounds, and conversation didn't matter. There's something so intimate about a record-listening party. Other bar-goers, mostly analogue-loving couples in their 20s, had their lists waiting, and Mr Choi tended to their requests. Everyone had a ball.

Even luxury hotels are in on LP bars. Make your choice, grab a beer or coffee, put the needle on the record and sit back to take in that warm analogue sound.

A fine selection of liquor and vinyl at Ryse in Hongdae, Seoul

BEST RECORD BARS IN SEOUL

Andrea Black

- **Park Hyatt Seoul:** This luxury hotel has renovated its underground restaurant, the Timber House, into an LP bar with 2000 records.

- **Ryse:** Hip hotel in Hongdae with the Side Note Club on the top floor, housing curated shelves of vinyl (inexplicably, there's a disc-cutting lathe there, too) surrounded by framed prints of the Beastie Boys and Run DMC by hip-hop photographer Ricky Powell.

- **Music Complex Seoul:** If you can't wait until evening, head to this giant listening cafe in Insa-dong where each table has a turntable and headphones, and the walls are lined with vinyl; there are 12,000 albums to choose from.

MANDY ALDERSON

WHERE MAYAN AND CATHOLIC RITUALS COLLIDE

CHAMULA, MEXICO

My first words: 'I think I've found copal heaven.'

Before stepping through the doors of what appeared to be a quaint white church on the edge of a small village square, I thought I'd simply come across yet another charming *iglesia* (church). But stepping inside was a whole other experience.

In the dimly lit space, the air felt heavy. It was thick with the smoke of copal incense and the low but emotional murmur of prayer. After my eyes and mind adjusted, I took in the glow of what seemed like, and probably were, a thousand small white candles. They were everywhere – stuck with wax to the floor, to table tops and into the many small altars for the numerous Catholic saints who bore witness from the walls. The tiled floor was thick with pine needles, laid fresh every morning. Tzotzil Maya gathered and chanted with *curanderos* (healers) to carry out cultural rituals of hope and healing. Meanwhile, Catholic saints were dressed in Maya clothes, with mirrors hanging from their necks, so that when people made their confessions, they saw not only the priest, but also themselves as someone they could not lie to. A local form of moonshine called *pox* (medicine in the Tzotzil language) was generously consumed by those who believed it would release negative spirits or energies from their body.

Wandering carefully and respectfully up to the main altar, silent, barely breathing (either from absolute awe or the fear of coughing) and mindful not to knock a candle onto the floor covered in dried pine needles, I felt like I'd stepped into an incredibly private yet somehow peaceful and perfectly organised chaos where over 500 years of opposing religion blended and thrived.

Iglesia de San Juan in Chamula is approximately a 15-minute drive from San Cristobal de las Casas in Chiapas, Mexico, a state often referred to as the cultural heart of Mexico. The village of Chamula itself is unique in its autonomy from the rest of the state of Chiapas. It is governed by its own authority, and external police and military are forbidden to enter. Sitting at 2200m (7000ft) above sea level in the Chiapas highlands, the population is almost 100 per cent Indigenous with Tzotzil language and culture living strong.

Iglesia de San Juan Chamula, near San Cristobal de las Casas in Chiapas, Mexico

Castro street scene

ANDREW COLLINS

CELEBRATE LGBTQIA+ CULTURE IN CASTRO

SAN FRANCISCO, USA

It might just be the world's most recognisable queer neighbourhood; it's certainly one of the most colourful and historic. The first thing you'll notice as you approach this hilly San Francisco district of Victorian and Edwardian houses and storefronts is the 6-by-9m (20-by-30ft) rainbow flag, waving from the top of a towering flagpole at Market and Castro Sts. It rises above Harvey Milk Plaza, which is named in honour of the iconic 1970s activist and politician, whose inspiring life and tragic assassination were depicted in the 2008 Gus Van Sant Oscar-nominated biopic *Milk*. The flag also honours the late Gilbert Baker who, while living in San Francisco in 1978, created the rainbow flag.

These are among several landmarks that celebrate the neighbourhood's vibrant LGBTQIA+ legacy. Perhaps most dramatic is the Castro Theatre, an ornate 1400-seat movie palace from the 1920s; at the time of writing it was undergoing a major restoration. It's expected to reopen in summer 2025, when it will once again host queer and multicultural film festivals, music concerts and drag shows. At 575 Castro St, you can admire works inside Queer Arts Featured, an artist-led gallery located in the storefront that once housed Harvey Milk's camera shop, and around the corner, be sure to explore the fascinating photos and artifacts at the excellent GLBT Historical Society Museum. But perhaps the easiest way to get to know the Castro's rich queer legacy is simply by popping inside one of its many longtime gathering spots, such as Twin Peaks Tavern and Moby Dick gay bars, and the iconic all-night diner Orphan Andy's, all of which have served the community since the 1970s.

KASSIDY WATERS

DANCING A 65,000-YEAR-OLD TRADITION

SYDNEY/WARRANG, AUSTRALIA

I'm standing in complete blackout. The Sydney Opera House Theatre air is crisp. I'm waiting side stage to start our 90-minute dance theatre work. Shimmers of bodies and faces sweep past me. All our hands reach for the soft clay earth we call Ochre. We get the last of our laughs out. You can feel the energy start to calm as our minds focus on our breath and our intention as we paint up.

Our bodies are conditioned daily to undertake the athletic weight and artistry of a Bangarra Dance Theatre show. By sharing the stories of our First Nations Peoples and our unique and beautiful landscapes, audiences are invited to learn the complexities of our culture and our survival for over 65,000 years.

The flame in my belly ignites and after about five minutes, it's a fire that gives warmth to my body. If I close my eyes, I could be standing outside breathing the crisp morning air of eucalyptus on Wanaruah Country.

The smoke machines start to pour out a thick fog. I look down at my body and see the ochre is dry and starting to crack like our dry salt lakes. I see the silhouette of the dancers marking through choreography. I feel the readiness and see the staunchness. I see a generation ready to inspire and share truth. I see them. I don't want to be anywhere else.

So we continue to paint the ochre onto our bodies and dance. It is our medicine.

Kassidy Waters and Daniel Mateo of Bangarra Dance Theatre perform outside the Sydney Opera House

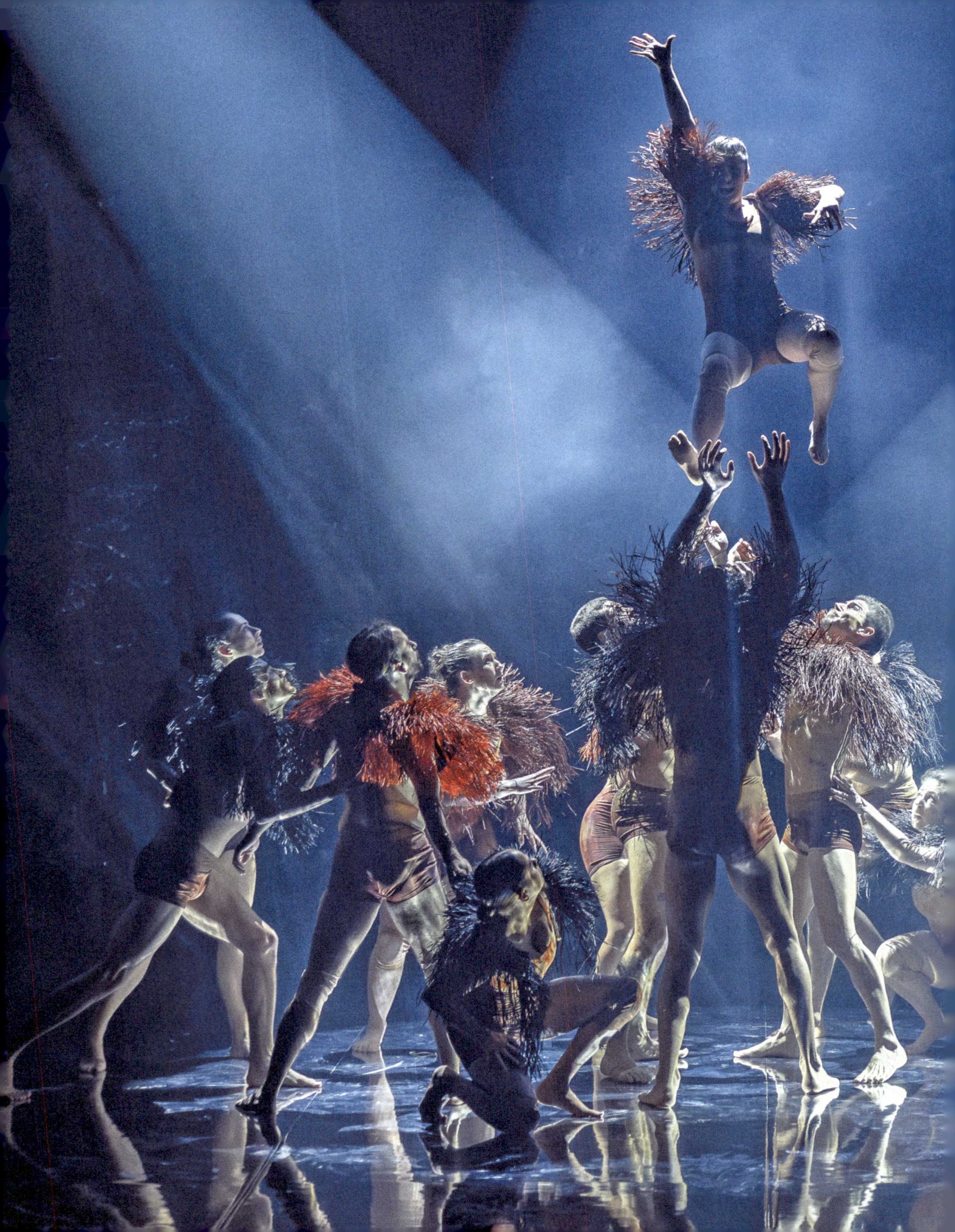

Bangarra Dance Theatre performance of *Horizon*

EMMA LALIBERTE

GET A GLIMPSE OF NOMADIC LIFE

MOROCCO

It was a beautiful fall day as we drove on a winding road between Fes and Midelt. Our guide, Youssef, loved to surprise us each day. From a tasty treat to a roadside view, we never knew what was around the next corner. Youssef phoned his friend, Rahal, who is a Moroccan Berber. The Berbers proudly call themselves the Amazigh, the 'free people', and they live a nomadic lifestyle, herding sheep and goats and moving with the seasons.

On this particular day, Rahal happened to be around, so we stopped in to say hello. Not only did Rahal greet us with open arms, he also welcomed us into his home, a traditional Amazigh nomadic home made of woven goat hairs and other textiles. A place where his family called home for a few months of the year until they packed up and moved their animals with the seasons.

We sang, danced, sipped tea and had great conversations with Rahal for well over an hour. Rahal told us all about his upbringing and way of life and serenaded us with his guitar. This surprise was well received and has never been forgotten, all thanks to Youssef and Rahal allowing travellers to experience their culture.

Top: Dancing along to Rahal playing traditional Berber music

Bottom: Rahal showing how to play one of the traditional Berber instruments

Dancing at dawn in Timor-Leste

LUCY SIEBERT

AN ENCOUNTER WITH THE ANCESTORS

TIMOR-LESTE

We were up at 4am – it was a chilly start at 1392m (4500ft) above sea level, but there was no time for coffee – even though we were in the heart of Timor-Leste's subtropical highlands and the coffee here is among the best in the world.

Instead, our group of seven dashed across the main street of Maubisse and drowsily heaved ourselves into two hardy Troopy 4x4s. 'Hurry,' our tour leader Anastacio Madeira urged us.

We were in a race against not only dawn – but also the ancestral spirits, who loom large over life in Timor-Leste. We had been invited to a cultural ceremony that had only previously been experienced by two other groups of visitors – but we needed to get to the remote mountain village before dawn.

Forty-five minutes of spine-cracking, bouncing ascents in the Troopys and we reached the summit. I could smell smoky fires and could just make out some shapes of the village buildings. But it was the eery sounds that meandered through the darkness that grabbed my attention: a yowl, bells jingling, gongs being beaten, singing, a horn being blown.

As a buttery pre-dawn light cast a gentle glow over the hills, I saw a group of about 20 figures making their way towards us – silhouettes of fine feathered headdresses and ceremonial tais fabrics.

The villagers sang and swayed as they greeted us, grasping our hands and pulling us into a circle where we joined the rhythmic dancing – kicking one foot in front of the other – for who knows how long. Time stood still. We danced, we laughed and each visitor made an offering to the ancestors. I offered a single cigarette on the timber altar.

More dancing, more gongs, more celebrations. We realised the sun had risen – dawn had passed, and Anastacio declared we were all family now. We could return any time – the villagers will remember us, he said.

In that moment in time, an experience shared with so few others, I knew that I too would remember the villagers forever.

INUKSUK MACKAY

EXPERIENCE THE DEEP RESONANCE OF INUIT THROAT SINGING

NUNAVUT, CANADA

As the sounds of Inuit throat singing echo through arctic landscapes, they carry with them stories of resilience, culture, and a deep connection to the land. This ancient art form, once on the brink of extinction, now thrives, captivating audiences worldwide. Adventurers can now experience a journey to witness the revival and celebration of throat singing, a cultural gem that has not only survived but flourished against all odds.

Throat singing, or *katajjaq* in Inuktitut, is more than a musical performance, it's a dialogue, a dance of breath and sound between two performers. Traditionally, Inuit women would engage in these vocal games, their voices intertwining in rhythms that mimic the sounds of nature – water flowing, wind whispering, animals calling. This practice, handed down through generations, is a testament to the Inuit way of life, deeply intertwined with the Arctic environment.

However, during the 20th century, Inuit throat singing faced severe suppression. Colonial policies and missionary efforts aimed to eradicate Indigenous practices, viewing them as obstacles to assimilation. Throat singing was banned, and many traditions were driven underground. Yet, despite these efforts, the spirit of *katajjaq* endured, preserved in the memories of elders who passed it on in secret.

Today, throat singing is experiencing a powerful renaissance, thanks to the efforts of Inuit women who have passed the practice on to their children and grandchildren. Modern-day acts like Silla and PIQSIQ blend traditional techniques with contemporary music, bringing *katajjaq* to new audiences through mesmerising performances and innovative recordings. Their work, amplified by social media, has sparked a global interest in this unique art form.

For those seeking an immersive experience, travelling to Nunavut offers the chance to engage directly with Inuit communities and their traditions. Throat singing festivals and music events are now vibrant spaces where culture, history and modernity converge. The Alianait Arts Festival in Iqaluit, Nunavut, is a must-visit, offering a week-long celebration of Inuit culture through music, dance, and art. Nunavut Music Week, another significant event, showcases local talent and invites visitors to witness the vibrant, living culture of the Inuit.

Top: Music duo PIQSIQ blend traditional throat singing techniques with contemporary styles

Bottom: The Arctic landscape of Nunavut, Canada, shapes the cultures and traditions of the Inuit

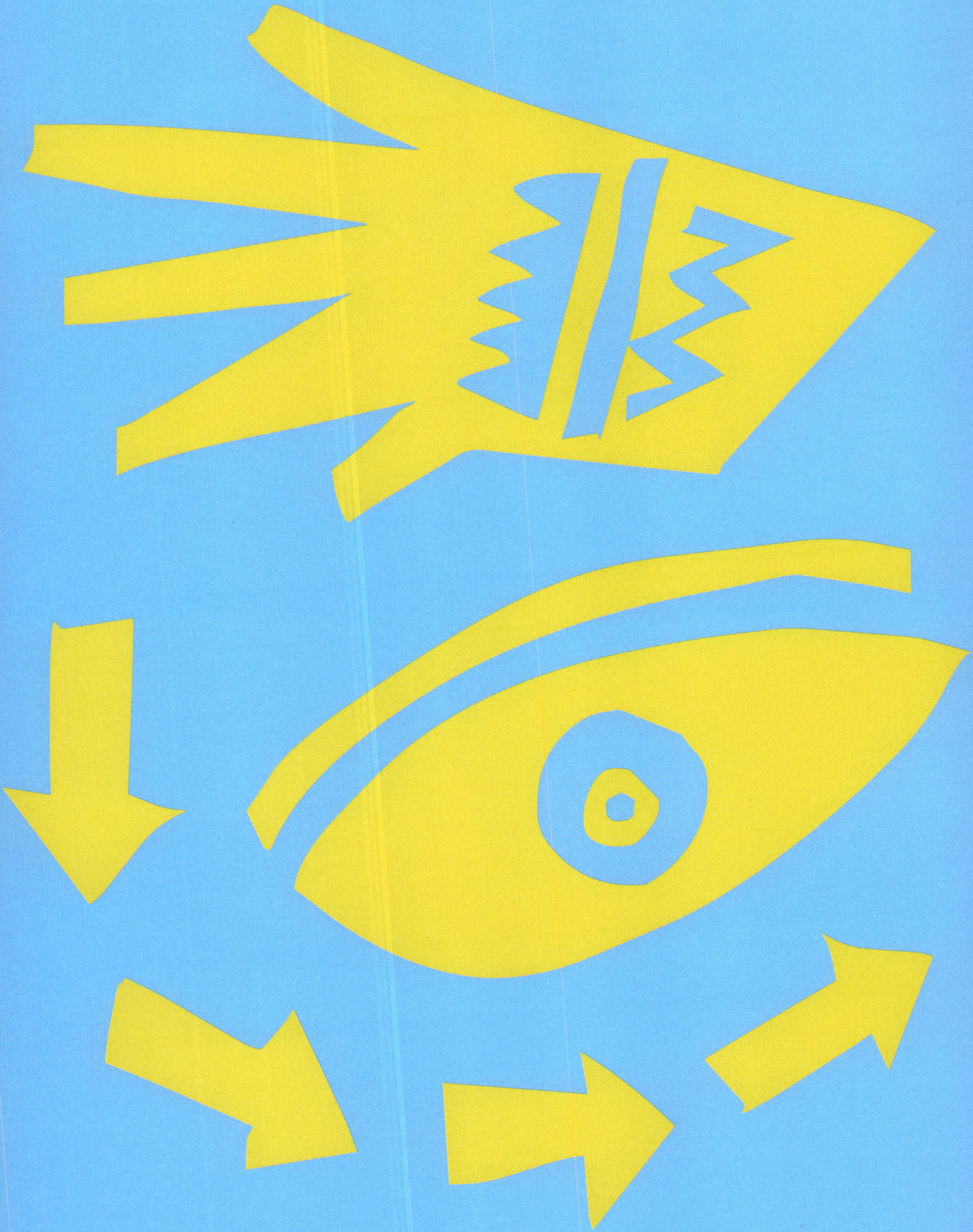

FESTIVALS & EVENTS

FESTIVALS & EVENTS

181	**WELCOMING THE DEAD AT DÍA DE MUERTOS**
182	**SONGKRAN – THE WORLD'S BIGGEST WATER FIGHT**
185	**THE LORD OF THE EARTHQUAKE**
186	**GATE-CRASHING AN INDIAN WEDDING**
189	**CELEBRATE BLOOMSDAY**
190	**RAMADAN IN THE HIGH ATLAS MOUNTAINS**
195	**WORLD OF WEARABLEART**

"What began as a traditional new-year ritual of gently sprinkling water on someone as a sign of good luck and goodwill has now developed into the biggest water fight on the planet."

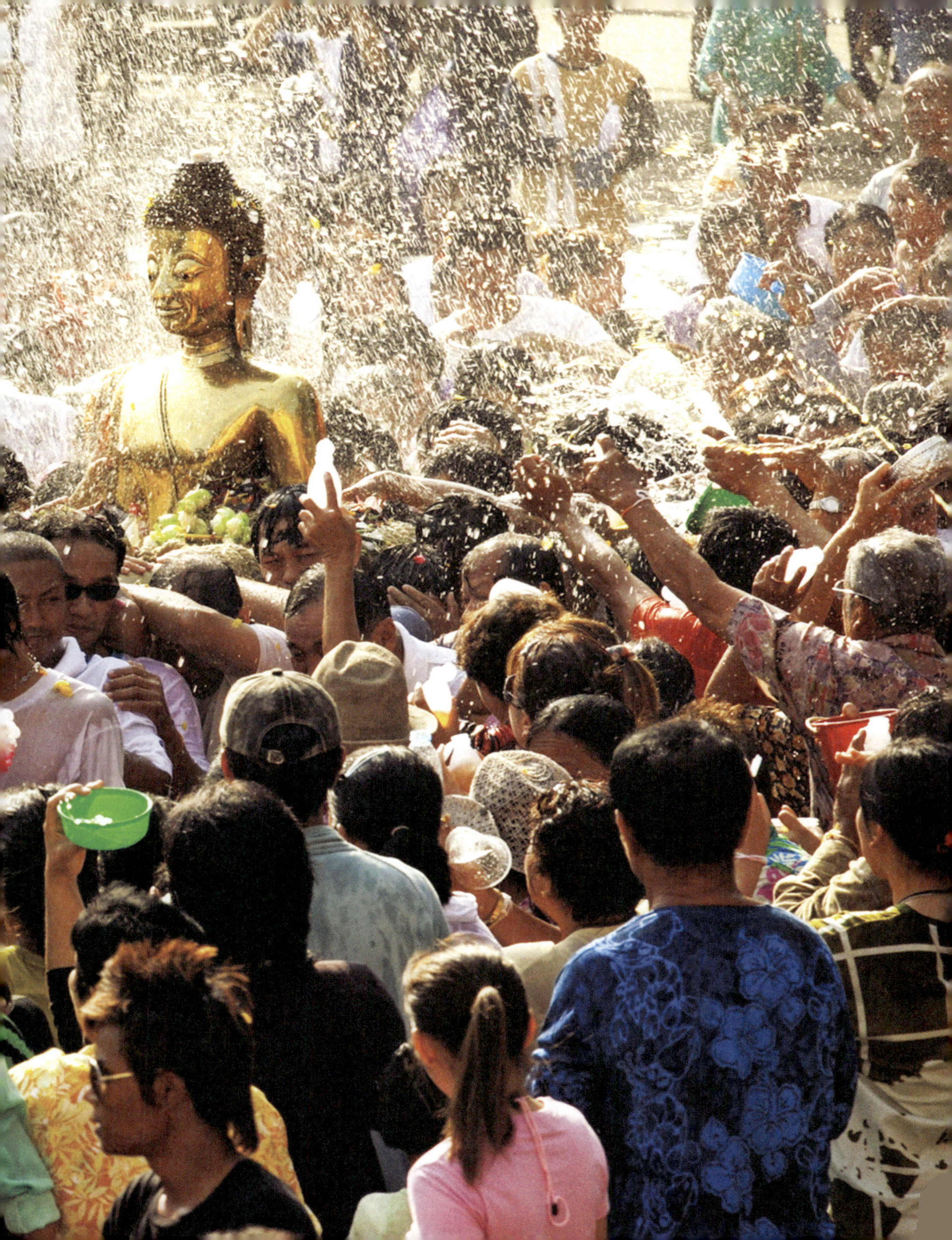

Top: Plaza de la Constitución (known as Zócalo)
Bottom: Women wearing Catrina makeup at the Día de Muertos parade

CRISTINA ALONSO

WELCOMING THE DEAD AT DÍA DE MUERTOS

MEXICO CITY, MEXICO

Something magical happens in Mexico City as October comes to an end. The streets are painted a lively orange with *cempasúchil* flowers – bright marigolds. They announce the upcoming visit of our dearly departed on 1 or 2 November, known as Día de Muertos (Day of the Dead).

To welcome the dead back to the realm of the living, we set up altars with their pictures, flowers, candles and favourite food and drink – perhaps a glass of tequila for them to make a toast. All around the city, altars are an expression of love and creativity. From homes to museums to hotels, they range from the sweet and simple to the spectacular. Some of the most stunning altars in town await at Museo Anahuacalli, in Coyoacán, and Zócalo, the city's massive main square, although my favourite will always be the one at my mother's house, with our family members' photos and plenty of candles.

Día de Muertos is not only a spiritual holiday, it's also a feast for the senses. Every year, I make a trip to the city's Mercado Jamaica, a massive flower and plant market, where I walk among mountains of fresh *cempasúchil* in orange and deep purple. Pumpkins and traditional candy also line the aisles, including sugar skulls of all sizes.

During this season, biting into *pan de muertos* is mandatory. This fluffy, buttery bread, found in bakeries, coffee shops and restaurants all over the city, is baked with a touch of orange blossom and sprinkled with sugar. It's one of the reasons millions of people look forward to this holiday every year.

Día de Muertos is at its most stimulating and spellbinding during the city's impressive parades, including the Monumental Alebrijes Parade, during which dozens of imposing fantastical creatures take over Paseo de la Reforma, the capital's main avenue. Throughout this season, the colourful, festive atmosphere is a reminder that Día de Muertos is an understanding of death as a natural part of our journey through this world and, most of all, a celebration of life.

BRETT ATKINSON

SONGKRAN – THE WORLD'S BIGGEST WATER FIGHT

BANGKOK, THAILAND

What began as a traditional new year ritual of gently sprinkling water on someone as a sign of good luck and goodwill has now developed into the biggest water fight on the planet. During the annual Songkran festival, the streets and laneways of Thai cities, including Bangkok and Chiang Mai, are ground zero for hundreds of locals armed with giant Super Soakers. It's also common for passing *tuk-tuks* to be surprised by liquid fusillades or for street food vendors to playfully throw buckets of water over their local rivals. In neighbouring Laos, Cambodia and Myanmar, Songkran is also a wildly popular way to combat the incessant tropical heat of mid-April.

My own Songkran experience saw me ambushed along Bangkok's Silom Rd by a local couple with matching Angry Birds water blasters. The basic water pistol I was wielding was comprehensively outgunned, so I retreated to a street food stall to fuel up on squid-on-a-stick, and bought both protective eye goggles and a much more serious weapon. Another street-side entrepreneur was selling on-the-go refills from a 166L (44-gallon) water drum, and I was soon locked, loaded and ready to re-enter the fray.

Bangkok's humidity inevitably rose to an inexorable peak, and the afternoon devolved into utter urban mayhem. Salvos hit me from everywhere and nowhere, and snipers crouched under the escalators leading to Bangkok's Skytrain platforms. As a tropical mist rose slowly from the tarmac battlefield, everyone from toddlers to Thai seniors was sporting the same delirious grin, signifying unbridled fun.

Locked and loaded for the biggest water fight

A procession carries a statue of Señor de los Temblores through Cusco

PATRICK O'NEILL

THE LORD OF THE EARTHQUAKE

CUSCO, PERU

If you're in Cusco on the Monday before Easter (Holy Monday), be sure to take in the solemn procession of townsfolk parading through the streets behind a statue of Jesus, throwing bright-red *ñucchu* flowers in its wake.

The celebration honours the patron saint of Cusco, a late 16th-century statue of Christ known as Señor de los Temblores (Lord of the Tremors, or Taytacha Temblores in Quechua). It is named after a terrible earthquake that rocked the city in 1650, which supposedly struck at the exact moment the Jesus statue was being carried out into the public for the first time. Miraculously, the tremors stopped. Credited with preventing the worst damage and devastation, the Christ statue is now a symbol of safety and protection for the town and its inhabitants. It was also believed to have helped stave off a later plague.

The red *ñucchu* flowers thrown by the procession represent Christ's blood, and a crown of the same blooms adorns the statue's head.

Cusco's faithful Catholic population believes that by worshipping and honouring the Lord of the Tremors, the town will remain protected from the worst seismic tremors that regularly rattle Peru.

CHETAN SHANKER JHA

GATE-CRASHING AN INDIAN WEDDING

INDIA

As a tour leader in India, I want to ensure that my guests are imprinted with indelible memories. So, I always try to spontaneously gate-crash an event when I have a curious and adventurous group!

Cultural and religious events, such as weddings, are invariably accompanied by lots of music, singing and dancing. People dress in colourful traditional attire, including proud dhoti-clad men I like to call 'the Turbanators'. There are also gracious women sporting sparkling ornaments, richly embroidered saris and *lehengas* (skirts), all flaunting their style-statements.

Indians are very hospitable, and my group is always warmly welcomed by the gyrating souls; in fact, the travellers become instant celebrities. And they just can't help but jump on the bandwagon of jubilation. Soon it's all selfies, sweets, smiles, handshakes and laughter galore. And we are often invited for a dinner or luncheon!

In India, no one asks for any money to engage in these rich festivities, and the moments create ecstatic memories for the many group members who participate, irrespective of age. Many people take home the memories of a lifetime. My guests always enjoy these unplanned, shimmering additions, which have a joyful ripple effect throughout their holiday experience.

Bright colours and intricate henna designs are abundant at a vibrant Indian wedding

INDIAN WEDDING 101

Jenny Varghese

Indian weddings are vibrant, multi-day celebrations with varied customs and rituals depending on the community and geography. Some pre-wedding events include the *sangeet* (musical night), *mehendi* (henna application) and *haldi* (turmeric ceremony). The main wedding ceremony is followed by a grand reception. Prepare for dancing at almost all the events! Women wear colourful saris, *lehengas* or salwar suits, while men don *sherwanis*, *kurtas* or Indo-Western suits. Guest lists typically range from 300 to 500, but can exceed 1000 on occasion. Indian weddings bring together families and communities, where everyone is always well-fed and entertained, truly embodying the term 'Big Fat Indian Wedding'!

Bloomsday celebrations at Davy Byrnes, Duke Street

Opposite: *Ulysses* re-enactment, Glasnevin Cemetery

FIONA HILLIARD

CELEBRATE BLOOMSDAY

DUBLIN, IRELAND

I don't know of any other city in the world that has embraced a book or writer to the same extent as Dublin and its annual love-in with James Joyce and his 1922 novel *Ulysses*. Indeed, anyone exploring the Irish capital on 16 June is in for a time-travelling treat – expect to see men and women strolling around in Edwardian finery, smell the faint whiff of fried pork kidneys in the air and hear Joycean ramblings echoing throughout the streets. It's all part of the charm of Bloomsday, a day when Dublin tips its (straw boater) hat to Joyce's meandering stream-of-consciousness story.

From Howth to Sandycove, calendars roll back to Thursday, 16 June, 1904 – the date *Ulysses'* main protagonist, Leopold Bloom, crisscrossed the city, encountering a kaleidoscope of people and places over the course of the day. Every year, traditional Bloomsday gatherings and events run from early morning to evening at various venues and locations mentioned in the book and include *Ulysses*-themed walking tours, readings at Sweny's Pharmacy on Lincoln Place and at Glasnevin Cemetery, lectures, exhibitions and fried kidney breakfasts at the James Joyce Centre on North Great George's St, and commemorative glasses of burgundy and gorgonzola sandwiches at Davy Byrne's on Duke St. Meanwhile, on the south coast, there are theatrical performances at James Joyce Tower and Museum and Sandycove, the setting for the book's opening scene, music and al fresco celebrations at Cavistons in Glasthule and a lively Bloomsday buzz in nearby Fitzgerald's Bar, where each of the stained-glass windows depict a chapter from the novel.

EVAN DAVIES

RAMADAN IN THE HIGH ATLAS MOUNTAINS

OUARZAZATE, MOROCCO

In Morocco, the town of Ouarzazate is known as 'the door to the desert'. In late April 2022, I was on my way to Tangier on a bike when I found myself there, though I was heading north from the Sahara into the High Atlas Mountains.

I pulled into town, thirsty and exhausted from a hard day of riding in the sun. It was the middle of Ramadan, and the streets were quiet during the day. I checked into a quirky, movie-themed, mudbrick hotel in a quiet part of town and, except for me, the hotel was empty. But by the time I checked in, got cleaned up and went to have a look around town, it was evening and Ouarzazate was bustling.

The first person I saw said hello and introduced himself as Mohammed. He said he would show me around town. As I walked with him, he recounted the history of Ouarzazate and then told me it was home to Atlas Studios, where many famous movies such as *Troy* and *Kingdom of Heaven* were filmed. The next person I met was the stunt double for Brad Pitt in *Troy*.

I cruised the market with Mohammed and watched a local soccer game before Iftar (the fast-breaking evening meal during Ramadan). I joined Mohammed and his sister for the meal, followed by a couple games of *swivvy*, a Moroccan card game I struggled to pick up, with Mohammed's friends late into the night.

RAMADAN: THE BASICS

Hena Jusic

Ramadan is the holiest month in the Islamic calendar and is practised for the entirety of the ninth month (the dates move forward nine days each year in the Western Gregorian calendar) to signify when the Quran (holy book) was revealed to the Prophet Mohammed. During this month, Muslims around the world fast – abstaining from drinking and eating – from sunrise to sunset. This is a time of internal reflection, community and consciously deciding to be the best versions of ourselves.

Drinking and dining after sunset during Ramadan in Morocco

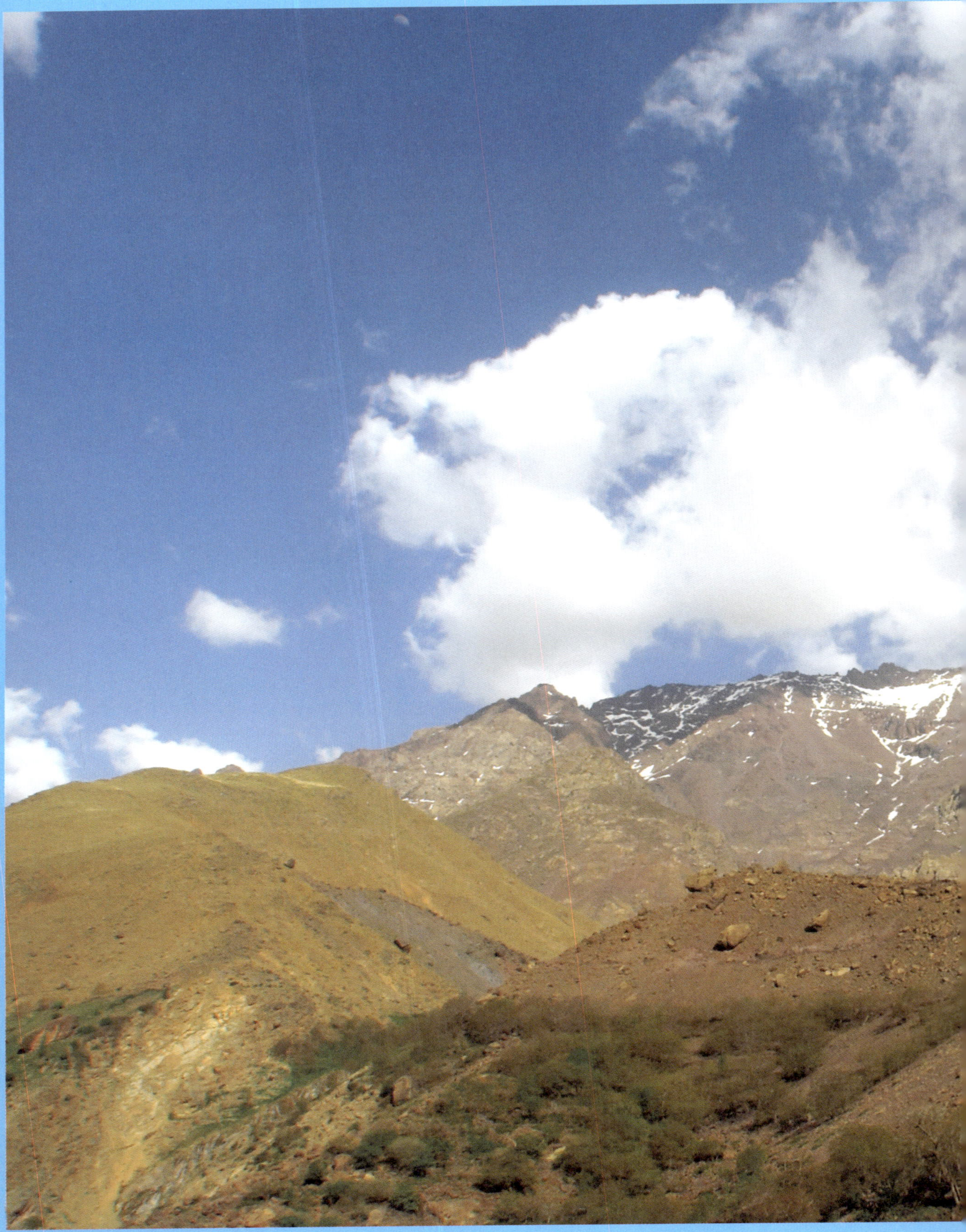

High Atlas mountain range, Morocco

Top: Wild, wacky, weird and wonderful: Wellington's World of WearableArt is the ultimate fashion show
Bottom: Bizarre Bras entrant aBRAcalypse Now by Wendy Moyer on display at the WoW Museum

LEE ATKINSON

WORLD OF WEARABLEART

WELLINGTON, AOTEAROA/NEW ZEALAND

The annual World of WearableArt (WOW) Awards Show in September/October is not your average prize giving. Nor is it a fashion parade. Think Cirque du Soleil gone 'through the looking glass', imagine Salvador Dali on the catwalk, blend Sydney's Mardi Gras and Rio's Carnaval and throw in some pyrotechnics and a dash of cabaret, and you'll have a better idea of this amazing spectacle that fills Wellington's TSB Arena to near capacity each year.

First shown in 1987, World of WearableArt originally began as a promotion for a small rural art gallery in Nelson at the tip of New Zealand's South Island. Back then, Nelson sculptor Suzie Moncrieff had the idea of taking art off the wall and putting it onto the body, turning an exhibition into a live theatrical show. The result is WOW, and it is now the largest theatrical production in the country and one of the biggest events on Wellington's calendar, showing to sell-out crowds each night.

Each year the competition attracts hundreds of entries from designers across New Zealand and around the world. The theatrical costumes are made from anything and everything – from bicycle tubes to rubber gloves, cardboard, plastic bottles and paper clips, even plastic collar stays (the plastic bits that keep shirt collars in shape).

Around 150 finalists are selected for the awards show, which is then choreographed into a two-hour theatrical production covering six themed sections and performed by a cast of dancers and acrobats, who model the entries. 'It's my big sculpture,' said creator Dame Suzie Moncrieff of the show, describing it as a magical romp. 'It's a montage presented in magical ways. We take the people of the audience out of their ordinary lives and give them some dream time.'

Whether you liken it to a psychedelic dream, a magical romp or a two-hour journey into an alternative reality, it has the wow factor down pat.

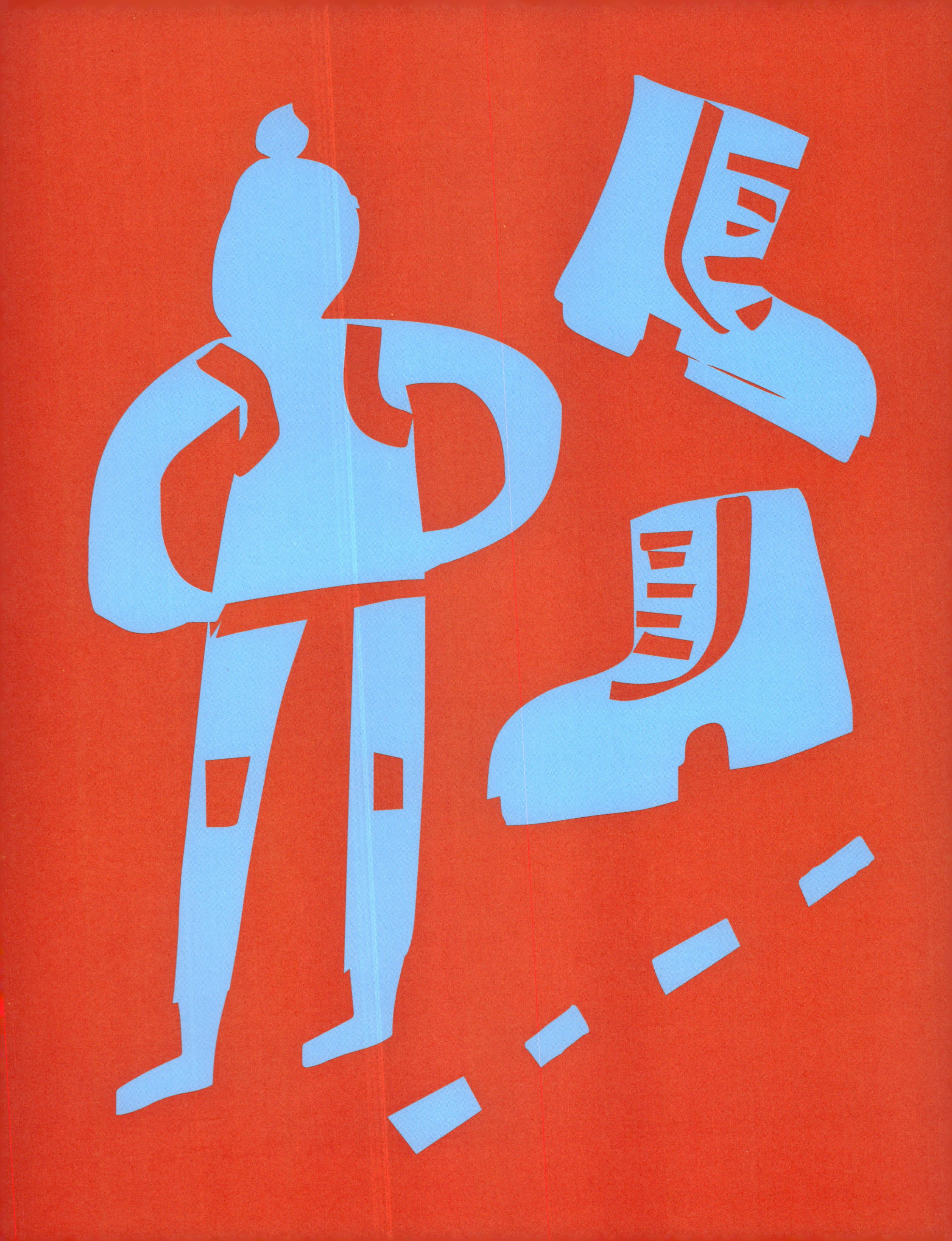

SLOW TRAVEL

SLOW TRAVEL

200	SLOW DOWN ON SKYE
205	CYCLING AROUND THE VICTORY LAKE
206	SHOW OF WONDERS ON THE *CALIFORNIA ZEPHYR*
210	PICNIC IN AVIGNON
213	WALKING THE GREAT WALL
214	TA XUA'S SEA OF CLOUDS
217	LIVING THE HIGH LIFE ON THE *GLACIER EXPRESS*
218	A GREAT WALK ON WATER
220	DRIVING SCENIC HIGHWAY 1
225	WENDY WHITELEY'S SECRET GARDEN
226	BIKEPACKING TO TORRES DEL PAINE

"Take a trip to see the local *fae* (fairies) with an easy stroll to Fairy Pools".

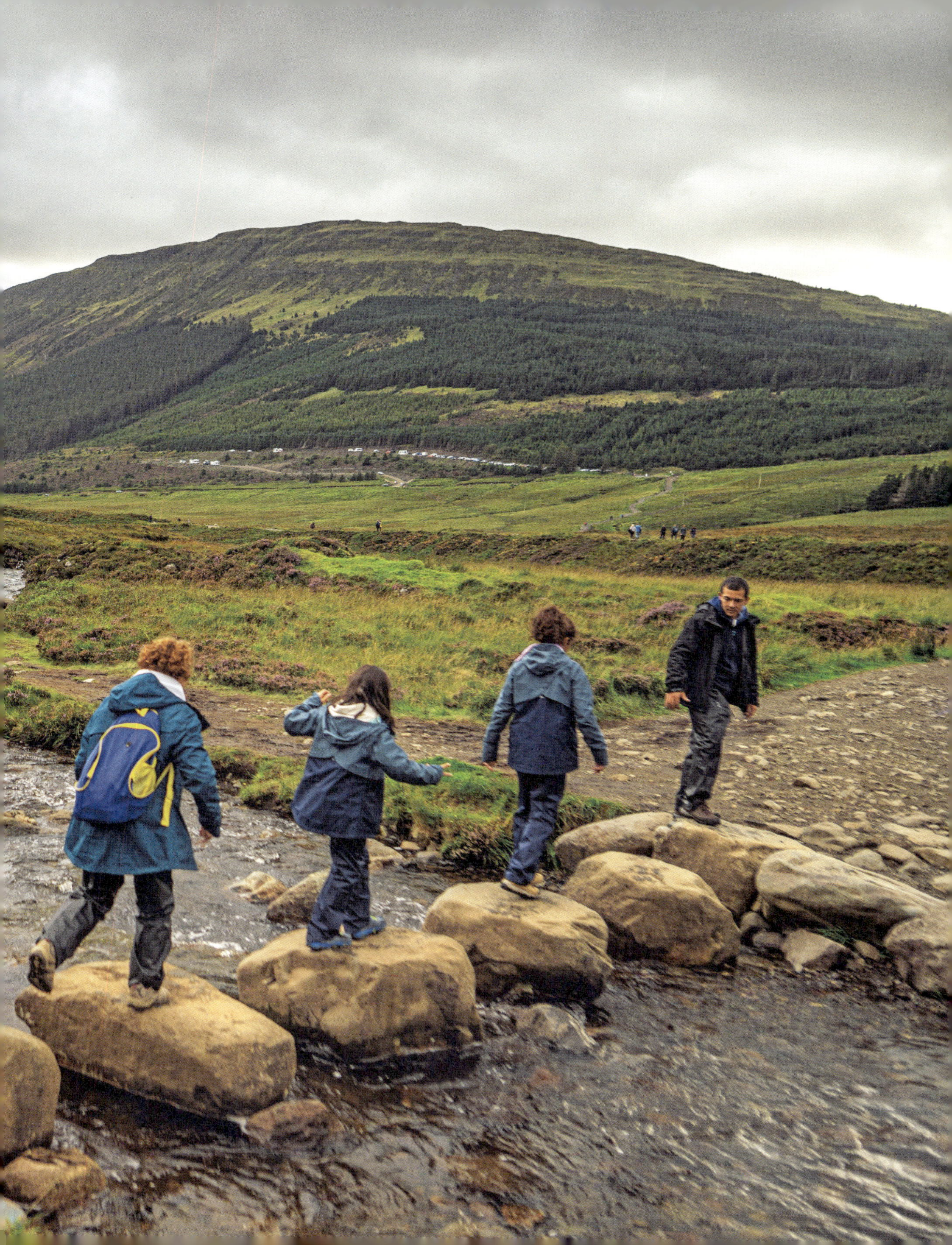

ROSANNA DUTSON

SLOW DOWN ON SKYE

ISLE OF SKYE, SCOTLAND

Skye holds a mystic thrall over all those who step upon it. Though it's becoming an ever more popular tourism destination, its immense, wild landscape cannot be taken for granted as just another stop along the travel route.

If you're lucky, you'll return to the isle many times. If you don't, here are a few recommendations to sample the best of what Skye has to offer.

Take the Old Man of Storr walk – climb many (many!) steps above the mountain mists for a spectacular view of the Old Man, a 55m-high (180ft-high) pinnacle of basalt rock that stands starkly along the Trotternish Ridge. Or take a trip to see the local *fae* (fairies) with an easy stroll to Fairy Pools at the foot of the Black Cuillin range. The crystal-clear blue pools start out gorgeous and just get better. This is a must-do wild swimming experience for those who can brave the frigid waters. Scour the rocky beach at An Corran north of Staffin for a dinosaur footprint or two, then head to the Staffin Dinosaur Museum to learn more about these Jurassic tracks.

The island's main town is pretty Portree, with hotels and boutique BnBs. Eco pods are also popular across the island and make for a more immersive experience of Skye, away from the busier town centres (small as they may be). The Lodge on the Loch has a herd of Scotland's iconic highland cows that can be easily spotted from the roadside.

Fairy Pools, Isle of Skye

The Old Man of Storr overlooking Loch Leathan, Skye

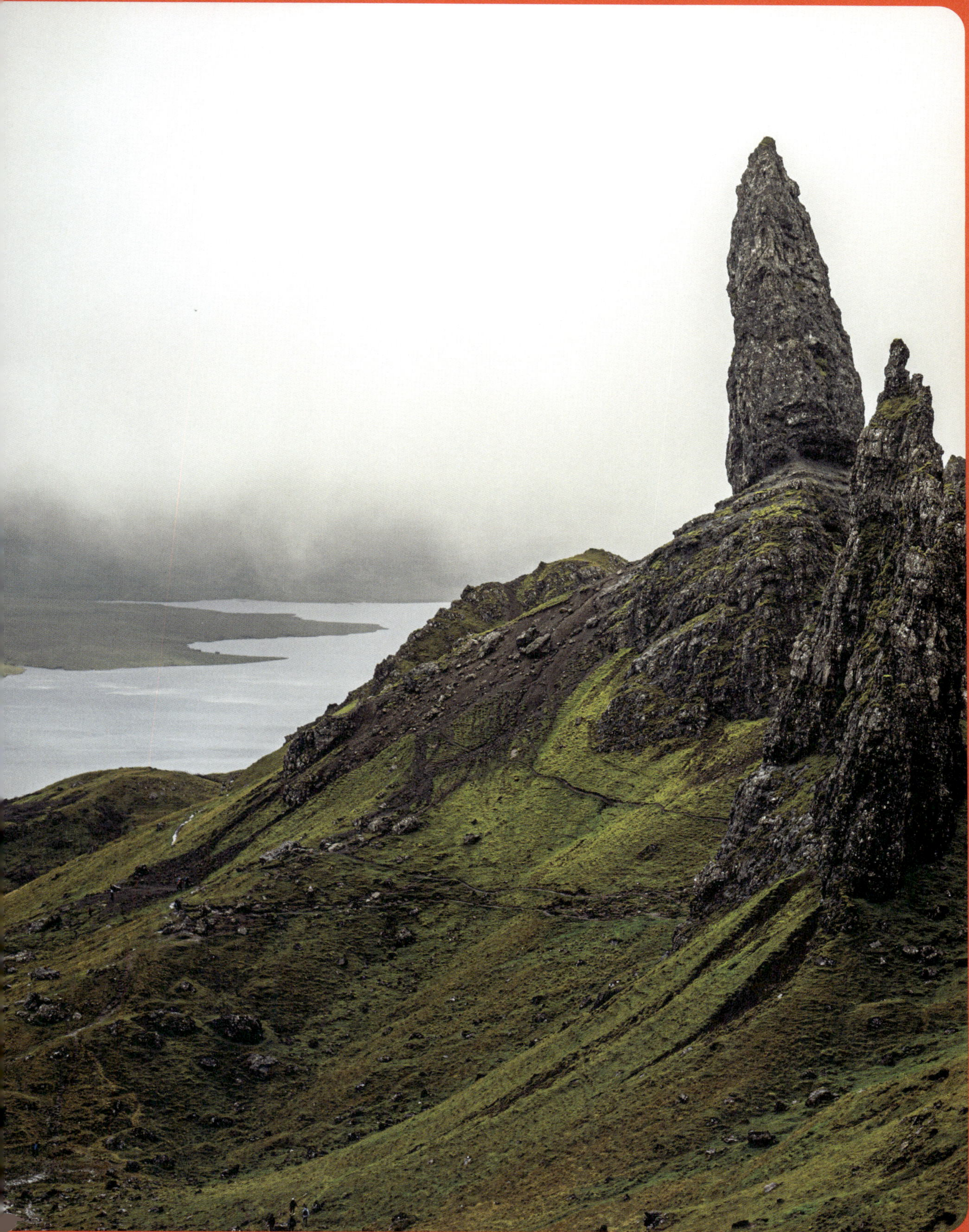

Udaipur's Fateh Sagar Lake is a popular exercise spot for locals and tourists alike

ANAND KAPIL

CYCLING AROUND THE VICTORY LAKE

UDAIPUR, INDIA

Known as the Venus of the East, Udaipur is undoubtedly one of India's most stunning towns, and the city wears its past like a crown. The people of Lake City are proud that their city draws tourists from all around the world.

We biked around Fateh Sagar Lake in the city as part of our cycling excursion across Rajasthan. The ride began just after daybreak. It was a nice surprise to see hundreds of residents walking, running, cycling and swimming in this massive body of water in the centre of the city, almost like we were at a fitness event.

The occasional greeting made us feel like we were a part of the city as we pedalled, with the lake on one side and the hills on the other. We had to walk our bikes across Central Arena St after pausing at a few fantastic photo spots.

This was arguably the most enjoyable way to see the city from a local's perspective. Many local club swimmers joined us for a hot cup of masala chai as we talked. We got the feeling from our hosts that Indian hospitality is unique. In incredible India, the proverb *atithi devo bhava* (our guests are a shadow of God) is quite accurate.

We were welcomed back to our hotel after a distinctive local breakfast of flattened rice and herbs. Our first day in the charming city of Udaipur was off to a wonderful start.

TIM RICHARDS

SHOW OF WONDERS ON THE *CALIFORNIA ZEPHYR*

CHICAGO, USA

To enter the Great Hall of Chicago's Union Station is to discover a magnificent temple to train travel at the heart of the USA's long-distance rail network. Opened in 1925, replacing a 19th-century predecessor, the station's interior is a glamorous collection of neoclassical pillars and arches, illuminated by a curved skylight and accentuated by decorative lamps and elegant timber benches.

This splendour is a mere curtain-raiser to the main event: stepping aboard the *California Zephyr*. This Amtrak sleeper train makes the two-night journey west to Oakland, California (for San Francisco). Arguably the world's most scenic regularly scheduled train, the *Zephyr* truly delivers after Denver when the journey becomes a nonstop show of natural wonders.

From the station's Metropolitan Lounge, where I chatted to an amiable Amish family whose train had been delayed, we passengers were led along dark platforms to our train, composed of imposing two-level silver carriages, which Amtrak calls Superliners. My compartment was, therefore, a Superliner Roomette, which seemed like a great name for a 1970s rock band. It was a snug area containing two armchairs that were converted into bunk beds by night.

I wouldn't spend much time in that space, however. My focus was the scenery, which I could enjoy from the train's lounge car; its curved roof was partly inset with windows, maximising the view. Once we departed Denver on the following day, this became a vista worth close attention. Gone was the flat farming country of Iowa and Nebraska, which we passed through after Chicago. Ahead of us in Colorado was the high terrain of the Rocky Mountains.

Around 10am, we passed through the Moffat Tunnel, situated 2816m (9240ft) above sea level and a whopping 10km (6.2 miles) long. We wound through the mountains at a slow and steady pace that involved spirals and tunnels to allow the train to ascend. There were plenty of craggy peaks to admire on the way and companions to talk to as we took in the spectacle. At a table in the lounge car, I chatted with a British couple who were crisscrossing the States by rail. They were the first of many fellow travellers I'd get to know on this journey. There was a similarly sociable vibe at mealtimes in the dining car, as passengers sat with random dining companions.

California Zephyr in Glenwood Canyon

Chicago's Union Station is a temple to train travel
Opposite: Rugged scenery along the *California Zephyr*'s route

SHOW OF WONDERS ON THE *CALIFORNIA ZEPHYR*

After conquering the Rockies, the *California Zephyr* met up with the Colorado River, which we followed for the rest of the day. The result was a feast of rugged scenery featuring rust-red rock formations that resembled backdrops for a movie set in the Wild West.

Night fell as we left the river and headed into Utah, but there was more mountainous terrain to come. On the final morning, we passed out of Nevada into the grand Sierra Nevada range of northern California with its imposing high mountains covered with trees. On any other train journey, these would be the undoubted highlight, but given the glories of the Rocky Mountains and the Colorado River on the previous day, they almost seemed par for the course.

LAURA DOGUET

PICNIC IN AVIGNON

AVIGNON, FRANCE

I never would have predicted that a simple picnic in Avignon would become one of my most cherished memories of Europe.

The weeks prior had been nonstop: hopping from country to country, with jam-packed days of sightseeing in major cities and probably a bit too much nightlife for my own good. As a result, funds were quickly diminishing, and my body was telling me to slow down.

I had planned to visit Avignon in the south of France as a pit stop en route to Cinque Terre from Barcelona. I had heard it was a nice city, but I was pleasantly surprised by its medieval charm and relaxed vibe. Wandering around, I felt instantly lighter. I met some friendly people at my hostel, and we decided to have a chilled (and very affordable) picnic by the picturesque Pont D'Avignon bridge – aka Pont Saint-Bénézet – over the Rhône River. The wholesomeness of this plan was just what I needed!

The first step, of course, was to visit our local supermarket and revel in the incredible selection of cheeses. Boursin with garlic and fine herbs is my personal favourite and a must-try (I'm somewhat qualified to recommend this as my dad is French). If you try this, be sure to check out the specialty cheeses from Provence, too, because the more cheese, the better. Next, grab as many baguettes as you can comfortably carry, something to drink (red wine is recommended but not essential) and wander through the town to find a quiet spot by the bridge.

We timed our picnic with the sunset, which was some kind of magic. It was one of those moments where you appreciate the small things, life's unexpected pleasures, and everything else becomes secondary.

PICNICKING AROUND THE WORLD

Olivia Brown

* **United States:** Sacramento is home to California's largest farmers' market, making it the perfect pit stop before a whimsical picnic in the **McKinley Park Rose Garden**. Stock your basket with local produce and wine made in the Napa Valley before finding an idyllic spot among thousands of beautiful rose bushes and palm trees. To really see the flowers flourish, aim to visit between March and May.

* **Japan:** Book a private *hanami* (flower viewing) picnic in the tranquil grounds of the 1200-year-old **Shiogama Shrine**, two hours north of Fukushima. Unwind and relax with a sake in one hand and a traditional *obento* lunchbox in another, while a local musician serenades you with a private *shamisen* (Japanese lute) performance.

* **The Netherlands:** Take a break from walking the charming streets of Amsterdam and enjoy your lunch on the well-clipped lawns of **Vondelpark**. Lay down a blanket on a secluded patch of greenery by the river and watch the world go by – or if you're lucky, relish in an open-air concert in the summertime.

Top: A French supermarket fridge filled with Boursin cheese
Bottom: Avignon's Jardin des Doms is the perfect place to stop for a picnic

The section of China's Great Wall near Gubeikou has been reclaimed by nature over time

MONIQUE CHOY

WALKING THE GREAT WALL

GUBEIKOU, CHINA

It's a Wonder of the World for a reason. The Great Wall of China stretches over 20,000km (12,400 miles), snaking along the ridgeline of mountaintops from Gansu in the northwest of China all the way to the Bohai Sea. It was constructed over two millennia to separate the settled agricultural civilisations of the Chinese empire from the nomadic peoples to the north-west, reaching its formidable pinnacle during the Ming dynasty (1368–1644).

The sections of the Wall close to Beijing are among the most accessible for travellers. Some of these have been restored to evoke the glories of the past, including Badaling, Mutianyu and Juyonguan. These are nice enough places to experience the Wall if you don't mind squeezing around tour groups, fashion shoots and ice-cream sellers. There's a carnival atmosphere, with chairlifts and gondolas to take you up to the ramparts and even a wheeled toboggan ride to take you down.

But if you want a little wilderness and solitude on the Wall, stepping just a little off the beaten track will take you to Gubeikou, a cobblestone village 130km (80 miles) from Beijing. Here, neat grey-stone streets overflow with vegetable gardens in summer and village life runs to a leisurely pace. The town is dominated by the impressive fortress gate where you can climb up on to the Wall. This unrenovated section is overgrown with weeds and crumbling away to reveal the intricate layers of its construction. In some places you'll have to scramble up rubble, over steep inclines and through mud.

The upside? You'll have this wonder almost entirely to yourself as it snakes into the distance with incredible views across the valleys on either side. You'll pass through ruined parapets, like the 24-Eyes Tower (a ruined fortification with 24 windows) and eerie bastions where the peril and isolation that must have been felt by the soldiers stationed on this military installation become almost palpable.

A 10km (6-mile) walk will take you to the town of Jinshanling. Guided hikes are available, but it's not hard to do the walk independently. Take a train to Gubeikou from Beijing, where the lovely Great Wall Box House Guesthouse will welcome you with home-cooked vegetarian meals and friendly cats.

NGUYEN MAI

TA XUA'S SEA OF CLOUDS

TA XUA, VIETNAM

Imagine standing on a mountain peak at sunrise, surrounded by a mesmerising sea of clouds. I had the chance to experience this awe-inspiring phenomenon in Ta Xua, Vietnam – a place renowned for its stunning vistas when the valley is shrouded in thick clouds, creating a surreal and otherworldly landscape.

The trekking road to the top of Ta Xua is winding and rocky; the majestic undulating rocks along the way and the extremely narrow trail in the middle of the abyss create a feeling of both adventure and overwhelm. This remote and off-the-beaten-path destination left me with many impressions, and the images remain with me. Walking through the forest's rich vegetation and mossy landscapes felt like stepping into a fairytale. The high cliffs required me to raise my foot to the level of my chest. Fatigue settled so that, like a young girl, I yearned to say 'Stop here!' But my porter kept saying, 'Climb a mountain not so the world can see you, but so you can see the world.' This resonated with me as I embraced the challenges and beauty of the journey.

It was a challenging yet rewarding experience. The sunrise, revealing picturesque hills and mountains through the parting clouds, made the two-hour trek to the top well worthwhile. It showed me the wonder of Vietnam and its most magical and serene moments.

A different world above the clouds

Top: A Swiss village seen from the passing train

Bottom: The *Glacier Express* passes over the lofty Landwasser Viaduct

TIM RICHARDS

LIVING THE HIGH LIFE ON THE GLACIER EXPRESS

ST MORITZ, SWITZERLAND

'Living the high life' suggests luxury, perhaps involving a glass of bubbly followed by fine food. But there's a more literal interpretation involving altitude; both are combined aboard the *Glacier Express*, which travels between Switzerland's glamorous ski centres of St Moritz and Zermatt.

Sipping a glass of Laurent Perrier champagne as I rolled out of St Moritz, I enjoyed the so-called 'Excellence Class' aboard this famous train, which takes eight hours to cover 291km (180 miles). Excellence Class – at a hefty supplement to the first-class fare – is a cut above standard rail travel. The stylish carriage's decor is finished with natural materials such as walnut and Alpine quartzite, and the floor is laid with hand-tufted carpet.

The train travels through Alpine scenery, featuring glacial streams, mountains rising above valleys dotted with grassy slopes and pretty villages. Though it was springtime when I travelled, there was snow along the way as we passed through 91 tunnels and over hundreds of bridges – and the world became pure white when we reached our highest altitude of 2033m (6669ft) above sea level.

Scenery aside, the most notable feature of Excellence Class was the dining, a leisurely meal of several courses. The first was a starter of cheese tarts and mixed spiced nuts. Around noon, we enjoyed smoked trout matched with a local white wine. Later, I tried a regional dish called *capuns*, which is composed of small rolls made from spätzli dough wrapped in chard leaves and served in a rich cheese sauce. It was tasty, especially with a glass of local syrah.

As I sipped my wine and admired the dramatic landscape, I wondered which was more impressive: the technical achievement of the railway or the external natural glory. But given that both are also available for anyone to experience in first or second class seats at a more moderate price tag, I thought – why choose? It was an all-round special rail experience, wherever you sat on the train.

ANDREW BAIN

A GREAT WALK ON WATER

WHANGANUI RIVER, AOTEAROA/NEW ZEALAND

Not all of New Zealand's Great Walks require footsteps. The hallowed list of the country's preeminent hiking trails curiously includes one paddling trip: the Whanganui Journey, an 87km (54-mile) or 145km (90-mile) voyage by kayak or canoe on the Whanganui River.

It's difficult to overstate the significance of New Zealand's third-longest river. In 2017, after years of lobbying by local Māori, the 290km (180-mile) waterway was granted 'personhood' status by the New Zealand parliament, making it the first river in the world to be recognised as a living being. To paddle it is to discover a remarkable – and remarkably beautiful – gorge.

The longer version of the Whanganui Journey begins in Taumarunui, in the shadow of the North Island's Central Plateau volcanoes, heading downstream to Pipiriki over about five days. Like many, however, I came to paddle the shorter course from Whakahoro – three days in which my only constant company was this living river.

By the time the river has reached Whakahoro, it's already travelled around 100km (62 miles) from its headwaters on Mount Tongariro, cutting a deep line into the green hills. Beneath slopes creased like dress pants, I stepped into my canoe – the usual Whanganui Journey vessel of choice – pushing off from the bank and beginning to drift.

Between Whakahoro and Pipiriki there are seven campsites and huts (plus another three upstream of Whakahoro), including Tīeke/Kāinga, a functioning Māori marae (meeting space) that doubles as a hut for paddlers. It's a privilege and a cultural experience to stay here, so check the Department of Conservation webpage about the marae for guidance on protocols.

Another highlight of the paddle is the chance to tie up at Mangapurua Landing and make the 3km (1.8-mile) return walk to the Bridge to Nowhere. Like a concrete monument to failed ambition, the 40m-long (131ft-long) bridge was built in 1935 when this area knotted with forest was being developed as part of a scheme to allow WWI veterans to settle and farm the isolated valleys. After just four years the plan was abandoned – the land was too rugged and remote – and only the arched bridge remains.

Near the gorge's end, there are a few timid rapids to navigate, including a final shallow bit of white-water as the Whanganui Journey approaches its finish in Pipiriki. Tip out in this one and you might finish this Great Walk on foot.

CHANGING FACES OF THE WHANGANUI RIVER

There are said to be more than 200 named rapids on the Whanganui River, and some 500 waterfalls that pour into it, but it's no wild white-water ride. At the heart of the gorge through which the paddle travels is a stretch of water so serene and still it's as though the world has hit pause.

Moss-coated cliffs plummet into reflections so perfect and pure that it's hard to tell where the walls end and the water begins. If you get a sense of vertigo from the puzzling effect on your brain, you won't be the first. Interspersed with rapids, it provides a curious contrast. At times, you could do your hair in the reflections; at other times, you're fighting to stop your hair from getting wet.

Floating on the Whanganui River

ANDREW COLLINS

DRIVING SCENIC HIGHWAY 1

COASTAL CALIFORNIA, USA

Perhaps most famous for the incredible 145km (90-mile) stretch along the 90m (300ft) seaside bluffs of Big Sur, this majestic coastal drive offers countless thrills and engaging diversions along its entire 1056km (656-mile) length. Starting just inland amid groves of leviathan redwood trees in northern California, the road soon plunges dramatically toward the coast, passing through the rugged timber town of Fort Bragg and the sophisticated but secluded vacation village of Mendocino, with its posh inns and farm-to-table restaurants. It's here that I like to make a short detour east on Highway 128 to investigate the Anderson Valley's exceptional wineries – sipping a glass of pinot noir on the gorgeous garden patio at Goldeneye is my definition of heaven.

From this point south, Highway 1 is rarely more than a few miles from the pounding Pacific surf. The road snakes atop massive coastal ramparts through Sonoma and Marin counties. Right before the road crosses the iconic orange frame of the Golden Gate Bridge, I enjoy stopping at one of the scenic pullouts in the Marin Headlands to snap a photo of it set against the city's gracious skyline. Then continue along as this mostly two-lane ribbon of blacktop curves south along intermittently lonely and populous stretches through the collegiate surf town of Santa Cruz, breezy Monterey (with its outstanding Monterey Bay Aquarium) and the fashionable pine- and cypress-shaded streets of Carmel before traversing the dazzling scenery of Big Sur.

Make time to visit the fabulously ornate Hearst Castle (the unique Cottages and Kitchens Tour is my favourite) before continuing through the sunny winemaking regions of San Luis Obispo and Santa Barbara counties. Take a break in Ventura to take a wildlife cruise offshore, exploring Channel Islands National Park before continuing along the highway's final stretch of secluded shoreline between Oxnard and Malibu. These final 200km (125 miles) access the glamorous attractions of Los Angeles and the affluent resort towns – such as Laguna Beach and Dana Point – of Orange County. End your journey with a peaceful walk through the historic Spanish Colonial cloisters of Mission San Juan Capistrano, which are near where Highway 1 ends at the Interstate 5 freeway. I like to complete the day with a dinner of classic Mexican fare within the 230-year-old walls of nearby El Adobe de Capistrano.

Bixby Bridge on Highway 1, Big Sur

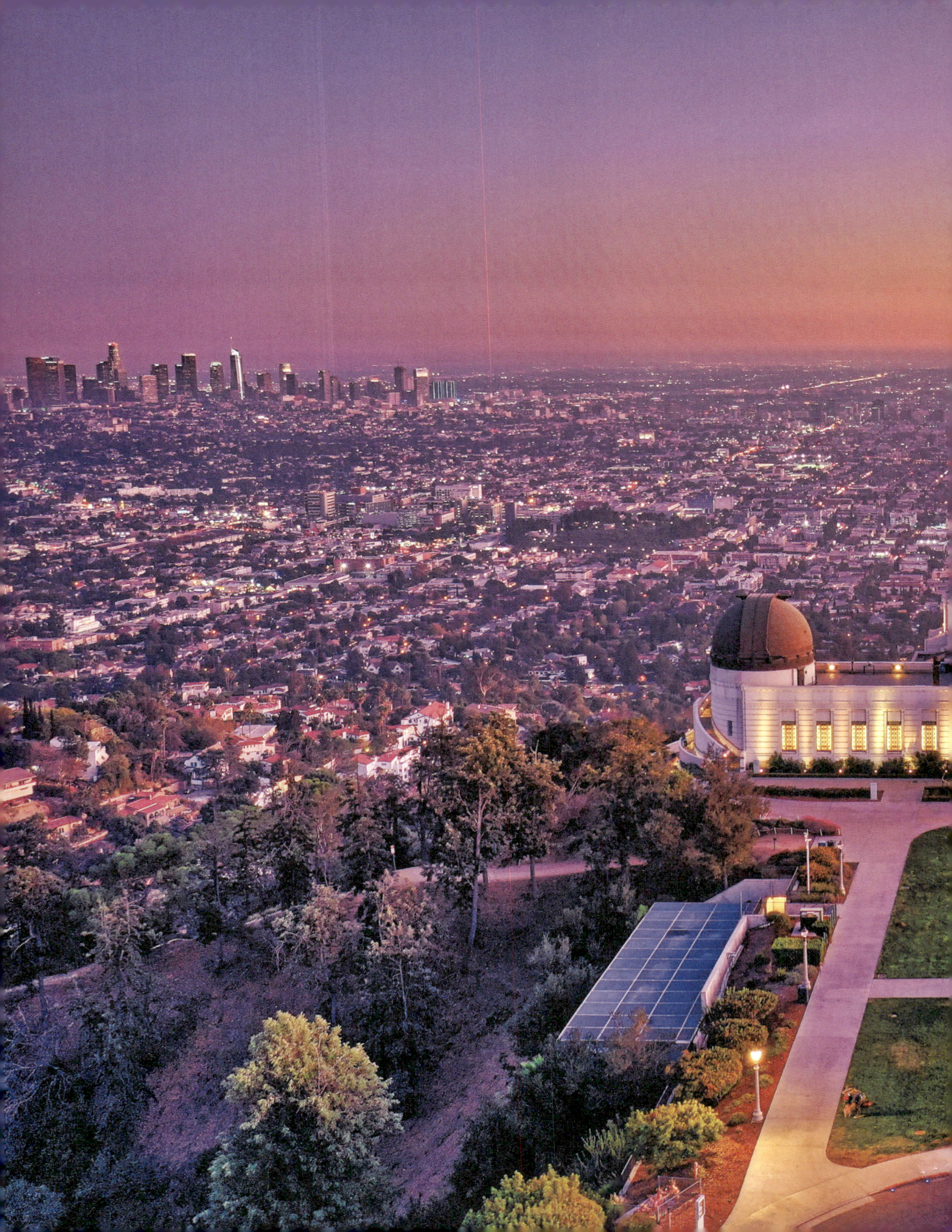

Griffith Observatory, Los Angeles

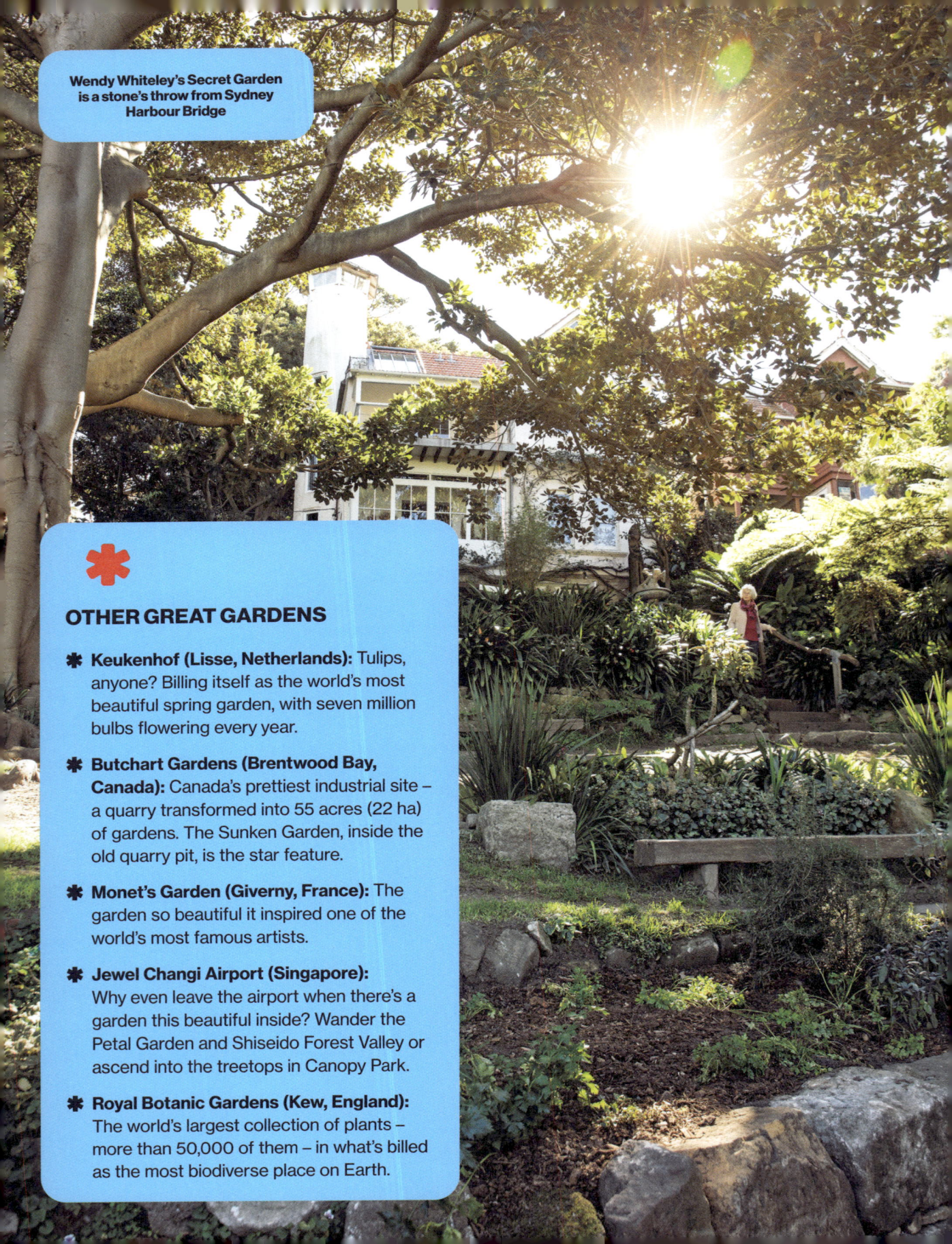

Wendy Whiteley's Secret Garden is a stone's throw from Sydney Harbour Bridge

OTHER GREAT GARDENS

* **Keukenhof (Lisse, Netherlands):** Tulips, anyone? Billing itself as the world's most beautiful spring garden, with seven million bulbs flowering every year.

* **Butchart Gardens (Brentwood Bay, Canada):** Canada's prettiest industrial site – a quarry transformed into 55 acres (22 ha) of gardens. The Sunken Garden, inside the old quarry pit, is the star feature.

* **Monet's Garden (Giverny, France):** The garden so beautiful it inspired one of the world's most famous artists.

* **Jewel Changi Airport (Singapore):** Why even leave the airport when there's a garden this beautiful inside? Wander the Petal Garden and Shiseido Forest Valley or ascend into the treetops in Canopy Park.

* **Royal Botanic Gardens (Kew, England):** The world's largest collection of plants – more than 50,000 of them – in what's billed as the most biodiverse place on Earth.

ANDREW BAIN

WENDY WHITELEY'S SECRET GARDEN

SYDNEY/WARRANG, AUSTRALIA

Hidden in plain sight of the Sydney Harbour Bridge, Wendy Whiteley's Secret Garden is a thin slice of urban forest emerging from a tale of grief and growth. Created by Sydney artist Wendy Whiteley after the death of her famous artist husband Brett Whiteley in 1992, the garden was hacked out of a mess of lantana and sticky weed beside the couple's home in Lavender Bay at the northern end of the Sydney Harbour Bridge. Today, it's a lush sliver of greenery where the city feels momentarily on pause, even as the garden's trees frame the city centre and the Harbour Bridge.

Just a 15-minute walk from the northern end of the Harbour Bridge, past the madcap grin of Luna Park, the garden – which is free to wander – is an urban oasis pinched between apartment blocks and a railway line. Each time a break appears in its trees, including a Moreton Bay fig that stands tall over the garden beside Whiteley's turreted home, the harbour peeps into view like the ultimate garden water feature.

The secret garden was almost entirely planted by Whiteley and is now tended by two full-time gardeners and volunteers. Dotted with seats, tables, engraved stone tablets and sculptures, it wraps around a small sandstone cliff, and though the city centre is little more than 1km (0.6 miles) across the harbour, the only things that disturb the peace are the occasional train and the brush turkeys scratching at the leaf litter. And all the while there's that famous bridge, appearing almost like trellising through the trees. This might well become your new favourite Sydney view.

MARK WATSON

BIKEPACKING TO TORRES DEL PAINE

TORRES DEL PAINE, PATAGONIA

The road led us into a landscape that could have been straight off a postcard, with calm lake waters surrounded by glacier-smoothed hillsides and ancient moraines against a backdrop of the sheer peaks of the Torres del Paine. As we cycled into the park, guanaco grazed near the roadside and I wondered if we might spy a puma.

For a few months we had been bikepacking along the Andes, crisscrossing the border between Chile and Argentina, discovering the most interesting routes we can find through the remarkable natural landscapes Patagonia is famous for.

Along the way I concluded that bikepacking might be the ultimate way to travel. It affords a freedom to the traveller that is unique: untethered from the inflexibility of buses, but more independent than hitchhiking. You can design your own itinerary, stop when you want and infuse your travel experience with spontaneity while travelling responsibly and sustainably under your own power.

It can be visceral at times – exposed to unrelenting heat, rain or snow without the shelter of a vehicle – but you also feel much more connected to what's happening around you: the changing sights and sounds, people and culture and the flow of the terrain.

We had just explored what might be regarded as the crown jewels of southern Chile's bounty: the Torres del Paine. This trio of monolithic granite towers are famous for their height and verticality. After cycling for a few days across the remote, windswept pampa of the Patagonian Steppe, with little more than guanacos for company, we camped near the trailhead for Lago Torres – the viewpoint at the base of the towers. Eager to catch dawnlight on the peaks, we left in the dark – hiking by torchlight for three hours – while laden with camera and tripod, food and water.

The trail was easy at first as it ascended through native lenga forest, before climbing more steeply through talus to the Mirador Las Torres at the edge of a narrow lake. At its head, the rock towers were just starting to brighten, picking up the pink hue of the oncoming dawn. I set up my camera by the lake shore and fired off the first frames, capturing myself dwarfed by the scale of the magnificent valley. It's a raw but beautiful landscape of bare rock, ice and snow. Turquoise lake waters fill the bottom of a cirque left by a long-departed glacier. The ice that carved out this valley has left behind huge moraines, which flank the lake, and above them rise the peaks which were resistant to the glacier's grind.

As we waited, clouds layered the horizon, but when the sun finally rose it pierced a gap for a moment, enough to light the walls ablaze with orange, rendering clearly every detail in the torres: the soaring corners and aretes, the water-streaked slabs that flow smoothly into the lake and the icefields that skirt the towers' base. It was the light you dream for as a photographer.

Bikepacking under the dramatic spires of the Torres del Paine

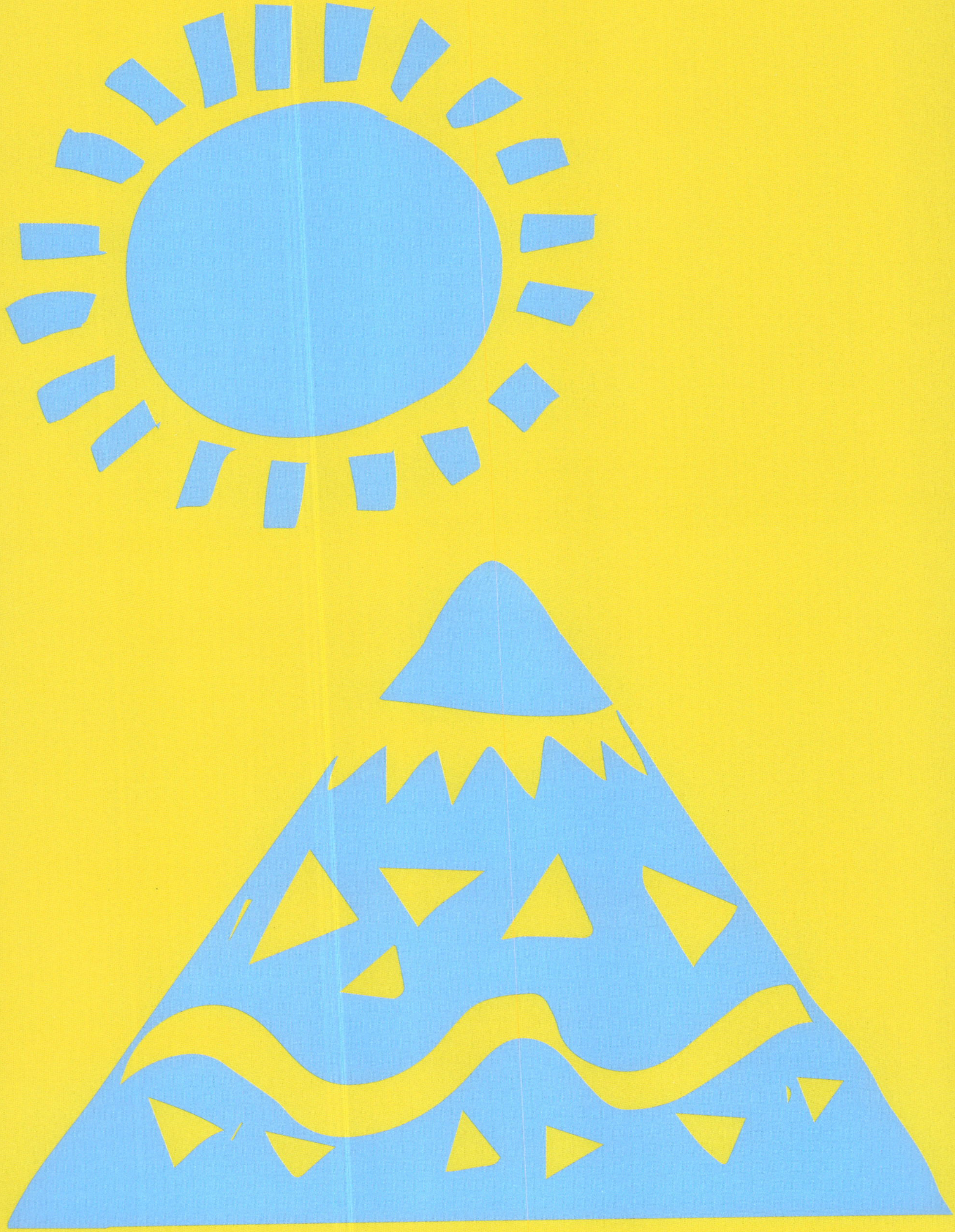

RESPONSIBLE TRAVEL

232	THE PEDALLING PILGRIMAGE
235	SUNRISE BLESSING AT AN OCEANSIDE TEMPLE
236	CAPTIVE COOKING
241	CONNECT WITH LOCALS MAKING PESTO
242	SUSTAINABLE COPENHAGEN
244	A RARE LOOK INTO A GLOBAL BIODIVERSITY FAILSAFE
247	RHINO ROYALTY

RESPONSIBLE TRAVEL

"Inside the thick concrete walls of an old prison yard, a group of people wander among one of Australia's largest kitchen gardens, stripping off beans, cutting greens and filling baskets with assorted garden produce."

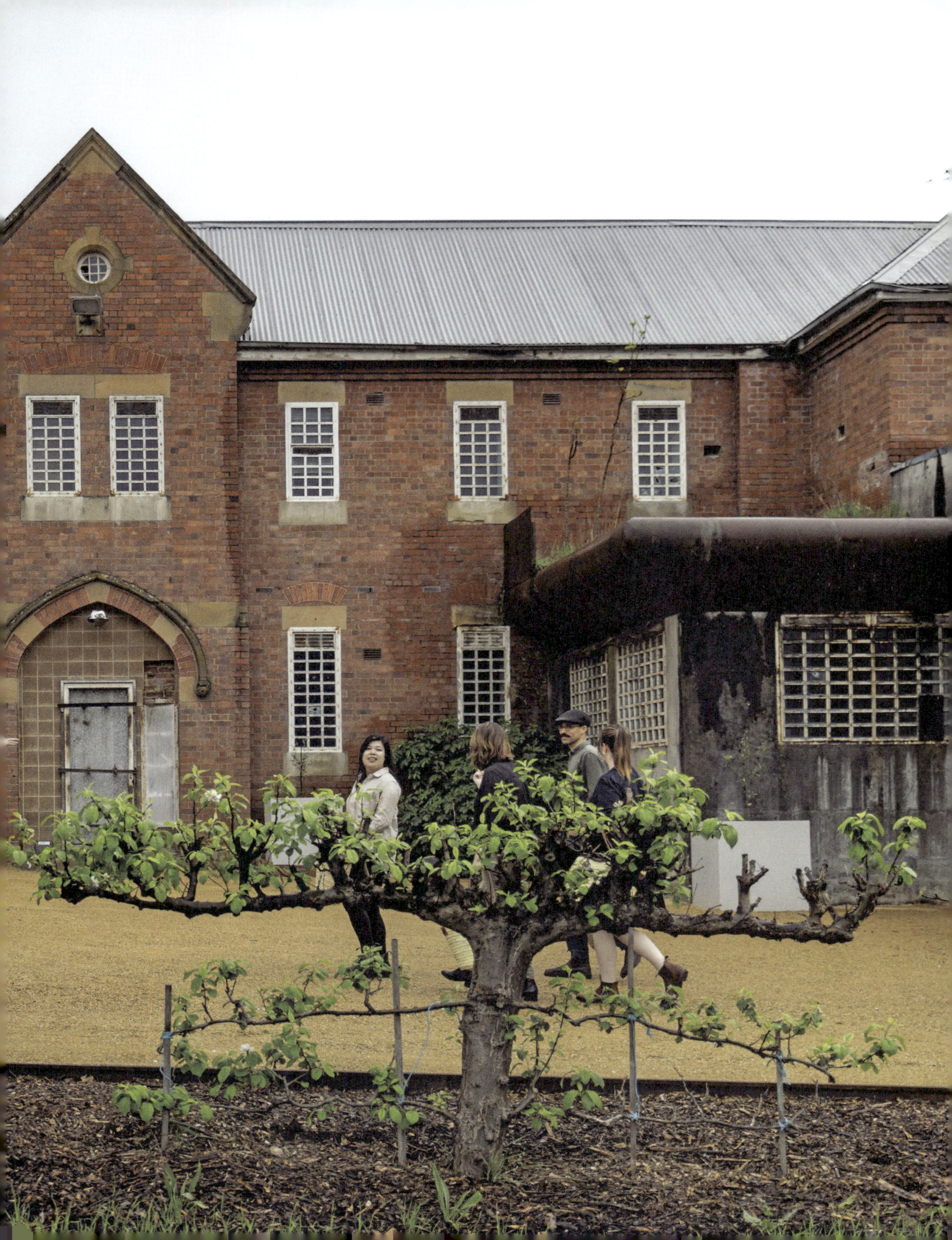

ANDREW BAIN

THE PEDALLING PILGRIMAGE

CAMINO DE SANTIAGO, SPAIN

Not all pilgrims are footsore. On Spain's hallowed Camino de Santiago, there are pilgrims who hike, but there are also those who come by bike. Under the regulations laid out by the Pilgrim's Reception Office, pilgrimages can be made on foot, bicycle or horseback. In 2023, more than one in every 20 pilgrims arrived at the finish point of Santiago de Compostela on two wheels.

While the full Camino Frances (the most popular of the pilgrimage routes) stretches 780km (484 miles) from the Pyrenean town of St Jean Pied de Port to Santiago, the rules deem that cyclists can qualify as *pelegrinos* (pilgrims) by covering a minimum of 200km (125 miles). This has made the city of León, just beyond the dreaded *meseta* (high plain) that demoralises so many pilgrims, a popular starting point. It was here that I began my own Camino by cycle.

For five days, I pedalled towards Santiago, rising over the Montes de León range and rolling through the Bierzo wine region. The *meseta* might have its mental challenges, but at this end of the Camino it's the climb to O Cebreiro that's most notorious. I rose up its slopes in a pool of sweat, barely outpacing the walkers, until I arrived in the hilltop town that marked my arrival into lush Galicia and the long final approach to Santiago.

The way ahead was green and lined with *pulperias* (octopus restaurants), where I paused for long lunches, delaying my audience ahead with the reputed remains of the Apostle James in his crypt beneath Santiago's cathedral.

MORE PILGRIMAGES

Olivia Brown

- **Glastonbury to Stonehenge, UK:** Embark on a four-day trek along the ancient Celtic way. Begin at the pagan town of Glastonbury and journey across rolling hills, iron-age hillforts and breathtaking English countryside. You'll conclude your pilgrimage at the iconic Stonehenge and be one step closer to spiritual enlightenment.

- **Kumano Kodo Trail, Japan:** Follow in the footsteps of peasants and emperors alike along a remote trail through the Kii Mountains, passing sacred sites, bamboo forests and serene mountain landscapes. Although the trail can be arduous, it is ultimately an enlightening experience spanning some of Japan's most untouched countryside.

- **The Inca Trail, Peru:** Considered the mother of all South American treks, the Inca Trail challenges you as you return to a great lost civilisation, trekking across mountainous landscapes and emerald-green terraces to the infamous Machu Picchu.

Summer cycling along wheat fields on the Camino de Santiago, Spain

Early morning sky after a blessing on Echo Beach, Bali

DYAN MCKIE

SUNRISE BLESSING AT AN OCEANSIDE TEMPLE

BALI, INDONESIA

The sun was rising, the waves could be heard crashing in the background, and a dog wandered by – this was Bali in its quietest hour. It was 6am, and I was there with eight of my closest girlfriends, ready to experience a side of Bali most don't, ready to embrace my 50th year. We fixed our colourful sarongs around our waists, ensuring we had done it correctly as we waited for the priest to open the temple gates. This temple can be visited by invite only; we felt like we were embarking on something truly unique.

Echo Beach is known for its reef breaks and beach bars, but standing among them is a majestic black temple with gold ornate doors: Pura Batu Mejan, a Hindu temple on prime oceanfront real estate. With keys in hand, the priest opened the gates and beckoned us to follow him. We stood on an expansive landing with panoramic views of the ocean and coastline. It was quiet and calming. The priest had prepared the offering *pejati* and awaited us on the rocky outpost among the crashing waves.

One at a time, we walked out along the rocks, ready for our purification. Three types of water were used: water from the springs inside the temple, seawater and water from a young coconut. He put my hands in the water to wash my face, to drink some and to wash my hair. No words were spoken. The procession was carried out in the hope of cleansing everything negative, both physically and spiritually.

ANDREW BAIN

CAPTIVE COOKING

NEW NORFOLK, AUSTRALIA

Inside the thick concrete walls of an old prison yard, a group of people wander among one of Australia's largest kitchen gardens, stripping off beans, cutting greens and filling baskets with assorted garden produce. They're not prisoners preparing mess; they're guests gathering the ingredients for a day at the country's leading cooking school, the Agrarian Kitchen.

'A very large proportion of what we use – 90 per cent-plus – comes from this garden,' said Agrarian Kitchen founder and owner Rodney Dunn, looking over the acre of no-till vegetables, spices and berries.

The garden, school and attached Agrarian Kitchen Eatery, which is regularly named among Australia's top restaurants, sit inside a former ward and the prison yard of Willow Court, Australia's oldest continually run asylum until its closure in 2000.

The Agrarian Kitchen began its classes in 2008 in Rodney and wife Severine's nearby home in Lachlan, opening its doors just as Tasmania began its meteoric rise as a food destination. Once known by the singular moniker of the Apple Isle, the state has rapidly developed a reputation for Australia's finest and freshest dining and produce, ranging from berries and seafood to the country's first black truffles and even avocadoes, saffron and kimchi.

Dunn, who apprenticed at Sydney's celebrated Tetsuya's Restaurant, leads the school, which has more than a dozen class options, from natural cheesemaking to fermentation and the weekly Agrarian Experience. In the latter, three courses are prepared from recipes designed around seasonality, with each participant preparing individual details from one of the 12 kitchen workstations for a lunch (with paired wines) that will last long into the afternoon. Noted chefs are also regular guest tutors, from Quay executive chef Peter Gilmore to Tasmanian chef, forager and TV presenter Analiese Gregory.

'It's giving people that I admire the run of my garden and seeing what they come up with, and having them sharing their knowledge with a group of people who may be fans,' Dunn said. 'It's creating a lovely kind of intimate cooking experience with some of the best chefs in the country.'

Learning all things cooking and produce at Tassie's Agrarian Kitchen

Harvesting fresh produce from the Agrarian Kitchen's garden

TASMANIA'S RISE TO GOURMET GLORY

Andrew Bain

Agrarian Kitchen founder Rodney Dunn has watched Tasmania grow as a culinary destination. 'When we started, there was this genesis of something that was going to be amazing, but even the people in Tasmania didn't realise it was special,' Dunn said.

'But there were these little glimpses of it – I remember seeing a menu that had a recipe from Chris Jackman (founder of Hobart's popular Jackman and McRoss bakeries) for "Lloyd George raspberry vacherin". I was like, "Wow, imagine being able to put raspberries on your menu that are a varietal". It blew my mind. And that was just the start of my foray into how special Tasmania was in terms of food and varietals and people growing things.

'Back then, people would go to France and Italy for food, but in Australia, I felt that Tasmania had a real opportunity to explore that.'

Appreciating the simple things in life: making good food in good company

NATALIE PLACKO

CONNECT WITH LOCALS MAKING PESTO

LEVANTO, ITALY

As we explored the colourful streets of Levanto, a cosy and charming Italian town on the coast, my family and I found ourselves in a small outdoor kitchen restaurant, greeted by a friendly local couple who welcomed us with beautiful Italian accents and warm smiles.

We were there for a pesto-making class, something different from the usual touristy activities. The couple showed us how to make pesto from scratch, using fresh basil that had just been plucked from the garden. It was a hands-on experience, with mortar and pestle in hand, grinding away while chatting and laughing.

The aroma of basil filled the air as we chopped and crushed the basil, olive oil and other ingredients, and with every step we felt more connected to the tradition and culture of Italy. It wasn't about fancy restaurants or extravagant experiences; it was about slowing down and appreciating the simple pleasures of life – good food and good company and, of course, a good local limoncello.

As we sat down to enjoy the fruits of our labour, spooning generous portions of our homemade pesto onto fresh, locally baked bread, it felt like a true taste of Italy. It wasn't just about the food; it was about the memories we created together – laughing, learning and sharing stories with new friends.

At that moment, surrounded by the warmth of Italian hospitality, I realised that the best experiences aren't always what you expect. Sometimes, it's the authentic, down-to-earth, small moments that leave the biggest impression – like making fresh pesto with a local family in an outdoor kitchen in Levanto!

CRISTIAN BONETTO

SUSTAINABLE COPENHAGEN

COPENHAGEN, DENMARK

My Danish mate Mette still laughs about our first swim together at Copenhagen's Islands Brygge Harbour Bath. The city's harbour was a toxic, rubbish-strewn soup a few years earlier. And then there we were, Mette bobbing happily in its navy-blue depths, me looking unconvinced by the water's edge. I should have known better. The water was ridiculously pristine, bracing, and utterly liberating. Copenhagen has respected nature, and on that warm July afternoon, it was rewarding us.

But then, Copenhagen has a knack for making sustainability ridiculously fun. You can feel it cycling the orange curves of Cykelslengen (The Bicycle Snake), trampolining atop multilevel carpark Konditaget Lüders or revamping your wardrobe at unisex Henrik Vibskov Boutique. This is my favourite boutique in the city, stocked with some of Denmark's edgiest, most idiosyncratic streetwear. After all, nothing says 'Copenhagen' quite like tearing down CopenHill in a killer Vibskov flying hoodie.

Technically, CopenHill is not a hill but the world's cleanest waste-to-energy power plant. The 'Hill' part refers to its giant sloping roof, designed to ski down or hike up. Danish architect Bjalke Ingels calls it 'hedonistic sustainability'. I call it brilliantly bonkers. In the warmer months, an afternoon at CopenHill is usually followed by a carefree cycle north to Reffen, a harbourside street-food village big on recycling, food-waste minimisation and organic, local ingredients. I grabbed the Mikkeller beers while Mette found the deckchairs. DJs were spinning, evening sunshine on our faces – it was bliss.

Skiing down CopenHill

TERESA NOWAKOWSKI

A RARE LOOK INTO A GLOBAL BIODIVERSITY FAILSAFE

PLATEAU MOUNTAIN, SVALBARD

The safety net for the world's food supply sits on an icy archipelago in the Arctic Ocean. The Svalbard Global Seed Vault holds more than a million seeds from around the world, waiting to come into use should a climate crisis, biodiversity loss or other threat beset one of the many smaller seed vaults that dot the globe.

Few are allowed inside the secure storage facility. No one works there on a day-to-day basis, and the doors open just a handful of times each year for new seed shipments. However, thanks to a virtual tour, you can now visit anytime and in a climate-friendly way.

Your tour opens on a concrete triangle poking out of a snowy mountainside, its only adornment an artwork of steel, mirrors and prisms that emits a pale green glow. It looks like the refuge of a James Bond villain, but its managers – the Norwegian Ministry of Food and Agriculture, regional gene bank NordGen and independent international organization Crop Trust – are working towards a noble cause. It's one so universal that seeds from longtime foes like North Korea and South Korea sit side-by-side.

You can also witness the countless shelves of seed boxes without experiencing the frigid temperature – minus 18°C (0°F) – necessary to conserve them. From the entrance, it's a 120m (393ft) journey to reach the digital boxes. You'll have to pass through processing areas and a long tunnel to eventually arrive at the three seed chambers that rest beneath up to 60m (196ft) of rock at their deepest points. Inside, a mosaic of plastic, cardboard and wooden boxes line their shelves.

So far, a country has withdrawn seeds only once: in 2015, seeds from the vault restarted a seed bank in Aleppo that had been abandoned during the Syrian civil war. A key way to ensure the rest of the deposits can remain safely tucked away is combatting the climate crisis that threatens global biodiversity. In the meantime, rather than opening the doors out of necessity, we can continue to click them open from the comfort of home.

FIVE MORE VIRTUAL TOURS TO SEE THE WORLD FROM YOUR ARMCHAIR

* **DMZ Border Area:** Get a rare glimpse of the demilitarized zone (DMZ) buffering North and South Korea, thanks to a partnership between Google Arts & Culture and South Korean cultural institutions. Explore important historical and natural sites, browse images of the DMZ Botanic Garden's archive and hear sounds recorded in the area.

* **US National Marine Sanctuaries:** Dive into the United States National Marine Sanctuary System without getting wet. This project from the Office of National Marine Sanctuaries and the Ocean Agency lets you experience life underwater in the Florida Keys, Monterey Bay and more. You can even swim alongside a playful sea lion.

* **Surface of Mars:** Space tourism may be lifting off for the ultra-wealthy, but for those who can't stomach the price tag or climate implications, Google and the NASA Jet Propulsion laboratory have you covered. See the actual surface of Mars, thanks to data and images recorded by the Curiosity Rover.

* **Iguazu Falls:** Located on the border between Brazil and Argentina, the Iguazu Falls make up the largest waterfall system in the world. AirPano's virtual tour gives you a unique lens on the destination with photos taken both on the ground and from 150m (492ft) in the air – a bird's eye view that reveals the waterfalls' towering natural majesty.

* **Virtual Angkor:** Monash University's Virtual Angkor project uses historical research and simulation technology to bring to life what the sprawling Cambodian metropolis of Angkor might have looked like at the height of the Khmer Empire's power in the 1300s. See depictions of the city's architecture, daily life and more.

The Svalbard Seed Vault rises starkly from the snow

White rhinos at sunset, Ol Pejeta Conservancy

ANDREW BAIN

RHINO ROYALTY

OL PEJETA CONSERVANCY, KENYA

On the plains of the Serengeti or Kruger National Park, millions of animals combine to create some of the planet's finest wildlife viewing, but head further north, to Kenya's Ol Pejeta Conservancy, and it's just two individual animals that steal hearts and headlines.

It's here in this privately owned, not-for-profit park that the world's last two remaining northern white rhinos roam in the 24/7 company of armed guards, protecting the ill-fated pair – they are both females, mother and daughter – against any poaching.

The presence of these rhinos, Najin and Fatu, lends Ol Pejeta, a 360-sq-km reserve in the shadow of Mt Kenya, an air of mystique and greatness, even though visitors don't get to see the secured rhinos. Instead, they get a more low-key and personal safari experience than those in more big-ticket parks, but still in the company of Africa's Big Five animals.

Beside the main tented camp at Sweetwaters Serena, a waterhole draws in giraffes, elephants, zebras and impala – it's a hypnotising walk from tent to restaurant each mealtime – and baboons sound the daily dawn alarm. But it's out among the conservancy's thick bush and regular clearings that the wildlife really gets into stride.

On a single dawn game drive, I passed grazing Thomson's gazelles, Grant's gazelles, lumbering giraffes, black rhinos and herds of zebras gathered in their barcode stripes. Most dramatic of all was a lion trying on his moves with a disinterested lioness just a few metres from the road and our vehicle. And never, at any moment, were there more than four or five other game vehicles around us. Bliss in the Ol Pejeta bush.

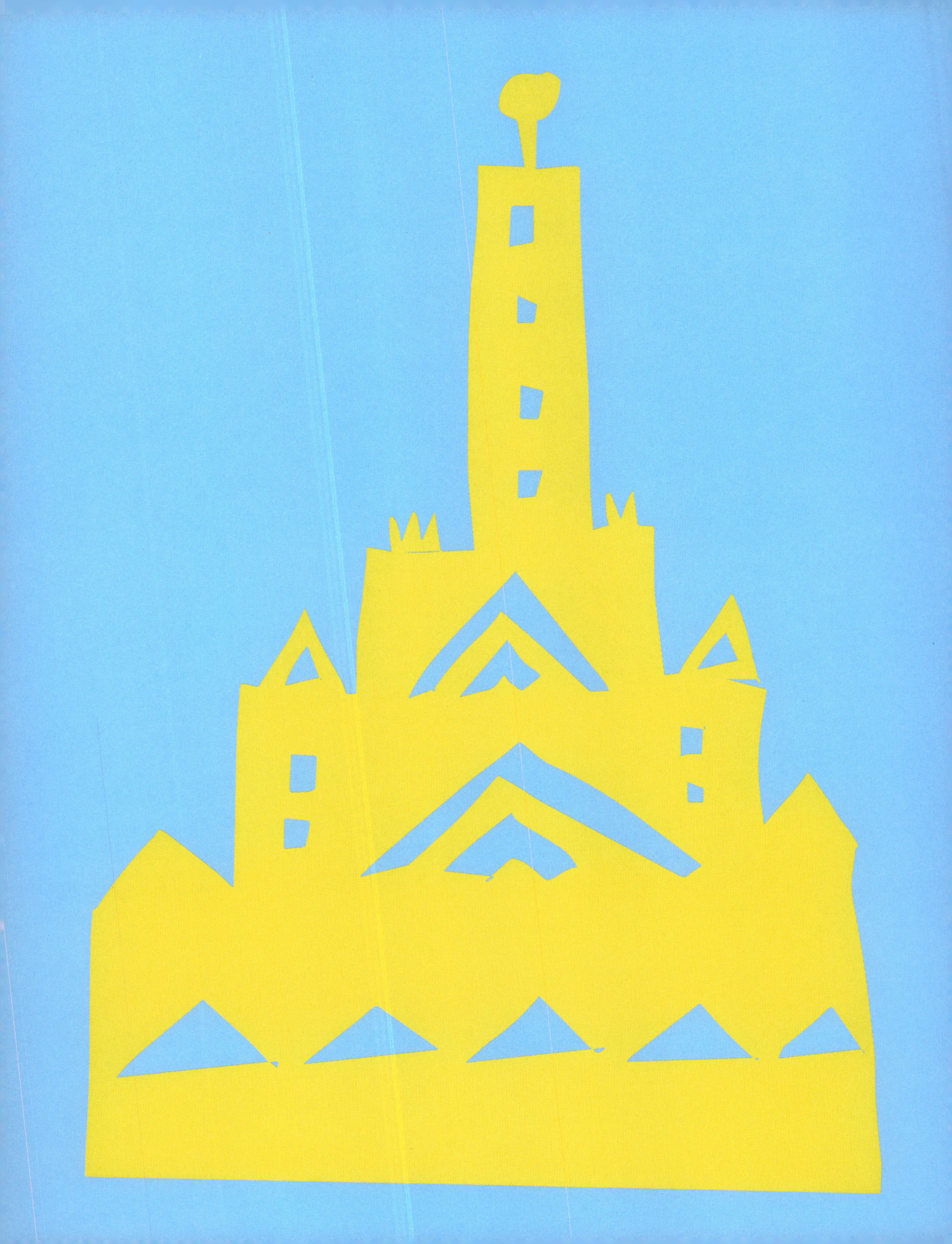

ARCHITECTURE

ARCHITECTURE

253	ICONIC BUILDINGS OF FRANK LLOYD WRIGHT
254	CAMBODIA'S HIDDEN MID-CENTURY HAVEN
257	FAMILY TIME IN A FUJIAN *TULOU*
258	ETHIOPIA'S NEW JERUSALEM
262	A SALT ON THE SENSES

"Sometimes featuring hundreds of rooms over multiple levels, these unique ancient apartment blocks are shaped like a ring or rectangle, often with a shared courtyard in the middle."

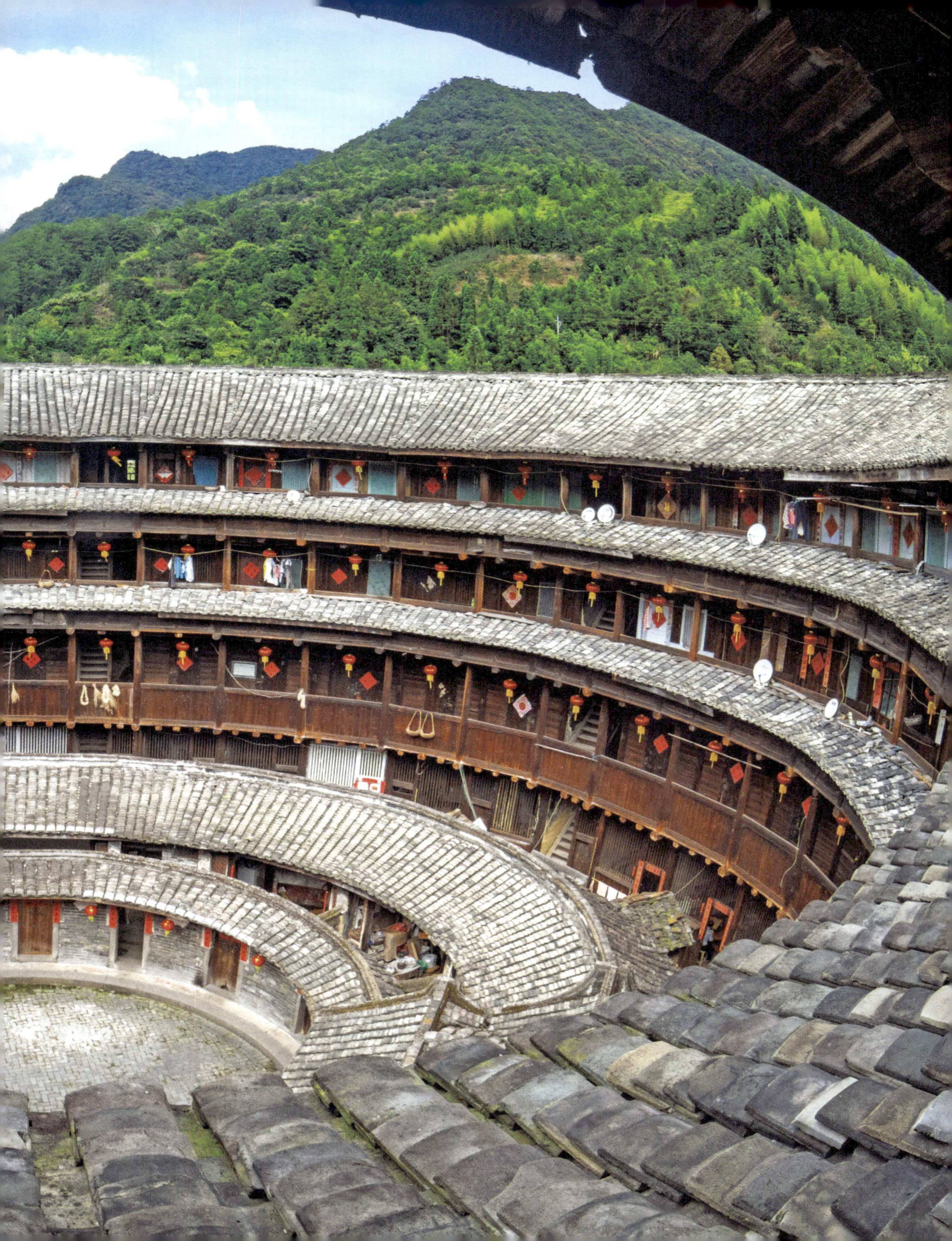

Top: The spiralling ramp and levels of New York's Guggenheim Museum
Bottom: Taliesin West in Scottsdale, Arizona

ANDREW COLLINS

ICONIC BUILDINGS OF FRANK LLOYD WRIGHT

USA

There's something instantly recognisable, and even a bit soothing, about the linear profiles, earthy tones and angular leaded-glass windows and light fixtures of the buildings dreamed up by Frank Lloyd Wright. The visionary architect credited with establishing the Prairie School style designed more than 1000 buildings over the course of his celebrated 70-year career, many of which you can view or even visit on a guided tour. Exploring these singular structures and learning about Wright's topsy-turvy life and larger-than-life personality offers a memorable lesson in harmonious, site-specific architectural design theory. Of course, these buildings are also just a delight to look at.

Wright's most enduring works open to the public include his two flagship homes and campuses. The original Taliesin is an 800-acre (324-ha) UNESCO World Heritage Site in Spring Green, Wisconsin, and his breathtaking stone-and-steel desert retreat, Taliesin West, is in the foothills near Scottsdale, Arizona. Wright passed away in 1959 while residing at the latter, just months before completing one of his most celebrated public designs, Manhattan's renowned Guggenheim Museum, with its iconic spiralling ramp and overhead oculus skylight.

Among Wright's residential designs for other clients, the one I return to at every opportunity is Fallingwater in the Appalachian foothills near Pittsburgh, with its dramatic cantilevers reaching out over a roaring waterfall. Martin House in Buffalo, New York, is another beautiful home that is well worth a trip, as is the Mayan Revival–style Hollyhock House in Los Angeles. Just outside Chicago, in Oak Park, you can explore Wright's roots on foot past several of his early designs in the compact, leafy neighbourhood where the architect established his first home and practice in 1898. And in Wisconsin, Taliesin is the most significant stop on the Frank Lloyd Wright Trail, a designated 320km (200-mile) route that connects a mix of prominent residential and commercial designs extending from Racine to Madison to Richland Center.

ANDREA BLACK

CAMBODIA'S HIDDEN MID-CENTURY HAVEN

PHNOM PENH, CAMBODIA

Palm Springs and Los Angeles may get all the attention, but when it comes to mid-century architecture, there's a surprising city with a plethora of buildings. I discovered this on a 1960s Khmer architecture tour in Phnom Penh, Cambodia, admiring the work of Vann Molyvann.

For a period after gaining independence from France in 1953, Cambodia experienced a cultural renewal. It was a time of optimism and experimentation, and at the centre of this progressive time was a building boom, out of which New Khmer Architecture emerged, with Cambodian-born architect Vann Molyvann, who studied at the Ecole Des Beaux Arts in Paris, leading the way. His structures, including the Olympic Stadium built in 1963, reinterpreted European modernism and mixed it with Khmer elements, incorporating local traditions and materials and taking the climate into account.

We wandered the stadium, then visited Molyvann's 100 Houses project, a stilted social housing development commissioned in 1965. Next were his designs at the Royal University of Phnom Penh. Open-air walkways and gathering areas under the building shade the students from the heat. In the lecture halls of the Institute for Foreign Languages, breeze blocks allow the cooling winds to waft. The library is a circular building sitting on a pond with concrete columns descending like spiders' legs, a design that Molyvann based on the shape of a straw hat.

But the cultural movement was short-lived. The Khmer Rouge forcibly depopulated the capital city, and residents fled to the countryside. It's estimated that 90 per cent of Cambodia's artists died under Pol Pot's genocidal regime. Molyvann spent 20 years exiled in Europe.

The impressive work of Vann Molyvann, as seen on the Olympic Stadium in Phnom Penh

Top: Squeezing between two *tulous* at Chengqilou

Bottom: Looking up at the top floor of Yuchang Tulou, built in 1368

DAVID NAGLE

FAMILY TIME IN A FUJIAN *TULOU*

HUKENG, CHINA

I could *not* stop eating the aubergine. I'd never tasted anything like it – the balance between the crisp outside and the soft middle, how the flavours of ginger and onion played with each other. Dishes were piled before me, and an intricate chess move was needed to find the next free space. More smells from the kitchen beckoned, luring me into my next choice, like a cartoon character to a pie cooling on a window ledge.

Sure, it had a lot to do with the culinary skills of Grandma Lin, but I think it was also due to the setting. There I was, perched at an antique table in an open courtyard, watching as Grandma Lin commanded the kitchen. It was a kitchen her family had used for generations, sitting at the centre of a fort-like building that was hundreds of years old. It overlooked a babbling river in Hukeng, Fujian province, south-east China.

Served on the side of exponentially delicious dishes were stories of the Hakka people from owner Stephen, and how their food and these *tulous* (earth buildings) are their greatest creations. Sometimes featuring hundreds of rooms over multiple levels, these unique ancient apartment blocks are shaped like a ring or rectangle, often with a shared courtyard in the middle. They were designed to keep whole communities safe from roaming bandits.

Grandma Lin's food was fuel for days spent exploring Yongding County on the back of a motorbike. My local guide wove through the traffic and pointed out clusters of *tulous*. Some sit abandoned, all crumbling doorways and dusty paths, while others still burst with family life – washing hanging off the balconies, lanterns framing ancestral halls and children's shouts echoing around the ring. Food and family are at the centre of Hakka culture, so stay in places like Tulou Fuyulou Changdi Inn and you'll find, just like with the aubergine and the *tolous*, there's a delicious soft heart under the firm outer shell.

ANDREW BAIN

ETHIOPIA'S NEW JERUSALEM

LALIBELA, ETHIOPIA

Ethiopia has no lack of intriguing religious connections. A heavily guarded church in the far-northern town of Aksum is claimed to hold the Ark of the Covenant (think *Raiders of the Lost Ark*) containing the Ten Commandments, and former Ethiopian emperor Haile Selassie is worshipped by Rastafarians. But the country's most striking religious sight is in the town of Lalibela, where 11 incredible churches were carved out of rock in the 13th century.

Built by angels during the reign of King Lalibela (or so the legend goes), the World Heritage–listed churches in the country's north were planned as a second representation of Jerusalem – essentially, a proxy pilgrimage site at a time when Christians had to cross through dangerous Muslim territories to reach Jerusalem.

Loosely organised into two clusters on either side of the River Jordan (an artificial gorge cut through the middle of the town to symbolise the holy river), the rock-hewn churches are remarkable constructions, not so much carved into the rock as freed from it. Trenches were cut around their exteriors, leaving solid blocks of rock, which were further carved out to create rooms, doors, columns, windows and other features. Built into the earth, they were constructed from the top down rather than the typical bottom up. So unusual are they that the first European to sight them – a Portuguese man named Francisco Alvarez in 1520 – wrote that 'it wearied me to write more of these works because it seems to me they will not believe me'.

I was quickly on Alvarez's side as I wandered among the churches, which were like no other structures on Earth – think Petra in 11 distinct portions. How would you explain to a Middle Ages world that believed in cathedrals rising towards heaven, not down into the Earth?

Nowhere was I more struck by the unreal reality of Lalibela than by the edge of an artificial cliff beside the isolated Bet Ghiorgis (House of St George), which stands alone a few hundred metres from the two main clusters of churches.

Standing at this edge, Bet Ghiorgis's cruciform shape looked a bit like a cross-shaped block punched into a square hole. But that hole was once hard rock, and rising from its centre was the 13m-high (42ft-high) church. The last of Lalibela's churches to be built, it was also the most advanced, complete with pillars built into the walls and stone gutters that have helped preserve Bet Ghiorgis in better condition than its counterparts.

My days in Lalibela disappeared wandering through the collection of churches, which are all distinct and fascinating. In the cluster on the northern bank of the river, I was drawn to the pillared Bet Medhani Alem (House of the Saviour of the World), which was built to the exact same dimensions as the Temple of Jerusalem. Said to be the world's largest monolithic church, its 36 rock pillars are all original – none have collapsed in 800 years.

And while I'm not particularly spiritual, as I entered nearby Bet Golgotha Mikael (House of Golgotha Mikael), I couldn't help but feel that I was just a curtain away from heaven. King Lalibela's remains are said to be interred in a chapel inside this church and to enter this chapel is to guarantee passage to heaven. Alas, only priests are allowed behind the curtain (women can't enter Bet Golgotha Mikael at all). I remained a mere mortal.

It is said that these structures were carved by angels

THREE ROCK-CUT CHURCHES

Andrew Bain

❋ **Bet Medhane Alem:** Dominating the cluster on the northern bank of the river is the pillared Bet Medhane Alem (House of the Saviour of the World). Built to the same dimensions as the Temple of Jerusalem, it's said to be the world's largest monolithic church, with all 36 pillars still original – none have collapsed in 800 years.

❋ **Bet Golgotha Mikael:** In nearby Bet Golgotha Mikael (House of Golgotha Mikael), men are just a curtain away from heaven. King Lalibela's remains are claimed to be interred in Bet Golgotha Mikael's Selassie Chapel, and to enter the chapel is said to guarantee passage to heaven, though only priests are allowed behind the curtain (women can't enter Bet Golgotha Mikael at all).

❋ **Bet Ghiorgis:** Lalibela's prize church is the isolated Bet Ghiorgis (House of St George), standing alone a few hundred metres from the two main clusters. It's the very image of Lalibela, with its cruciform shape looking like a cross-shaped block punched into a square hole. Head inside the church to view the original olivewood boxes, noting the wooden screws holding down the lids, one screw turning clockwise, the other anticlockwise. Legend says the boxes were built by King Lalibela himself. Cut 13m (42ft) into the earth, Bet Ghiorgis was the last of Lalibela's churches to be built, and is the most advanced, complete with pillars built into the walls and stone gutters that have helped preserve the church in better condition than its counterparts. From the edge of the cliff cut around it, it's a sight the equal of Petra or the Giza pyramids – a true and lasting monument to human ingenuity.

A moment of peace outside a church carved from stone

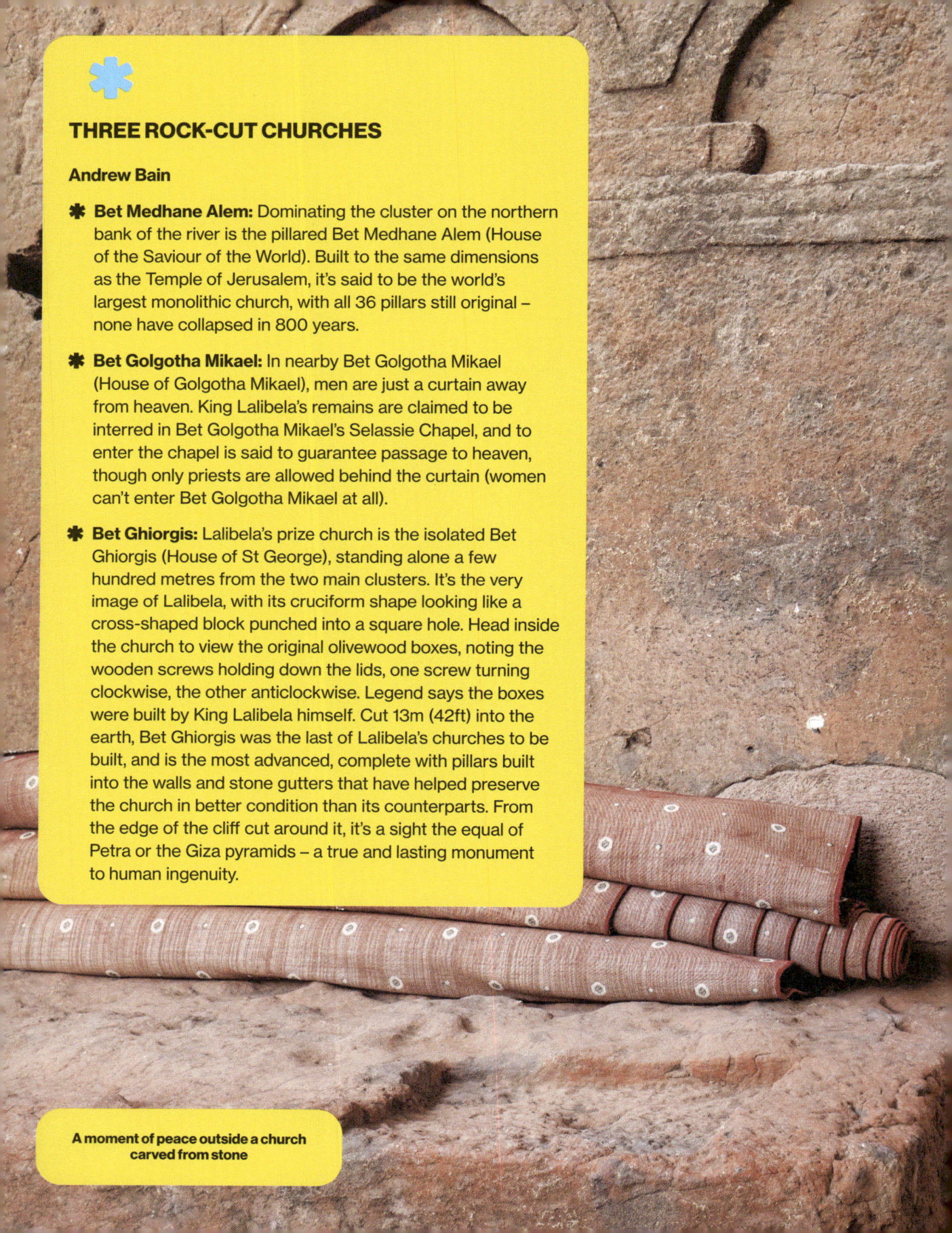

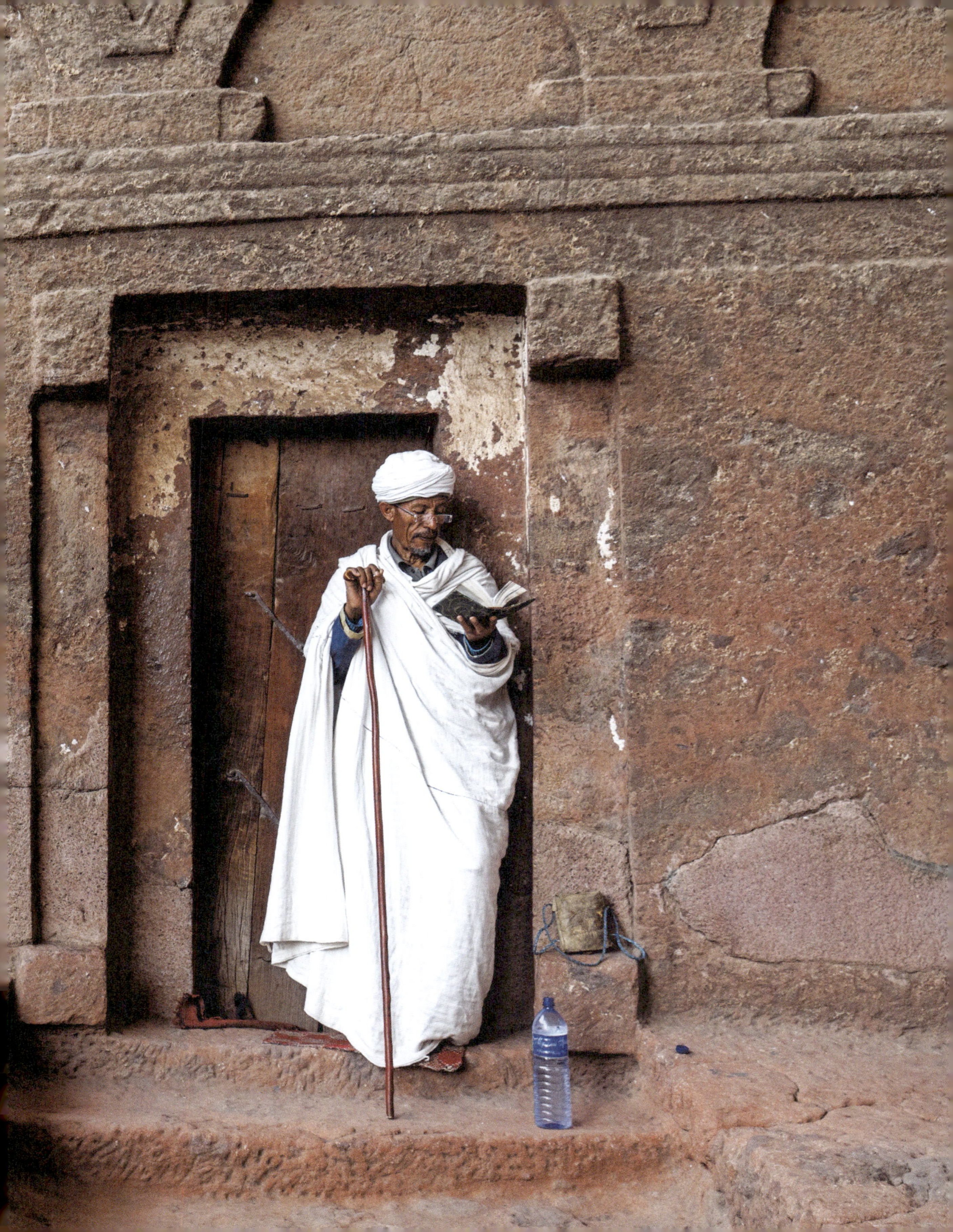

ANDREW BAIN

A SALT ON THE SENSES

ZIPAQUIRÁ, COLOMBIA

In the mountains of Zipaquirá, an hour's drive north of Bogota, the slopes are hollowed by salt mines. One of the world's largest rock salt deposits, Zipa mountain, was mined by the Indigenous Muisca people as early as the 5th century BCE, bringing them great wealth, and continues to be worked today.

Like all mining, it's difficult and dangerous work, prompting miners in this staunchly Catholic country to convert disused tunnels into a subterranean cathedral dedicated to the patron saint of miners – a place to pray before entering the mines each day.

First whittled into the mountain in the 1950s, the cathedral was eventually declared structurally unsound, so in the 1990s miners spent another four years carving out a new and grander cathedral 200m (650ft) underground.

Open to visitors, the Zipaquirá Salt Cathedral is entered through 14 Stations of the Cross – chapels notched into the rock that portray events in the Passion of the Christ. It's a grand entrance, with miners extracting 35,000 tonnes of salt and the stations taking up to a year to sculpt out of the hard halite rock.

The walls are gouged and scratched with drill marks and punctured with dynamite holes, and breezes whisk through the tunnels as they descend towards the main nave of the cathedral. Zipaquirá's most impressive feature, the nave, is lined with four cylindrical columns representing the four gospels – Matthew, Mark, Luke and John – and features a large sculptural re-creation of Michelangelo's *Creation of Adam*, albeit this time with God's hand larger than man's. In work as treacherous as mining, you have to do what you can to appeal to God, after all.

The Zipaquirá Salt Cathedral has been whittled into the Zipa Mountain

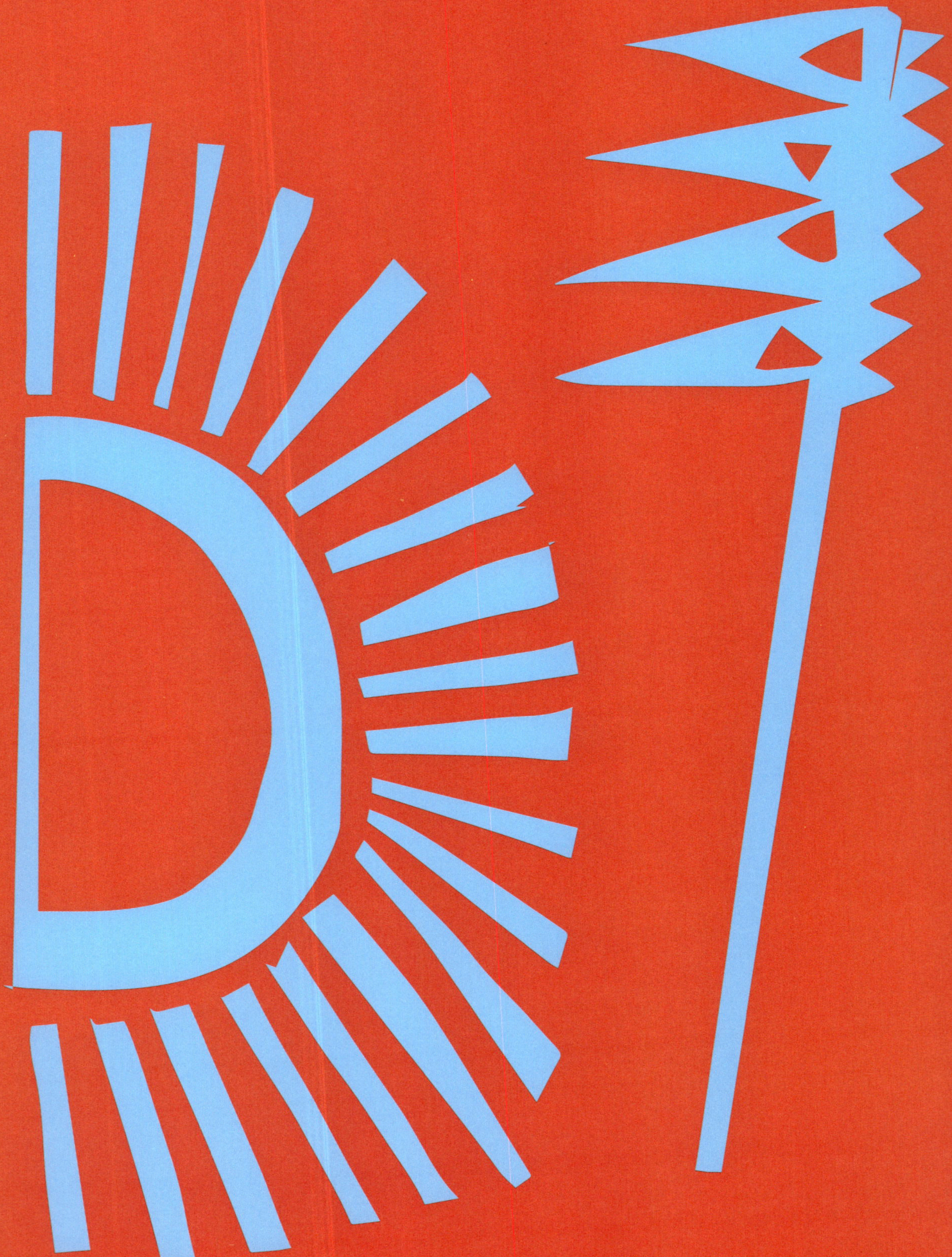

HISTORY

HISTORY

269	SACRED SCROLLS OF ISLAM
270	MATERA'S DARK HISTORY
272	EVER CHECKED OUT A GHOST TOWN?
273	HERE BE DRAGONS
277	SUNRISE AT THE TOMB OF AN EGOTISTICAL EMPEROR
278	THE FORGOTTEN MARWAR DYNASTY
282	EXPLORE NYC'S LGBTQIA+ HISTORY

"The Museum of Islamic Art is a singular masterpiece: a place of reverence that houses some of the most important historic artifacts from the Islamic world."

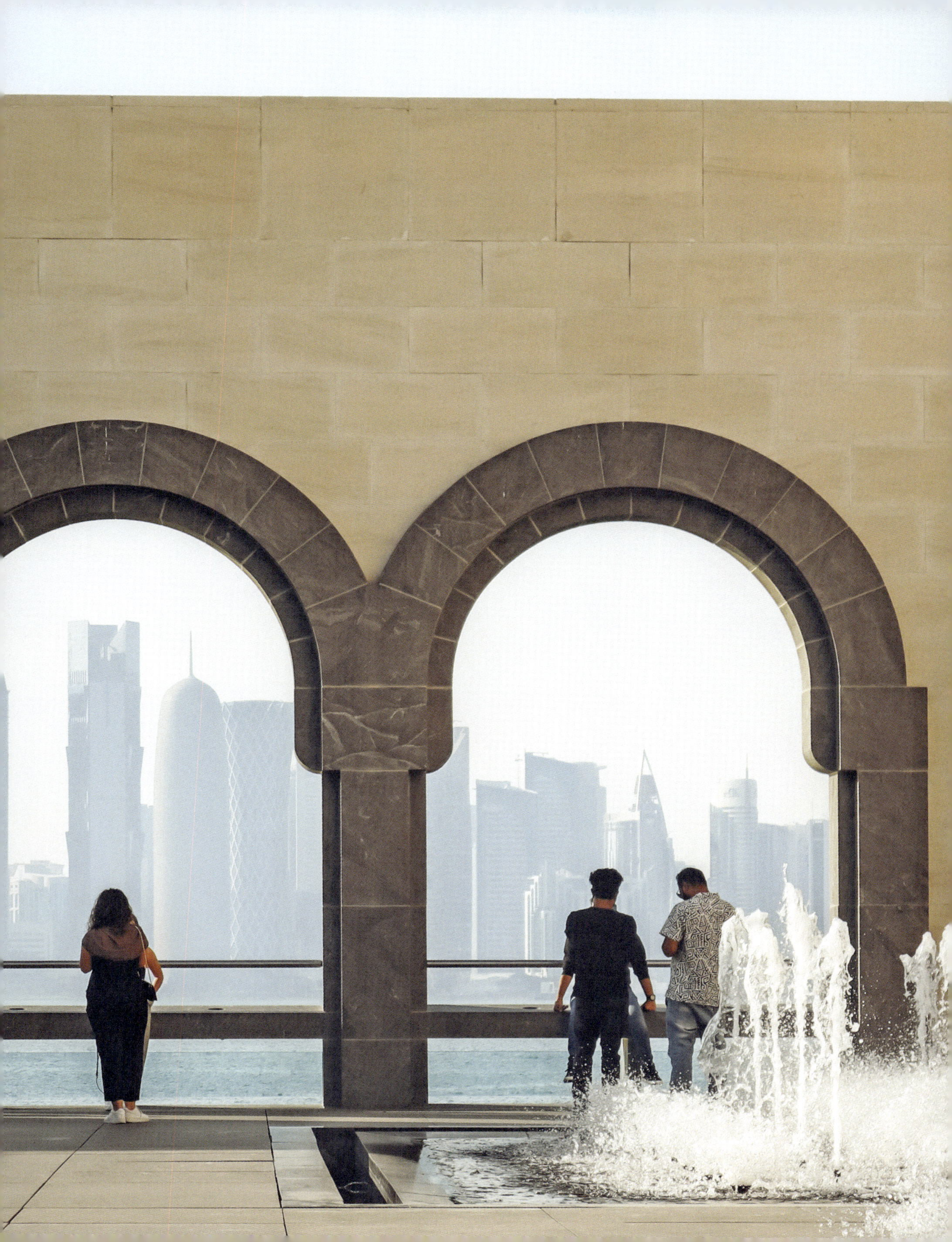

Top: The dazzling I.M. Pei-designed interior
Bottom: Exterior of the Museum of Islamic Art

JULIAN TOMPKIN

SACRED SCROLLS OF ISLAM

DOHA, QATAR

It is nearing 50°C (122°F) in Doha, and the storied Souq Waqif is soporific under the midday sun. I gravitated towards the water, fringed by palm trees all leading towards the Museum of Islamic Art. Built in the revivalist Islamic tradition – with more than a hint of the futuristic – the building's immense façade shimmers in the sunlight, its air-conditioned lobby beckoning like an oasis.

Designed by IM Pei, this iconic building stands like a citadel in the waters of Doha Bay, looking out to the Persian Gulf beyond. In a city defined by its architectural bling, the Museum of Islamic Art is a singular masterpiece: a place of reverence that houses some of the most important historic artifacts from the Islamic world.

While the grand domed hall, with its striking geometric patterns, is worth the price of entry alone, it is the historic collection that draws in millions of visitors each year – from regal jewels and ancient ceramics to traditional Islamic glasswork and ornately woven carpets dating back centuries.

But most awe is reserved for the museum's collection of rare Qur'ans: a truly staggering survey that includes the Abbasid Blue Qur'an, perhaps the world's most coveted edition. With most manuscripts painstakingly hand-etched, and dating to between the 7th and 19th centuries, the filarian and exquisite detail on display is arresting, and it is impossible not to be moved by the human pursuit of the divine on earth.

As I approached the fragments of the Timurid Baysungur Qur'an – the world's largest, with only a few pages having survived – I met a man named Fahmi who had travelled from Malaysia exclusively to pay reverence to these masterful manuscripts. 'Humankind can create such beauty,' he offered, wiping away a tear. 'These books are a reminder of that. A gift to all.'

ALISIA BUFANO

MATERA'S DARK HISTORY

SASSI DI MATERA, ITALY

Did you know that Italy has a dark history? Although it is a UNESCO World Heritage Site today, Sassi di Matera in southern Italy was once known as 'the shame of Italy'. This area is one of Italy's earliest known human settlements but also one of the region's poorest areas. Until the 1950s, families lived in caves carved into the limestone cliffs.

Today, the region welcomes visitors to explore the area and the preserved local history. Matera is best accessed by foot, so you can slowly explore the intricate alleyways and points of interest or stop at a bar to enjoy the views while sipping an espresso or granita. For an immersive experience of a cave-dwelling, the Storica Casa Grotta replica museum shares genuine stories of those who once inhabited these caves, the history of this time and the community's ingenious strategies for survival.

Another highlight is the Palombaro Lungo, an artificial underground cistern you can walk through, located right below the city. Close by, the Belvedere of Luigi Guerricchio is a stunning panoramic viewpoint where you can take iconic photos. Matera is also known for having over 150 places of worship carved into the rock. Climb a small stairway up a hill to Santa Maria de Idris, the must-see remnants of a small church with well-preserved hand-painted frescoes buried into the rock. The back of this monument overlooks a canyon with a stunning view, and if you look closely enough, you can spot the tiny remnants of the eerie cave openings, giving you a gentle reminder of Matera's sombre history.

Heading towards Santa Maria de Idris

Remnants of a once-popular resort town

ANTONIO RADIČEVIĆ

EVER CHECKED OUT A GHOST TOWN?

FAMAGUSTA, CYPRUS

Imagine this: you're in a country that's basically two countries with different eats, languages and vibes. These folks used to be BFFs, but now they're mortal enemies. Cyprus was split into northern (Turkish) and southern (Greek) parts in 1974, and the city of Famagusta was abandoned, becoming a ghost town overnight.

Once a glamorous seaside resort – and a hotspot for Hollywood big shots in the '60s – in the '70s, the city turned into a battlefield. Today, it's practically lifeless and known as no man's land – a family legacy turned war zone.

But hold up, it's not all doom and gloom. You can swing by the Turkish side of Famagusta, savour amazing baklava and coffee and explore the streets, churches, mosques and city walls. All that good stuff will help you shake off the eerie vibes from the ghost town. Plus, the Mediterranean weather and the world's most gorgeous beaches near the 'City of Ghosts' will catch your eye. Add in some ancient Greek monuments, and you'll realise the island is buzzing – except for that one part that's totally lifeless, the eternal ghost city that will stick in your memory forever.

HEATHER KANG

HERE BE DRAGONS

VIENNA, AUSTRIA

I've had the same magical habit since I was a kid: whenever I get my hands on a globe I give it a spin, shut my eyes and gently land my finger on a random location, proclaiming that's where I will travel next.

Vienna's Globenmuseum captures the wonder of holding the whole world in your hands. Even though you can't touch many of the 250 globes on display here, you'll leave with a renewed appreciation for humanity's enduring desire to explore and understand our world.

Some of the globes here date back to the 16th century, well before the entirety of the planet had been mapped. The oldest on display show much of the Americas uncharted, and where cartographical knowledge was lacking, drawings of sea monsters and other fantastical creatures took its place.

Beyond terrestrial globes, the museum's collection includes celestial globes that map out the night skies and astronomy and cartography tools used over the centuries.

The Globenmuseum is part of the Austrian National Library and is housed a five-minute walk from the main library. The same building is home to the Esperanto Museum, dedicated to this constructed international language, and worth a visit.

An ancient globe on display in the Austrian National Library's main hall

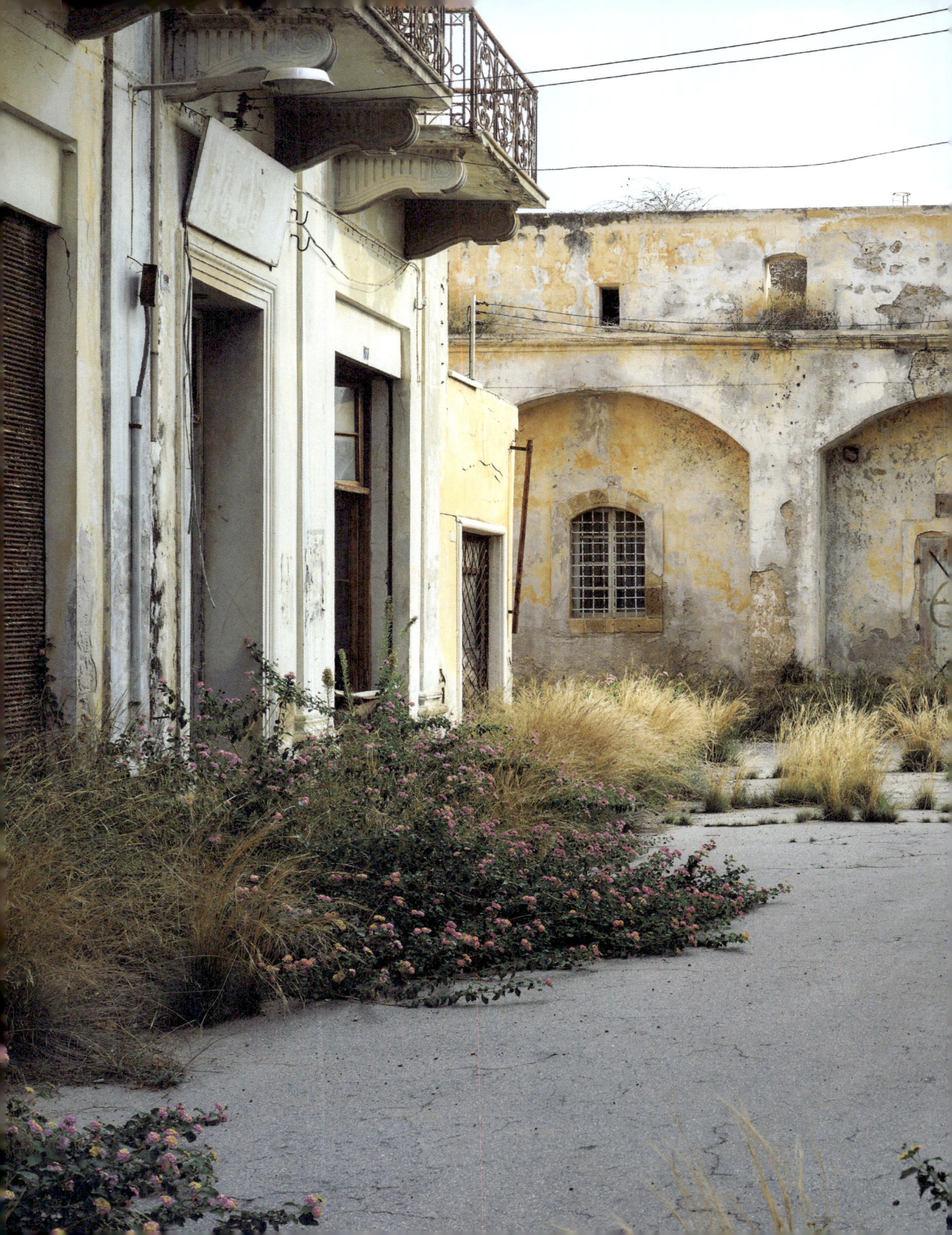

Nature reclaims Famagusta, Cyprus

Top: Sunrise on Nemrut Dag (Mount Nemrut)

Bottom: Giant statues commemorate Antiochus I of the Commagene kingdom

BRETT ATKINSON

SUNRISE AT THE TOMB OF AN EGOTISTICAL EMPEROR

NEMRUT DAG, TÜRKIYE

A journey up Nemrut Dag (Mount Nemrut) in south-eastern Türkiye usually involves a two-coffee start to the day. I always need at least a couple of cups of the country's strong and sweet Türk *kahvesi* to deal with a pre-dawn start and the winding road to the mountain's 2134m-high (7000ft) summit. Crowning this isolated mountain largely devoid of vegetation is a gravel-covered burial mound, rising into cobalt Turkish skies for around 50m (164ft), and a self-erected tribute to Antiochus I, the megalomaniacal last major ruler of the Commagene kingdom.

The great days of this minor Anatolian kingdom lasted only 125 years – from 163 BCE to 38 BCE, when Antiochus I was deposed by the Romans – but his legacy echoes across the centuries on the funerary terrace atop the mountain. Giant statues and enigmatic stone heads of the gods, eagles and lions look out over the expansive peaks of the Anti-Taurus Range and Mount Nemrut National Park. There's a representation of the egotistical Antiochus himself, and it's thought his tomb and that of three female relatives are secreted beneath the summit's leviathan burial mound.

Between May and September, when the serpentine road to the summit is usually snow-free, is my favourite time to visit, but even during the height of a Turkish summer, waiting for the sun to rise from the east can be cold and windy. I always wrap up warmly and take time to enjoy a third coffee served from local vendors also enjoying an Anatolian dawn. Once when I visited during the day, I had the spectacular summit all to myself.

MAHAVEER SINGH

THE FORGOTTEN MARWAR DYNASTY

JODHPUR, INDIA

Tourists flock to the blue streets of Jodhpur, soaking up samosas, *mirchi bada* (fried street snack) and lassis, as well as the colossal Mehrangarh Fort and striking Jaswant Thada historic site.

However, few visit one of the city's most incredible treasures. On the edge of Jodhpur, tucked away in a long-forgotten field, is one of India's true hidden gems: 46 cenotaphs built long ago to honour the lives of the queens of the former Marwar dynasty. Each ornate cenotaph is unique, reflecting both Hindu and Islamic architecture, with incredible craftsmanship on display. The area is so quiet that the grass has grown up around the cenotaphs, and some are starting to crumble a little, but these magnificent sandstone structures stand proud and literally glow in the light of sunset. In this peaceful, serene place with the wind gently flowing between the columns, you can truly soak in the powerful dynastic history of Rajasthan. And the best part is you'll have it all to yourself!

Each cenotaph, honouring the queens of the former Marwar dynasty, is unique
Opposite: Cenotaph silhouette at sunset

Intricate sandstone structures on the edge of Jodhpur

Opposite: Looking through a row of ornately carved archways

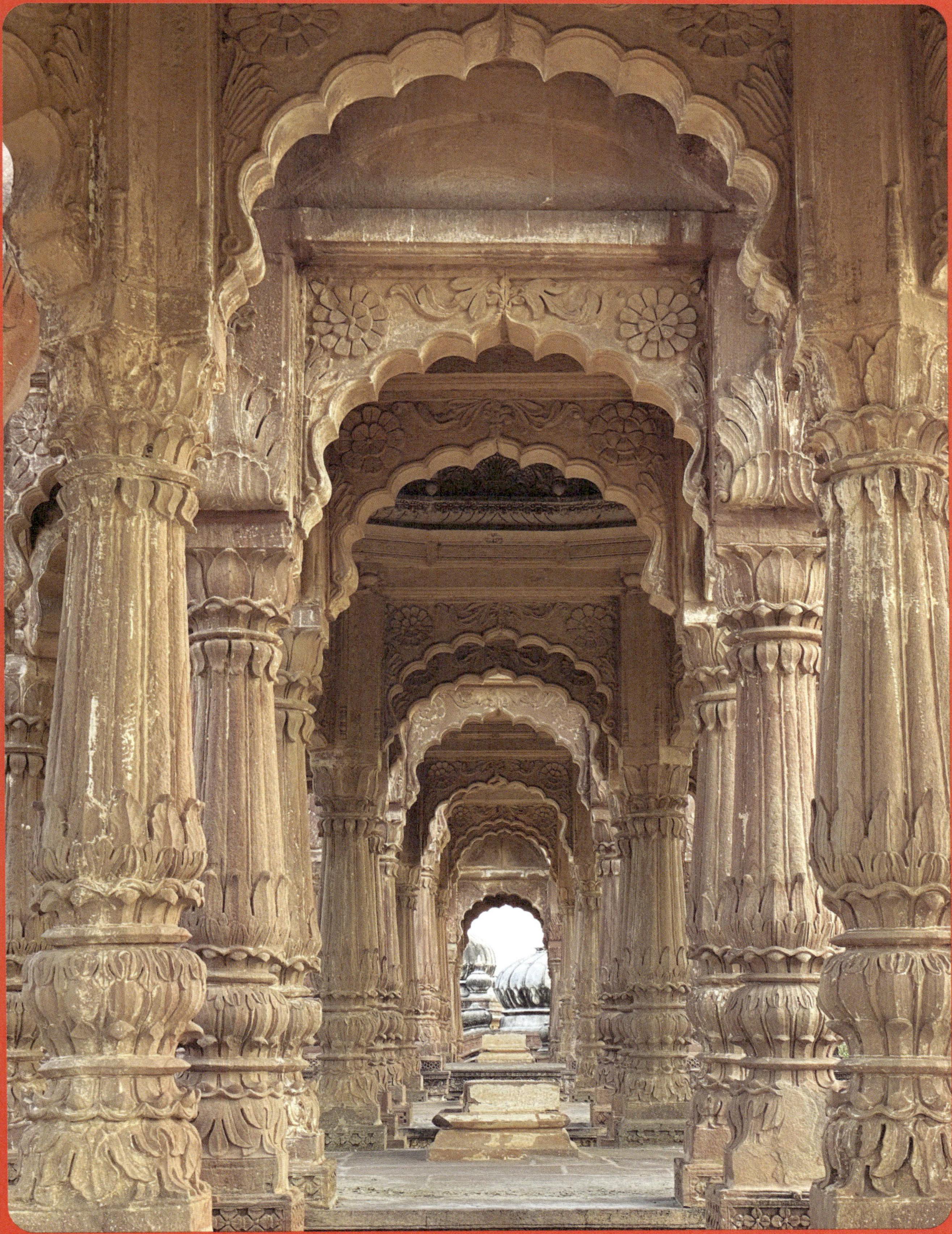

ANDREW COLLINS

EXPLORE NYC'S LGBTQIA+ HISTORY

NEW YORK CITY, USA

In the wee hours of 28 June 1969 in Manhattan's West Village neighbourhood, a group of mostly marginalised queer folks – many of them people of colour and transgender – became fed up with ongoing police harassment and courageously resisted a raid on a bar called the Stonewall Inn. The event sparked a watershed moment in the LGBTQIA+ movement: the following year, New York City (and several other cities around the world) held the first Pride demonstrations, and today the month of June is recognised as LGBTQIA+ Pride Month.

Although the original Stonewall Inn closed shortly after the riots and had several incarnations over the next few decades, new owners opened it once again in 2006, and it's been a welcoming hub for LGBTQIA+ folks and allies ever since, presenting piano cabarets, drag shows and dance parties throughout the week.

In 2016, the bar and a portion of Christopher Park, a small triangular sliver of benches and floral gardens across the street, were officially designated Stonewall National Monument by the US National Park Service. On the fence enclosing the park, signs and historic photos shed light on the Stonewall riots, and the early history of queer rights activism. The West Village is home to several LGBTQIA+ bars that have been open for decades, including the Cubbyhole lesbian bar and Julius' Bar. The latter dates to 1867, became popular as a gay hangout in the 1950s and was the site of its own 'sip-in' queer rights protest in 1966.

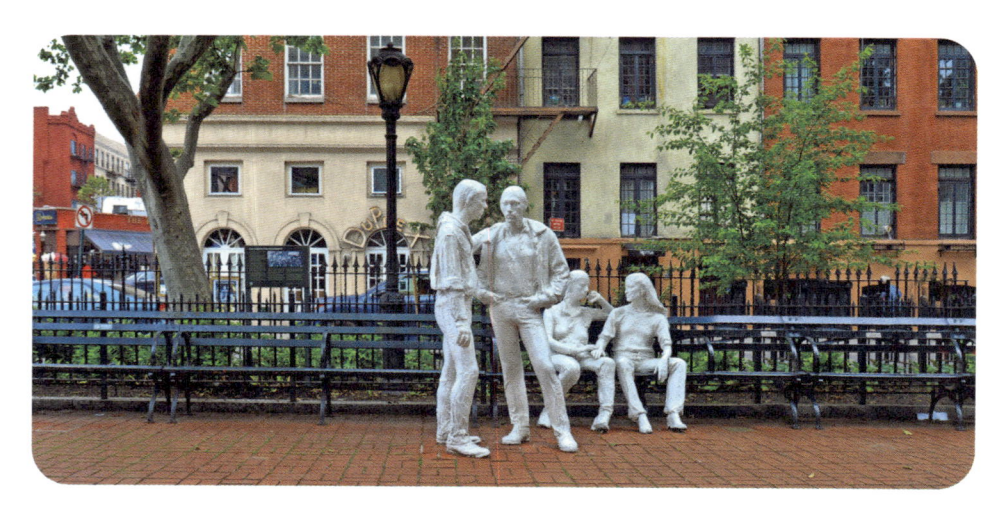

The iconic, historic Stonewall Inn
Opposite: Sculptures by Christopher Park commemorating the gay liberation movement and the Stonewall riots

INDEX

A

African landscapes, Ethiopia 98
Agrarian Kitchen, Tasmania, Australia 236–9
Alaska, USA 66–7
Amazon cruising, Nauta, Peru 56–7
Amazon flooded forest, Cuyabeno National Park, Ecuador 84–5
American barbecue 26–7
Antiochus I (emperor) burial mound, Nemrut Dag, Türkiye 276–7
Aotea/Great Barrier Island, Aotearoa/New Zealand 94–5
Aotearoa/New Zealand 94–5, 194–5, 218–19
Arches National Park, Utah, USA 100–1
architecture 252–55, 278–81
Argentina 81, 110–11, 248
arts and crafts 146–7, 150–1
Australia 42–3, 74–5, 121, 146–7
Austria 273
Avignon, France 210–11

B

bacari, Venice, Italy 20–1
baklava, Gaziantep, Türkiye 6
Bali, Indonesia 235
Bangalore, India 8–9
Bangkok, Thailand 182–3
baseball, USA 46–7
bear watching, Alaska, USA 66–7
big wave surfing, Nazaré, Portugal 48–9
Binmah Sinkhole, Oman 121
bird watching, Cambodia 64–5
Bloomsday celebrations, Dublin, Ireland 188–9
Bolivia 128–9
Boston, USA 46
Botswana 78–81
Brazil 144–5, 245

Bryce Canyon National Park, Utah, USA 100–3
Butchart Gardens, Brentwood Bay, Canada 224

C

California Zephyr (train) 206–9
Cambodia 64–5, 245, 254–5
Camino de Santiago, Spain 232–3
Canada 59, 224
canals, Delte el Tigre, Argentina 110–1
canoeing, Germany 36
cave-dwelling, Sassi di Matera, Italy 270–1
caves, Vietnam 108–9
Chamula, Mexico 162–3
Chicago, USA 46, 206–7
China 212–3, 256–7
churches
    Lalibela, Ethiopia 258–61
    Zipaquirá Salt Cathedral, Colombia 262–3
Coastal California, USA 220–1
coastal scenic drive, California, USA 220–1
Cocos Keeling, Australia 42–3
Colombia 262–3
cooking school, Tasmania, Australia 236–9
Copenhagen, Denmark 242–3
Cosigüina, Nicaragua 92–3
craft beer 8–9, 18–19
Croatia 40–1
crocodiles, Pakistan 69
Cusco, Peru 184–5
Cuyabeno National Park, Ecuador 84–5
cycling/bikepacking 38–9, 204–5, 226–7, 232–3
Cyprus 272
Czechia 18–19

D

Dalmatia, Croatia 40–1
dark sky stargazing 94–5, 97
Dead Sea, Jordan 113
Delta el Tigre, Argentina 110–11
desert experiences, Egypt 122–3
Dia de Muertos, Mexico 180–1
diving 117, 121
DMZ Border Area (between North and South Korea) (virtual tour) 244
Doha, Qatar 269
Dublin, Ireland 24–5, 35, 188–9

E

Ecuador 70–3, 84–5
Egypt 122–3
elephants, Botswana 76–7
England 224, 233
Ethiopia 98–9, 258–61
Everest region, Nepal 130–3

F

fall foliage, New England, USA 124–5
Famagusta, Cyprus 272
fine dining, Lima, Peru 10–13
Finland 126–7
flamenco dance, Seville, Spain 156–7
forest of future books, Oslo, Norway 152–3
France 97, 210–11, 224
Frank Lloyd Wright (architect) buildings, USA 252–3
Fremantle, Australia 146–7
fruit bats 80
Fukian tulou family life, Hukeng, China 256–7

INDEX

G

Galápagos Islands, Ecuador 70–3
gardens 224–5
Gaziantep, Türkiye 6
geology, Southwest USA 100–3
Georgia 142–3
Germany 36
ghost towns, Famagusta, Cyprus 272
Glacier Express (train) 216–17
Glastonbury to Stonehenge, England 233
Globenmuseum, Vienna, Austria 273
Great Wall of China 212–3
Greece 150–1
Gubeikou, China 213

H

Hiroshima, Japan 148–9
holy animals 68
holy crocodiles, Pakistan 68–9
Hukeng, China 257
humpback whales, Niue 82
Hungary 97
Hydra, Greece 150–1

I

ice dipping, Finlay and Norway 127
Iceland 104–7, 121
Iguazu Falls, Brazil/Argentina (virtual tour) 245
Inca Trail, Peru 233
India 8–9, 186–7, 278–9
Indian weddings 186–7
Indonesia 62–3, 235
Inuit throat singing 174–5
Ireland 24–5, 34–5
Isle of Skye, Scotland 200–1
Italy 20–1, 270–1

J

Japan 50–1, 148–9, 211, 233
Jewel Changi Airport, Singapore 224
Jodhpur, India 278–81

Johnstone Strait, Canada 59
Jordan 113

K

Kansas City, Missouri, USA 36–7
karaoke, Hiroshima, Japan 148–9
Kasanka National Park, Zambia 80
kayaking, Johnstone Strait, Canada 59
Kenya 246–7
Keukenhof, Lisse, Netherlands 224
Kilimanjaro National Park, Tanzania 114–15
Korean record bars, Seoul, South Korea 158–61
Kumano Kodo Trail, Japan 233

L

Lalibela, Ethiopia 258–61
large-scale artworks 140–1, 154–5
Lava Show, Iceland 104–5
Levanto, Italy 241
LGBTQIA+ culture, USA 164–5, 282–3
light installations, California, USA 154–5
Lima, Peru 10–13
Lord of the Tremors, Cusco, Peru 184–5
Lukla, Nepal 131

M

McKinley Park Rose Garden, Sacramento, USA 211
Manghopir, Pakistan 69
Marburg, Germany 36
Maria Island, Australia 75
markets, Oaxaca, Mexico 5
Marrakech, Morocco 139
Marwar dynasty cenotaphs, Jodhpur, India 278–81
Mayan and Catholic rituals, Chamula, Mexico 162–3
Memphis, Tennessee, USA 26–7
Mexico 4–5, 119, 162–3, 180–1
Mexico City, Mexico 181
Moalboal, Philippines 116–17

Monet's Garden, Giverny, France 224
Morocco 170–1
Mount Everest, Nepal 130–3
mountaineering 114–15, 131
Museum of Islamic Art, Doha, Qatar 258–9

N

Nauta, Peru 56–7
Nazaré, Portugal 49
Nemrut Dag, Türkiye 276–7
Nepal 130–33
Netherlands 211, 224
New England, USA 124–5
New Norfolk, Australia 236–7
New York City, USA 282–3
Nicaragua 92–3
Niue 82–3
nomadic Berber life, Morocco 170–1
Norway 126–7, 244–5
Nunavut, Canada 174–5
Nuwara Eliya, Sri Lanka 15–17

O

Oaxaca, Mexico 5
Okavango Delta, Botswana 76–9
Old Pejeta Conservancy, Kenya 246–7
Oman 121
orangutans, Sumatra, Indonesia 62–3
orcas (killer whales) 58–9, 81
Oslo, Norway 152–3
Ouarzazate, Morocco 190–1

P

Painted Desert, USA 140–1
Pakistan 68–9
Paso Robles, California, USA 154–5
Patagonia 226–7
Peru 10–13, 56–7, 86–7, 184–5, 233
pesto-making class, Levanto, Italy 241
Phnom Penh, Cambodia 254–5

INDEX

Phong Nha-ke Bang National Park, Vietnam 108–9
Pic du Midi Observatory, France 97
picnicking 210–11
pilgrimages 232–3
Plateau Mountain, Svalbard, Norway 244–5
Plzen and Ceske Budejovice, Czechia 18–19
Portugal 48–9
Prek Toal Bird Sanctuary, Cambodia 64–5
Punta Norte, Argentina 81

Q

Qatar 269

R

Ramadan celebrations, High Atlas Mountains, Morocco 190–1
record bars, Seoul, South Korea 158–60
Reykjavik and Vik, Iceland 104–5
rhinoceroses, Kenya 246–7
Rio de Janeiro, Brazil 144–5
rock-cut churches, Lalibela, Ethiopia 258–61
Roden Crater, Arizona, USA 140–1
Royal Botanic Gardens, Kew, England 224

S

sailing, Dalmatia, Croatia 40–1
St Moritz, Switzerland 217
Salar de Uyuni, Bolivia 128–9
Salt Cathedral, Zipaquirá, Colombia 262–3
salt flats, Bolivia 128–9
San Francisco, USA 165, 206
Santo, Vanuatu 118
Sassi di Matera, Italy 270–1
saunas, Finland and Norway 126–7
Scotland 200–3
sea of clouds, Vietnam 214–15
Seoul, South Korea 159
Seville, Spain 156–7

Shiogama Shrine, Japan 211
shrines 69, 211
Simien Mountains, Ethiopia 98–9
Singapore 224
sinkholes 119–21
Skye, Scotland 200–3
snorkelling 42–3, 70–3, 116–17, 121
Songkran festival, Bangkok, Thailand 182–3
South Africa 38–9
South Korea 159, 245
Southern Utah, USA 100–3
Soweto, South Africa 39
space travel/space tours 97, 245
Spain 156–7, 232–3
spice bags, Dublin, Ireland 25
spirituality 69, 162–3, 190–1, 232–3, 235, 259–63, 268–9
Sri Lanka 15–17
stargazing 94–5, 97, 122
Stonewall Inn, New York City, USA 282–3
street art Rio de Janeiro, Brazil 144–5
Sumatra, Indonesia 63
sumo, Japan 50–1
Surface of Mars (virtual tour) 245
sustainability, Copenhagen, Denmark 242–3
Svalbard Global Seed Vault, Norway 244–5
swimming 34–5, 113, 118–21, 200
swimming with whales, Niue 82
Switzerland 216–17
Sydney/Warrang, Australia 166–7, 225

T

Ta Xua, Vietnam 214
Taliesin, USA 253
Tanzania 114–15
Tbilisi, Georgia 142–3
tea, Sri Lanka 15–17
temples, Bali, Indonesia 235
Texas, USA 26–7
Thailand 182–3
therapeutic relaxation, Dead Sea, Jordon 112–13
Timor-Leste 173
Tokyo, Japan 50–1

Torres del Paine, Patagonia 226–7
traditional dance 156–7, 166–7, 170–1
traditional music 138–9, 142–3, 174–5
traveller ethics xii–xiii
trekking see walking
Türkiye 6, 276–7

U

Udaipur, India 205
US National Marine Sanctuaries (virtual tour) 245
USA 26–7, 44–5, 66–7, 97, 100–3, 124–5, 140–1, 154–5, 165–6, 206–9, 214, 220–3, 245, 252–3

V

Vann Molyvann (architect) buildings, Phnom Penh, Cambodia 254–5
Vanuatu 118
Venice, Italy 20–1
Vienna, Austria 273–5
Vietnam 108–9
Virtual Angkor (Cambodia) 245
virtual tours 244, 245
volcanic activities, Iceland 104–7
volcanic climbs, Nicaragua 92–3
Vondelpark, Netherlands 211

W

walking/hiking 98, 131, 200–1, 212–3, 233
water fight, Songkran festival, Thailand 182–3
welcome the dead, Dia de Muertos parade, Mexico 180–1
Wellington, Aotearoa/New Zealand 194–5
Wendy Whiteley's Secret Garden, Sydney/Warrang, Australia 225
Whanganui River, Aotearoa/New Zealand 218–19
White Desert, Egypt 122–3
wildlife watching 56, 62–3, 66–7, 75, 76–8, 84, 98, 246–7

INDEX

World of Wearable Art, Wellington, Aotearoa/New Zealand 194–5

Y

Yucatan, Mexico 119

Z

Zambia 80
Zipaquirá, Colombia 262–3
Zselic Starry Sky Park, Hungary 97

PHOTOGRAPHY CREDITS

Cover Matt Cherubino for Intrepid Travel
Internal pages iv, 78 Ruan Vorster for Intrepid Travel; vi Goran Jovic for Intrepid Travel; ix, 191 (both) Adam Gibson for Intrepid Travel; x, 132–3 Patrick O'Neill for Intrepid Travel; xiii Mario Hernandez Vergara for Intrepid Travel; xiv–xv Lilli Morgan for Intrepid Travel; 2–3 Radiokafka / Shutterstock; 4 (both), 180 (bottom) Cristina Alonso; 7 resulmuslu / iStock; 9 Filip Jedraszak / Alamy Stock Photo; 11 Liam Neal for Intrepid Travel; 12 (top) Gavin Rodgers / Alamy Stock Photo; 12 (bottom) Intrepid Travel / Urban Adventures; 14, 28–9, 148, 149 Ryan Bolton for Intrepid Travel; 16 Travel Faery / iStock; 17 Mark Daffey for Intrepid Travel; 19 Michaela Jilkova / Shutterstock; 21 AlexandraFar / Shutterstock; 22–3, 41 Rachel Claire for Intrepid Travel; 24 Fiona Hilliard; 27 Martin Thomas Photography / Alamy Stock Photo; 32–3 Philippa Whishaw for Intrepid Travel; 34 Mark Henderson / Alamy Stock Photo; 37 Raja Sen / Unsplash; 38 (both), 79 Intrepid Travel; 43 WaterFrame / Alamy Stock Photo; 44–5 JustAbove / Shutterstock; 47 (top) Emma Krahmer / Shutterstock; 47 (bottom) Joseph Sohm / Shutterstock; 48 R.M. Nunes / Shutterstock; 51 (top) J. Henning Buchholz / Shutterstock; 51 (bottom) Ivan Roth / Shutterstock; 54–5 wildestanimal / Shutterstock; 56 (top) mariusz_prusaczyk / iStock; 56 (bottom), 67 Carol Atkinson; 58 Ralph Lee Hopkins / Alamy Stock Photo; 60–1 Alexopoulos Kyriakos for Intrepid Travel; 62, 63 Danielle McDonald; 64 (top) Mr Sak Sin; 64 (bottom) kathrinerajalingam / Shutterstock; 68 (top) Sahar Aman; 68 (bottom) Tuul and Bruno Morandi / Alamy Stock Photo; 71, 72–3 Cliff Bielawski; 74 (top) Martin Pelanek / Shutterstock; 74 (bottom) Willowtreehouse / Shutterstock; 77 Artistic photographer / Shutterstock; 80 Minden Pictures / Alamy Stock Photo; 83 Imagine Earth Photography / Shutterstock; 85 oscar garces / Shutterstock; 86–7 Jess Kraft / Shutterstock; 90–1, 129 (both), 227 Mark Watson; 93 robertharding / Alamy Stock Photo; 95, 96–7 James Rua; 98 Rowan Waters for Intrepid Travel; 99 Lou Day for Intrepid Travel; 101 (both), 102–3, 112 (both), 120–1, 198–9, 201, 202–3, 205 Ben McNamara for Intrepid Travel; 105 Courtesy of Lava Show; 106–7 Kotenko Oleksandr / Shutterstock; 109 Vietnam Stock Images / Shutterstock; 111 Marc Venema / Shutterstock; 115 (top) Bronwyn Lintott for Intrepid Travel; 115 (bottom) Fiona Liz for Intrepid Travel; 116 (top) Sean Steininger / Shutterstock; 116 (bottom), 271 Alisia Bufano; 118–9 Cindy Hopkins / Alamy Stock Photo; 122 Simona Weber / iStock; 123 Marjolein Hameleers / Shutterstock; 125 Jay Yuan / Shutterstock; 126 Mark Waugh / Alamy Stock Photo; 130 Lucy Piper for Intrepid Travel; 136–7, 172 Rachelle Mackintosh for Intrepid Travel; 138, 240 (both) Siena Nisavic for Intrepid Travel; 141 Jcilwa / iStock; 142 (top) ERIK Miheyeu / Shutterstock; 142 (bottom) Atis Everss / Shutterstock; 145 (top) Thales Botelho de Sousa / Unsplash; 145 (bottom) Milos Hajder / Unsplash; 146 (top) Marco Taliani de Marchio / Shutterstock; 146 (bottom) Leanne Irwin / Shutterstock; 151 kovalcookie / Shutterstock; 153 Katie Paterson; 154 Abaca Press / Alamy Stock Photo; 157 (top) Alexandre Rotenberg / Shutterstock; 157 (bottom) Corrado Baratta / Shutterstock; 158 (top), 160–1 Andrea Black; 158 (bottom) hwanchul / Shutterstock; 163 Rubi Rodriguez Martinez / Shutterstock; 164 Piotr Musiol / Unsplash; 166, 167–8 Daniel Boud; 171 (both) Emma Laliberte; 175 (top) Courtesy of PIQSIQ; 175 (bottom) Isaac Demeester / Unsplash; 178–9 Sukpaiboonwat / Shutterstock; 180 (top) Sipa USA / Alamy Stock Photo; 183 (top) drpnncpp / iStock; 183 (bottom) Brett Atkinson; 184 Arne Beruldsen / Shutterstock; 187 Digital Cloud / Shutterstock; 188 Phil Crean A / Alamy Stock Photo; 189 noel bennett / Shutterstock; 192–3 Ewen Bell for Intrepid Travel; 194 (top) pbpvision / Alamy Stock Photo; 194 (bottom) Imago / Alamy Stock Photo; 204 Anand Kapil; 207 Chris Enright / Alamy Stock Photo; 208, 209, 216 (top) Tim Richards; 211 (top) Laura Doguet; 211 (bottom) Roger Cannon / Alamy Stock Photo; 212 Christopher Moswitzer / Shutterstock; 215 Nguyen Mai; 216 (bottom) Koray Bektas / Shutterstock; 219 Image Professionals GmbH / Alamy Stock Photo; 221 Cristofer Maximilian / Unsplash; 222–3 Venti Views / Unsplash; 224 Destination NSW; 230–1, 237 (both), 238–9 Tourism Australia; 233 Ackab Photography / Shutterstock; 234 Dyan McKie; 243 Boris-B / Shutterstock; 245 Borkowska Trippin / Shutterstock; 246 Tomas Drahos / Shutterstock; 250–1 Sean Hsu / Alamy Stock Photo; 252 (top) Nicholas Ceglia / Unsplash; 252 (bottom) Kit Leong / Shutterstock; 255 NiceProspects-Prime / Alamy Stock Photo; 256 (both) David Nagle; 259, 260–1 Annapurna Mellor for Intrepid Travel; 263 Felix Lipov / Shutterstock; 266–7, 268 (top) Andrei Antipov / Shutterstock; 268 (bottom) Zosar_mohy / Shutterstock; 272 (both), 274–5 Steffen Lemmerzahl / Unsplash; 273 Nak Anna / Shutterstock; 276 (top) Efe Kurnaz / Unsplash; 276 (bottom) Birgul Zengin / Unsplash; 278, 279, 280, 281 Mahaveer Singh; 282 poludziber / Shutterstock; 283 Glynnis Jones / Shutterstock.

ABOUT THE AUTHORS

Born in the UK with a Southern Italian heritage, **Alisia Bufano** took her 'Where Are You From' story to the next level by relocating to Melbourne. Having journeyed through various roles, she currently manages Intrepid's Global Studio. Passionate about travel, she often seeks off-the-beaten-path trips to less popular destinations, always searching for unique experiences to feed her wanderlust.

Andrea Black is a Sydney-based writer specialising in travel across such publications as *T Australia The New York Times Style Magazine* and *The Weekend Australian*. Her book, Los Angeles Pocket Precincts is published by Hardie Grant Explore.

Andrew Bain is a Hobart-based writer (Australia) who is passionate about the outdoors and remote places, having walked, cycled and kayaked his way across large parts of the world over the last 25 years.

Writer and editor **Andrew Collins** lives with his partner, Fernando, in Mexico City and a rural village in New Hampshire but spends about half of his time travelling. He's the author of numerous guidebooks, including *Ultimate Road Trips: USA & Canada*, and you can catch up with his adventures on Instagram at TravelAndrew.

Annette Sharp is the Global Social Impact Manager at Intrepid, responsible for understanding and guiding Intrepid's impact on communities that we visit. Originally from beautiful Aotearoa New Zealand, Annette has a profound respect for the people of the Pacific Islands, embracing their kindness, strength and connection to their culture, land and family.

Antonio Radičević is from a small town on the Croatian coast where he was exposed to tourism from a young age, and his love towards travelling and learning about new cultures was born even then. All those experiences have helped him in his current role as Senior Product Executive for Intrepid Travel.

Based in Auckland, **Brett Atkinson** writes about travel, food and craft beer around the world. He's researched and written Lonely Planet guidebooks to 15 different countries, and is the author of *Ultimate Road Trips: Aotearoa New Zealand*. Instagram @travelwriternz

Chetan Shanker Jha is a Tour Leader for Intrepid Travel India; he has been leading Intrepid Tours for the last 20 years across India and Nepal. He comes from The Blue City, Jodhpur, in Rajasthan. His heart-line for trip leading is 'Welcome a stranger; send back a life-time friend'.

Cliff Bielawski, from Toronto, is the global video lead for Intrepid Travel. Formerly in the film industry, he spent three years embracing the surf life in Central America before merging his passions for travel and video production at Intrepid.

Highly caffeinated Italo-Aussie **Cristian Bonetto** has written over 50 guidebooks to places as varied as LA, Melbourne, Copenhagen and Venice. When he's not on the road, you'll find him procrastinating on Google Maps.

Cristina Alonso is a Mexican travel and food writer. She is the author of *Art and Fiesta in Mexico City*, published by Hardie Grant Explore. Her work has appeared in publications like *T Magazine, Travesías,*

ABOUT THE AUTHORS

Departures International, and *Travel+Leisure*. She travels in search of great food, cocktails, and authentic connections to the people she meets along the way.

Based in Melbourne, Australia, **Danielle Dominguez** is a travel book publisher, food and travel writer and hiking guide, who loves nothing more than adventuring near and far with her son, Giulio.

Danielle McDonald is an Intrepid copywriter whose love for storytelling is matched only by her love for travel. She's gone far and wide in the pursuit of adventure and lived in several countries around the world. She's now based on the Gold Coast, Australia, although she still feels most at home when she's on the road.

David Nagle, a Melbourne-based Brit, uses his love of film to bring the unique stories of people and places to the world in his role overseeing production at Intrepid Travel. He might say one of his favourite things about travel is being able to watch countless movies back-to-back on long haul flights with no one thinking he's strange.

Dyan McKie is the Senior Product Manager for Intrepid Travel who loves designing trips, is an avid reader and a seeker of gluten-free goodness around the world.

Emma Glencorse is a member of the Intrepid Sales team based in Melbourne, and has worked in the travel industry helping folks find their perfect journey for the better part of seven years.

Born and raised in Alberta, Canada, **Emma Laliberte**'s love for exploring, meeting new people, and experiencing new cultures has sent her all over the world. When she's not busy advocating for rescue animals or diving into social and environmental causes, you can find her planning the next travel adventure, which is always around the corner.

Evan Davies is a graphic designer from Melbourne that likes to travel by bike or foot where possible. Most of the time he's taking photos of signs, being overwhelmed by the landscape or eating copious amounts of food.

Fiona Hilliard is a travel writer from Dublin, Ireland and is author of *Beyond the Cobblestones in Dublin* (Hardie Grant Explore, September 2023). Outside of exploring Dublin, some of her favourite travel experiences have included stargazing in Wadi Rum, Jordan, and learning to cook local dishes in Oaxaca, Mexico.

Heather Kang is Intrepid's global content manager and lives in the forest in Canada. She has been working in and writing about travel for 18 years and still can't decide where to go next.

Hena Jusic is an Australian Muslim of Bosnian ethnicity currently studying law and criminology at Swinburne University of Technology.

Inuksuk Mackay is a renowned Inuit throat singer and artist, best known as one half of the duo PIQSIQ, where she blends traditional throat singing with contemporary sounds. Her work celebrates and preserves Inuit culture, bringing its unique vocal traditions to new audiences worldwide.

James Taylor is an Australian travel writer who has lived and worked throughout Europe since 2014. He spent almost four years in Iceland during its major tourism boom, and returns regularly for work and to see family and friends.

Jenny Varghese has had the privilege to find adventure in her multiple homes across hemispheres, having lived in Botswana, South Africa, India and now Australia. With an insatiable curiosity for cultures and cuisines, she eagerly awaits where life might take her to explore next.

ABOUT THE AUTHORS

A widely published journalist, author and academic, **Julian Tompkin** was born to the remote desert regions of Western Australia. When not on the road he divides his time between the cities of Fremantle and Berlin.

Kassidy Waters is a descendant of the Wanaruah People of the Hunter Valley in New South Wales, Australia. She joined Bangarra Dance Theatre in 2019 after training at NAISDA Dance College. Kassidy has worked closely with Legs on the Wall, Karul Projects, Jannawi Dance Clan, Vicky Van Hout and Wagana Aboriginal Dancers to name a few. All have played an important role in her cultural learning and performance growth.

Kati Pankka is a Tour Leader for Intrepid Travel in Europe, who's passionate about authentic local experiences and wellbeing of humans and the environment.

Laura Doguet is a content producer from Melbourne, Australia. As an avid traveller, food enthusiast and nature lover, she'll seize any opportunity to enjoy all three at once.

Travel writer **Lee Atkinson** has been writing about her travel adventures for newspapers, magazines and travel guides since 1991. She is the author of 16 travel books, including the best-selling *Ultimate Road Trips Australia*.

Lucy Siebert has worked as a journalist, editor and communications professional in travel and tourism for two decades. Hailing from South Africa, she believes that travel truly has the capacity to build deep connections and cultural understanding. Today she lives in country Victoria, about one hour outside of Melbourne.

Mahaveer Singh is an Intrepid Leader from Jodhpur, Rajasthan, who loves to dig a little deeper into the history, culture and sights of India to ensure guests have memorable experiences.

Mandy Alderson knew travel was in her future after a family road trip, complete with a mock passport, to World Expo in 1988. Many moons later, when she's not heading up Intrepid's Global Brand Management team, she's perfecting her cacio e pepe or real carbonara with her fiancé Pete while crafting her next adventure.

Based in Lyttelton, New Zealand, photographer and writer **Mark Watson** is an advocate of long distance self-propelled travel. Most recently he spent four years cycling from Alaska to Patagonia – a journey of over 52,000 km.

Megan Cuthbert has been working in travel publishing for more than 10 years. Originally from Canada, she now calls Melbourne, Australia home.

Monique Choy is an Australian travel writer living on Gadigal Wangal land in Sydney. She's written guidebooks on the Philippines, Aotearoa/New Zealand, India and Tibet. She aims to tread lightly, collecting only recipes as souvenirs. @moniquechoy

The daughter of Croatian parents, **Natalie Placko** attributes her European heritage to a love affair with food, people, culture and an optimistic attitude to life. As Intrepid's General Manager Global Brand, Natalie loves to share the joy of travel with others by inspiring travellers to be more curious, conscious and connected to the world around them.

Nguyen Mai is a Sales Consultant and Tourism Enthusiast for Intrepid Travel. As a young woman from Vietnam with an insatiable love for exploring the world, she's embarked on an exciting journey from traveler to worker bee in the tourism industry.

Olivia Brown is an editor-in-training and passionate bibliophile based in Naarm/Melbourne. Although she is more of an armchair traveller of fictional worlds, she is keen to explore the globe and embrace new cultures.

ABOUT THE AUTHORS

Patrick O'Neill is a graphic designer and photographer from Melbourne, living and working in Naarm/Melbourne. Working at Intrepid, he's had the whole world open up to him and has been fortunate enough to visit many amazing places, most recently hiking the Nangma Valley in Northern Pakistan.

Rachel Miller is a storyteller and passionate advocate for a more sustainable and just planet. She seeks to inspire action through her words in the areas of climate and conservation, gender equality and development. She is based in Melbourne, Australia, but feels most at home anywhere in the mountains.

Rosanna Dutson is a British-born Aussie living in Melbourne. Travelling to the UK and Europe always feels like coming home, and perhaps one day she'll finally make her retreat to a secluded cottage in the Scottish highlands, surrounded by dogs prancing through the heather.

A Product Manager from Melbourne, Australia, **Rowan Waters** has 20 years' experience in the travel industry and has been on as many small group adventure trips. He believes it's the adventures that make travel great.

Sahar Aman is a Pakistani-British writer and editor. She was born on the Isle of Man, and through her writing adventures, she has lived and travelled across Europe, Asia and North America.

Sajiya Shah is a travel enthusiast from Kathmandu, Nepal, who works as a Sales Manager at Intrepid DMC Nepal, where they aim to inspire, create, share, and lead exceptional travel experiences that benefit both people and the planet. This mission aligns perfectly with Sajiya's personal values and passion for travel.

Samnang Mao is an ex-tour leader of Intrepid Travel Cambodia and is currently a freelancer tour guide base in Siem Reap, Kingdom of Cambodia. Samnang likes travelling, meeting people, making new friends and sharing experiences with different people from over the world.

Teresa Nowakowski is a journalist based in Chicago who covers history, art, science, and anything else that strikes her fancy.

Tim Richards is a freelance travel writer based in Melbourne, Australia. He's never happier than when aboard a train, and has ridden the rails on six continents.

Vanessa Ondrade is a graphic designer currently residing in Toronto. When she's not designing things for Intrepid, you can find her playing the ukulele, trying out new baking recipes or mapping out her next trip.

Published in 2024 by Hardie Grant Explore, an imprint of Hardie Grant Publishing

Hardie Grant Explore (Melbourne)
Wurundjeri Country
Building 1, 658 Church Street
Richmond, Victoria 3121

Hardie Grant Explore (Sydney)
Gadigal Country
Level 7, 45 Jones Street
Ultimo, NSW 2007

www.hardiegrant.com/au/explore

All rights reserved. No part of this publication may be reproduced, stored in a retrieval system or transmitted in any form by any means, electronic, mechanical, photocopying, recording or otherwise, without the prior written permission of the publishers and copyright holders.

The moral rights of the authors have been asserted.

Copyright text, concept, maps and design © Hardie Grant Publishing 2024

Maps in this publication were made with Natural Earth @ naturalearthdata.com

A catalogue record for this book is available from the National Library of Australia

Hardie Grant acknowledges the Traditional Owners of the Country on which we work, the Wurundjeri People of the Kulin Nation and the Gadigal People of the Eora Nation, and recognises their continuing connection to the land, waters and culture. We pay our respects to their Elders past and present.

For all relevant publications, Hardie Grant Explore commissions a First Nations consultant to review relevant content and provide feedback to ensure suitable language and information is included in the final book. Hardie Grant Explore also includes traditional place names and acknowledges Traditional Owners, where possible, in both the text and mapping for their publications.

The Intrepid List
ISBN 9781741179149

10 9 8 7 6 5 4 3 2 1

Project editor
Megan Cuthbert

Editor
Monique Choy

Editorial assistance
Rosanna Dutson and Olivia Brown

Proofreader
Lyric Dodson

First Nations consultant
Jamil Tye, Yorta Yorta

Cartographer
Emily Maffei

Illustrations
Lee Hodges

Designer
George Saad

Typesetting
Megan Ellis

Index
Max McMaster

Production manager
Simone Wall

Colour reproduction and pre-press by Megan Ellis and Splitting Image Colour Studio

Printed and bound in China by LEO Paper Products LTD.

The paper this book is printed on is certified against the Forest Stewardship Council® Standards and other sources. FSC® promotes environmentally responsible, socially beneficial and economically viable management of the world's forests.

Disclaimer: While every care is taken to ensure the accuracy of the data within this product, the owners of the data do not make any representations or warranties about its accuracy, reliability, completeness or suitability for any particular purpose and, to the extent permitted by law, the owners of the data disclaim all responsibility and all liability (including without limitation, liability in negligence) for all expenses, losses, damages (including indirect or consequential damages) and costs which might be incurred as a result of the data being inaccurate or incomplete in any way and for any reason.

Publisher's Disclaimers: The publisher cannot accept responsibility for any errors or omissions. The representation on the maps of any road or track is not necessarily evidence of public right of way. The publisher cannot be held responsible for any injury, loss or damage incurred during travel. It is vital to research any proposed trip thoroughly and seek the advice of relevant state and travel organisations before you leave.

Publisher's Note: Every effort has been made to ensure that the information in this book is accurate at the time of going to press. The publisher welcomes information and suggestions for correction or improvement.

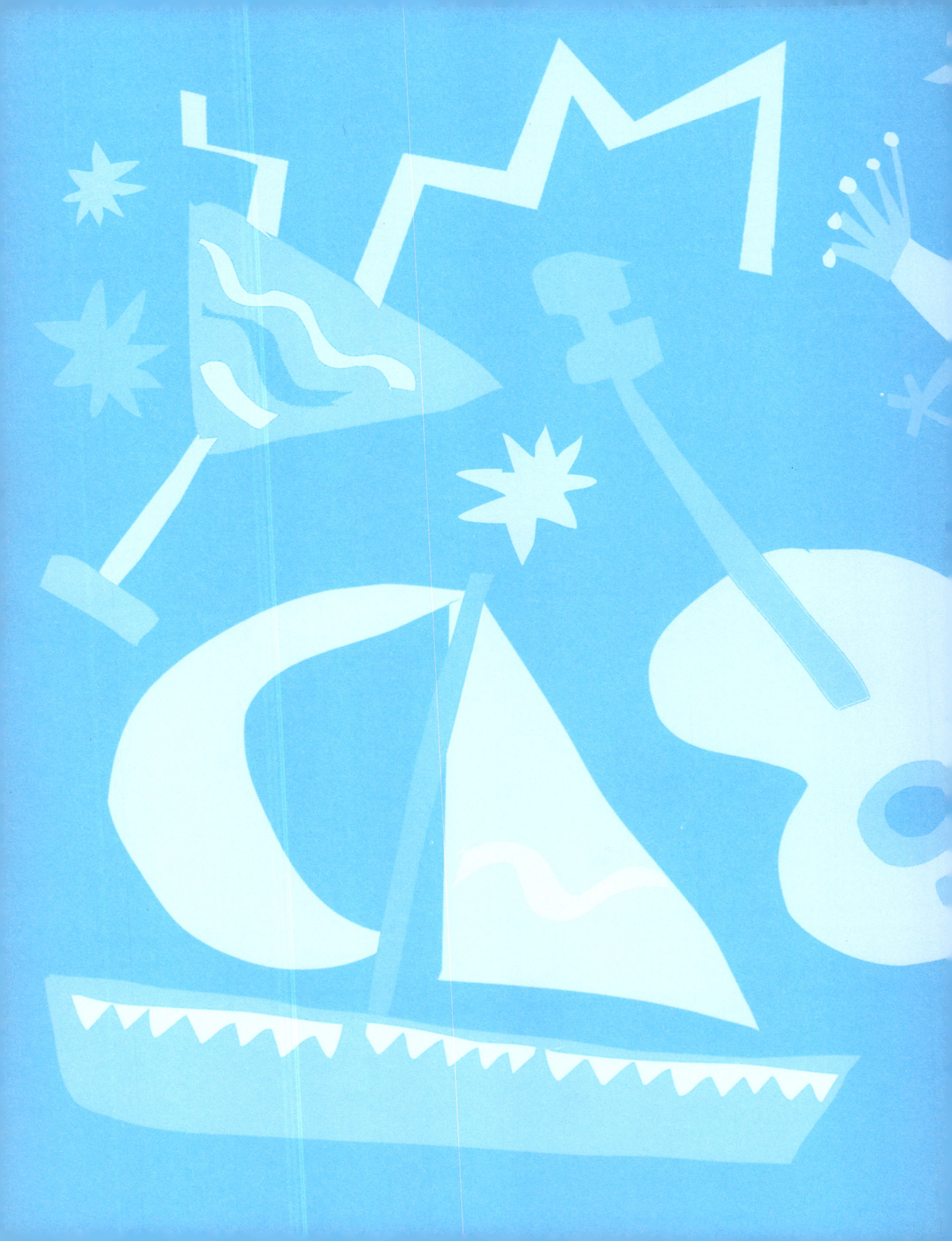